SONGS IN THE KEY OF BLACK LIFE

SONGS IN THE KEY OF BLACK LIFE

A RHYTHM AND BLUES NATION

MARK ANTHONY NEAL

ROUTLEDGE   NEW YORK AND LONDON

Published in 2003 by
Routledge
29 West 35th Street
New York, NY 10001
www.routledge-ny.com

Published in Great Britain by
Routledge
11 New Fetter Lane
London EC4P 4EE
www.routledge.co.uk

10 9 8 7 6 5 4 3 2 1

Library of Congress Cataloging-in-Publication Data

Neal, Mark Anthony.
    Songs in the key of black life : a rhythm and blues nation / Mark Anthony Neal.
       p. cm.
    Includes bibliographical references (p.) and index.
       ISBN 0–415–96570–5 (hard cover : alk. paper) — ISBN 0–415–96571–3
    (soft cover : alk. paper)
       1. Rhythm and blues music—History and criticism. 2. African Americans—Music—
    History and criticism.

ML3521 .N42 2003

                                                                                  2002153219

Dedicated to
Gloria Taylor-Neal
Misha Gabrielle Neal (Ya-Ya)
Camille Monet
and
AC and Lil' Lena

In Memory of
Willie B. Taylor
and
Benjamin James Moore (BJ)

you be like damn, it's that big man we all love to like
game air tight, while you caught in the hype
—Heavy D, "Big Daddy"

CONTENTS

AND BLUES

ACKNOWLEDGMENTS

Initial props to my editor, Matt Byrnie—this is your world now. To my homie publicist Patty Garcia, thanks for holding it down for them "Soul Babies"; now's the time for some next-level "shit." As always, peace to Bill Germano, who first peeped bruh's work a while ago.

To my UAlbany peeps Randy Craig, Don Byrd, Jeff Berman (who gets a special shout out), Cary Wolfe, Pierre Joris, Jennifer Fleischner: thanks for representing for a bruh on the professional tip. Much luv to my UAlbany running partners Bret Benjamin and Mike Hill (and their respective Lauras). Quick shout to the "Women of Women's Studies," *Vivian Ng*, Janell Hobson, and my B-Lo-bound homie Lillian Williams. Most thanks though to my Blackalicious partner in crime Ms. Lisa "L-Boogie" Thompson, who has brought all the flava to UAlbany's English department. Quick holla to my students past and present, Ms. Nicole Renee July (who still thinks I work for her), Sanjay (you coming up in the world, bruh), Ms. Karima Fitzgerald (like Cee-lo say, you "gettin' grown"), Cariann Colman, my blues "nigga" Lon Normadin, Heidi Xu (she of the perfect score), Habiba Ibrahim ("whose world is this?" it's yours, it's yours, it's yours), Mrs. Wendy Taylor (who during many moments during the course of a year reminded me why I do this in the first place), Ms. Ozioma and finally Ms. Faith "I can't call you baby-girl no mo'" Corbett, who should know by now that it's her world now.

Got to give some major love and props to the folks in the field who put it down and keep me wide open: Tricia Rose, Joy James, Michael Awkward, Craig Werner, my British alter-ego Maurice Bottemley, Ed Pavlic (who told me a while ago that I wasn't having enough "fun" with this music), those "Spelman Women" Beverly Guy-Sheftall and Bahati Kuumba (with a special shout to the Baldy Center and the Progressive Black Masculinities think tank), Farah Jasmine Griffin, Davey D, my Popmatters homie Cindy Fuchs, Norman Kelley, Ingrid Banks, Jennifer Devere Brody, John "Harlem World" Jackson, Aishah Shahidah Simmons, my Boogie-Down homie Thomas Glave, Kevin Powell ("Step into a World . . ."), Charlie Braxton and the "James Brown" of literary journalism, Jabari Asim. Gotta throw some luv toward the women who have been editing me these last few years: Kate Tuttle (Africana.com), Zahia Carter, Esther Ivereem (SeeingBlack.com), Sarah Zupko (Popmatters.com), to whom I owe much of this book, and especially Karen Zarker, who has edited my "Critical Noire" columns for Popmatters with great care.

On a more personal tip, got to acknowledge the brotherly love of my "Detroit Nigga" Michael Eric Dyson, who with his lovely wife and partner, Marcia, have been major supporters of a brotha's career. Another major shout to my other "Detriot Nigga" Todd Boyd—we on some next-level "shit" now fo' sho'. Peace to my Austin homie S. Craig Watkins, who has been nothing short of a thoughtful and supportive friend and distant colleague and one of the few bruhs in the trenches who I can talk to about both the professional challenges and the challenges of raising "little brown girls" in this world. Much love to one of my Chi-town homies, Sharon Patricia Holland, who gave bruh a breath of air three years ago, and I ain't half-stepped since. Ain't got nothin' but good words and major praise for Robin D. G. Kelley, who continues to play his role as one of the most influential of his generation (that would be the post-soul generation) of black scholars with grace and humility (we still waitin' for the Monk book tho'). Lastly, a cross-country holla to my "Hindu homie" Dipa Basu.

In the spirit of Donald Byrd (the trumpeter), I've got to acknowledge the "places and spaces I been." As I am writing this, I am looking forward to a brief sojourn to my intellectual birthplace, SUNY-Fredonia, where great folks like the Courts, the Krauses, Linda Phillips, the Torrains, Kathleen Bonds and EDP, and others played such valuable roles in my development. Praises to Pastor James and Duryee Memorial AME church, which has become our (mine, Misha's, and Mommie's) spiritual home. Many thanks to staff at Newton Medical III, who have a bruh seriously plotting to be on this earth for another thirty or forty years. Gotta show some luv for the "Ladies of the 'Bucks" (the Wolf Road Starbucks in Colonie), especially Lisa, Natasha, Ms. Judy, Heather, Blanca, the Jennifers, and Laura. Finally, a salute to "dem Davis Boys" Bob and Mike, who hold it down in real time with the Soul Patrol, which continues to be the place where I learn the most about *this* music we call ours.

To the Fam: Mama Soul (Masani Alexis De Veaux), who knew that six years later I would still be seeking the light you first shone on me damn near a decade ago. So much of this book is about you—about us, really; Grandma Elenor is eighty-nine at the time of this writing and still gets the spirit when the spirit needs to be got—thank you for being you and for providing for this rich clan of folks that I call family; same goes for AC's people in Danbury, Augusta, and of course NYC. Nothin' but affection for my homegirl Janette McVicker, Charles Banks, Gary White (how Phoebe and that baby?), Jason Smith, Mojavi Wright, the Burghers (Gopal and Denise), my brother-in-law Wesley Taylor and his wife Jacqueline, and my mother-in-law Odessa Taylor, who will probably never understand how important she (and the departed Willie B.) have been to me. When I think of Nic, Terri, Wil, and David, it's nothin' but good thoughts about brilliant minds, generous spirits, and folks who were never really "students," but were the folks I counted on to keep me grounded, focused, and not too full of myself. I especially miss you, Nic, but I know you got to do your thing, so we'll talk about those book contracts in a few years.

Quick holla to my "Big Bruh" Julius Adams, whose counsel and friendship has been so instrumental in me becoming the man I am today. There are three brothas—brothers literally in many regards—who I talk to via the phone or e-mail virtually every day. To my other Chi-town homie Richard "the R" Iton, much respect for the support and affirmation that you so willingly give. To my man Sebastian, it was perhaps a stroke of fate that you and Jiann and them boys Jason and Jamarr ended up moving "up the road," and for the first time in a while it's like we have real family around us. Of course you been one of my core "niggas" for a while, and now if Misha has her way you may be my in-law one of these days. Damn, FP, it's almost been thirty years, and even as family (hey Sonja, FP Sr., and Mama Alice), career, and this thing called life pushes us in so many directions you are still the brother that this only child has ever had (we love you Imani!).

To AC and Lil 'Lena, your baby boy ain't too grown yet, to acknowledge that he loves ya'll dearly. And Dad, thanks sharing yourself that afternoon we spent with the Dixie Hummingbirds, the Five Blind Boys, and the Mighty Clouds. Fay, you know it's all about you and has been since I first glimpsed you on that D train back in '82. I fell in luv with you that day, and been in luv with you since, so don't trip when your Yogi just tryin' to get his work on. Every one of the songs I write about in this book, I've listened to at one time or another with Ya-Ya sitting in the backseat or on my lap. And even though I have to scold you those times when you insist on hearing "Shining Star" while Daddy is trying to get his Jeffrey Osborne on, you know you are Daddy's heart and I have fundamentally changed the way I live so that I can be around for the next thirty or forty years of your life.

Finally, this book was close to completion when one of my oldest friends Benjamin James Moore (BJ) died suddenly. I never got the chance to tell him, but he's one of the reasons I do what I do, as we formed a friendship over our mothers' desires to keep us off the street and on safe voyages to adulthood—there were literally hundreds of train rides shared from our homes in Throggs Neck to our high school in Brooklyn (shout out to Brooklyn Tech). It was during BJ's funeral that I touched base with my childhood and all those folks that helped a little nappy-headed black boy "get grown" in the world. Just want to take a moment to acknowledge the folks up in Throggs Neck and our tiny little enclave on Schley Avenue—those were indeed the very best of times.

Mark Anthony Neal
Colonie, New York (the 'Bucks)
October 1, 2002

PROLOGUE

I was listening to music at the moment the terror was first shared with me. I was in my regular space—Starbucks—reading Danzy Senna's *Caucasia* in preparation for class the next day, with nothing else on my mind but Senna's character Birdie Lee, the still unlistened-to advance of Macy Gray's *The Id* in my bag, and Young Hova's (Jay Z) *The Blueprint*, which dropped on that day, September 11, 2001. In the background was the usual Starbucks mix, which at any given time includes Nina Simone, Frank Sinatra, Shelby Lynn, Marvin Gaye, Moby, and the Pastels ("Been So Long")—the kind of pretentious and programmed eclecticism and hipness that the corporate coffee house chain has long been associated with. When the severity of the attacks finally became clear to me, I packed up my stuff, checked my e-mail, and made cursory phone calls to make sure "fam" and "peeps" were good and safe. On my way to pick up my daughter from day care I made one stop: Circuit City, where I purchased a copy of Hova's *The Blueprint*. I was among the 493,000 who did so in the week that followed the 9/11 attacks. Afraid to watch anything remotely connected to the attacks with the three-year-old in the room, I spent much of the next week watching *Dora the Explorer*, *The Power Puff Girls*, and VH-1, the latter of which I had rarely watched before 9/11. With the help of VH-1 and a regular mix of Five for Fighting, Enrique Iglesias, Brian McKnight, and Macy Gray I self-medicated on introspection, remorse, and disbelief. Never a raving patriot, in fact decidedly fearful of those who were, I found myself unable to feel . . . anything . . . a state that channels such as VH-1, Lifetime, TV Land, and the Family Channel seem to specialize in facilitating.

The option, of course—actually plugging out of the televisual world was not one—was to watch the continuous looping replays of the dastardly terrorist deeds that read like that old *SNL* skit about Buckwheat getting shot. The same day (9/11) I peep the cover art to the Coup's forthcoming CD *Party Music*, with lead vocalist Boots firing off the detonator that explodes a bomb atop the WTC. Damn, talk about timing. While their label and web-site designers move fast to remove the visuals from the public domain I am struck by the image from the Coup, the hypertext visuals of CNNABCMSNBCCNBCNBCFOX (remember, we are a global community) and this notion of "Party Music." As if in real time, Boots raps about being "anti-imperial, Anti-trust, Anti-gun if the shit won't bust, Anti-corporate . . ." on the track "Ride the Fence" and relishes in his claim that he has "5 Million Ways to Kill a CEO." Some have legitimately argued that hip-hop is music bred from post–Civil Rights urban crisis and in this regard the Coup's (and Dead Prez's, and Michael Franti's, and Bahamadia's, and so on) regular flow of capitalism's-got-to-go speaks powerfully to the kinds of postindustrial (damn, that's cliché about now) crises faced in urban communities in the last three or four decades. In a world of fake gangstas and corporate hustlers (as if Jay Z were more damaging than Kenny-boy Lay) there's something righteous about the Coup's willingness to drop dime on "champagne sippin' money fakers" and the Forbes 500 mafia. Crisis music? Ya damn skippy, but yet the spirit of "Party Music" ("two thousand, zero, zero, party over . . . ?") is so disconnected from the crisis at hand.

On 9/11, I asked, "Who the hell is Lee Greenwood?" Sitting around a campfire prayer vigil three days later in the Adirondacks, about fifty or so people let me know. I wondered quietly if knowing the lyrics to Greenwood's "God Bless the USA" was required for immigrants at the Americanization ceremonies that mark their transition into American citizenship. Suddenly I too was caught up in the 9/11 mourning, though it was like the mourning was being choreographed somewhere. Clear Channel agreed. They put out a list for all of their affiliates suggesting what *not* to play during "this time of crisis." Clear Channel's list seemed rooted in denying any references to anything remotely associated with fire (the Tramp's "Disco Inferno"), death (Don McLean's "American Pie"), air travel (hence the absurd inclusion of Elton John's "Bennie and the Jets"), and New York City (Frank Sinatra's "New York, New York"). The choices ranged from the inane (Peter and Gordon's "I Go to Pieces" and Annie Lennox's "Walking on Broken Glass") to the innocuous (Kansas's "Dust in the Wind" or "I Feel the Earth Move," by Carole King). What exactly is the *music* for media conglomerates like Clear Channel who want to censor your right to mourn, celebrate, or get pissed off at the events of 9/11? The irony is that the firmly inside-the-box packaged programming that comes from conglomerates like Radio One and Clear Channel has specialized in a kind of middle-of-the-road distance from the more disconcerting aspects of daily life; hence mundane slogans like "no rap and no rock," lest middle-class, middle-management audiences be reminded from the hordes of uncouth and uncivilized youth whose music may, in fact, speak to the general disaffection of a significant segment of the American public.

The logic of the Clear Channel list was among the concerns and questions that I posed to a rather formidable collection of popular music scholars, critics, and musicians. A few bickering exchanges later, no answers were to be had, but the conversations yielded some very poignant comments about "getting back to the kids." It was like there was a collective "no more analyzing the music, how about we get back to the lives and the passions that inspire the music" that was spoken. And yet the questions remain:

If you're Dr. Dre, how do you go from "Fuck the Police" to a pro-nationalist/anti–Bin Ladin spin with requisite Million-Dollar donation? And if "Fuck the Police" was indeed birthed in the belly of terror known as the LAPD's "oops upside ya head" remix, how come it never deserved such a financial commitment?

"Born in the USA, I was born in the USA"—didn't anybody bother to call in the first time that was played in Anywhere, America, to let them know that it was a critique and not an affirmation? And since we are being so damn American, did anybody play Springsteen's "American Skin"? (How'd Cornel West put it, "America has been 'niggerized'"?) Is there room for music to be a critiqued anymore or does it all have to follow the party line (haven't heard "Rocking the Casbah" lately—it was on the Clear Channel list) or serve as a soundtrack to foreplay or a wake in order to get airplay?

And lastly, what did Representative Barbara Lee listen to the night she made her historic antiwar vote in the House? (What did Davey D listen to after he lost his radio gig for daring to give Barbara Lee and Boots Riley voices in the media via his indispensable web site?) Do we have the heart to make, buy, listen to, critique, and promote music of dissent in the face of so many erosions of civil liberties and civil rights (already so eroded before 9/11)? Are the FBI, CIA, and NYPD gonna be setting up surveillance at Greene Street studios?

Of course many of these questions are the product of my own, perhaps perverted response to the attacks and the top-shelf nationalist fury that appeared in the aftermath. My reality as an African-American man, a self-described "thug-nigga" intellectual, and morbidly self-conscious father and husband means that I am not simply jesting when I suggest that the appearance of hundreds of American flags instill a desire in me to run my ass down the street. The history is there. It will now be the history of those of Middle Eastern descent who now get regularly profiled in supermarkets, airports, and yeah, even my beloved Starbucks.

We've been in crisis for a while, and those marginalized on the margins (and I mean exactly that), struggling against racism, homophobia, sexism and misogyny, classism, and their real-time components like racial profiling and murder by "law enforcement" officers, queer bashing, rape and mutilation, and economic exploitation, know the drill and have done the dance. Sarah Jones knows the drill. Jones was of course sanctioned by the hyperconservative Michael Powell (son of Colin) and *his* FCC for the "vulgarity" of her song/poem "Your Revolution." In the past year, both Jones and Eminem have faced Powell's wrath, but where Eminem (a rabid homophobe) has become the poster boy of the ACLU and elicited an embrace from the most prominent "Queer" artist in the recording industry, Jones, who recently issued a countersuit against the FCC, has received a fraction of the attention that "Slim Shady" has. In my most perverse moments I will argue that such discrepancy is rooted in the different functions of the two artists. Whereas Eminem's "cause" further stimulates interest in his music and by extension "gangsta rap" (a misnomer in these days of mainstreamed "bling, bling") and increases the coffers of the Viacom empire (we love without our MTVBETVH-1MTV2), Jones's very trenchant critique of so-called gangsta rap might be interpreted as blocking the "flow" of transnational ("gangsta") capitalism.

When all was said and done I went back to a New York City song-writer. In the lyrics to her "New York Tendaberry," Nyro sings of New York, "you look like a city / but you feel like a religion to me." For those who live and feel their music as if a "religion" there's will always be music of crisis—the ongoing crisis of making sense of the lives we lead and the people we love—and no distinguished American president or five-hundred-station media conglomerate will change that.

INTRODUCTION

● ●

MUSIC ● N MY MIND

Forty years ago, *Blues People*, Amiri Baraka's (Leroi Jones) groundbreaking book on African-American music and culture, was published. Not everyone was feelin' the brother. In his oft-cited review of *Blues People*, Ralph Ellison wrote in the pages of the *New York Review*, "[Baraka] appears to be attracted to the blues for what he believes they tell us of the sociology of Negro American identity and attitude. . . . The tremendous burden of sociology which Jones would place upon this body of music is enough to give the blues the blues."[1] Baraka's desire was to examine the tradition of black popular music—jazz, the blues, gospel, and soul—within the context of the lived realities of the communities of black folk who produced and organically consumed this music. So groundbreaking was Baraka's effort that forty years later the book shows little wear and is still among the two or three books most crucial to understanding the relationship between America's race politics and the cultural production of America's black citizens. Baraka also had other designs. At the time of the publication of *Blues People*, it was the mainstream critical establishment that was largely responsible for bestowing "credibility" to black art outside the segregated confines of black life. Baraka and Ellison, for instance, were two of the few black critics who were given access to mainstream critical organs like *Down Beat*. Thus *Blues People* was also inspired by Baraka's burgeoning cultural nationalism and was part of his design to reclaim the critical terrain where black expressive culture was evaluated (and often condemned). The idea, of course, was to have critics whose aesthetic sensibilities were closer to those who produced the music. Even Ellison was forced to admit as much, arguing that "It would do well if all jazz critics did likewise," adding that it "would expose those who have no business in the field."[2]

Thirty years after the publication of *Blues People* (1963), Tricia Rose's definitive critique of hip-hop was published. At the time of *Black Noise*'s publication in 1994, the field of cultural studies was taking hold within the American academy and a generation of black "public" intellectuals, many of whom were affiliated with elite universities, were also emerging. As black public intellectuals and cultural critics were all called on to explain, decipher, repudiate, deconstruct, and defend hip-hop and black youth culture, a veritable cottage industry of African-American cultural criticism was created in which hip-hop culture and music served as clear subtexts to these conversations. On the strength of his book *From God to Gangsta Rap* (1995), which was one of the first scholarly studies of hip-hop aimed at mainstream readers, Michael Eric Dyson became known as the "hip hop scholar."[3] Black scholars' and critics' ability to talk about hip-hop in stridently sociopolitical terms—often at the expense of the music itself—is directly related to Baraka's efforts of forty years ago.

The past thirty years or so have witnessed large numbers of volumes written about jazz, the blues, and hip-hop music, with biographies of some of the biggest icons within these genres dominating the publications. Provocative bio-critiques of Billie Holliday (Farah Jasmine Griffin's *If You Can't Be Free, Be a Mystery: In Search of Billie Holiday*), Billy Strayhorn (*Lush Life: A Biography of Billy Strayhorn,* by David Hajdu), Muddy Waters (Robert Gordon's *Can't Be Satisfied: The Life and Times of Muddy Waters*), and Tupac Shakur (Dyson's *Holler if You Hear Me: Searching for Tupac Shakur*) are just a few examples of this trend. While books on rap and jazz, in particular, represent a wide spectrum of ideological and critical vantage points, there have been relatively few books written about rhythm and blues. There have been notable efforts like Nelson George's *The Death of Rhythm and Blues*, Peter Guralnick's

Sweet Soul Music, Robert Pruter's *Chicago Soul*, *You Send Me*, Daniel Wolf's biography of the late Sam Cooke, and, most recently, quality academic efforts such as Craig Werner's *A Change Is Gonna Come*, Suzanne Smith's *Dancing in the Street*, and my own *What the Music Said*, but few of these efforts have taken seriously contemporary rhythm and blues (what the music industry calls "urban contemporary"), instead focusing mainly on the "golden" era of soul music and its performers.

Serious consideration of rhythm and blues has been challenged for several reasons. During the 1950s, rhythm and blues was largely associated with honky-tonks, after-hours clubs, black youth, and "good rockin' tonight." In comparison, jazz was seen as a more highbrow form of black expression and thus was given more critical esteem. By the time Parliament Funkadelic recorded "One Nation under a Groove," R&B was regarded by some as "rhythm and bullshit." As hip-hop music began to demand more airplay, generate more sales, and dominate the black social imagination, it was seen as a window into the travails of black America, whereas R&B was simply seen as a "bunch of love songs." Though R&B was the second most popular genre of popular music in 2001 in term of sales, there has been little serious criticism on contemporary R&B. It is in this context that contemporary R&B has been given short (critical) shrift. *Songs in the Key of Black Life: A Rhythm and Blues Nation* represents my effort to take seriously the ways that black popular music, including contemporary R&B, reflects the joys, apprehensions, tensions, and contradictions of contemporary black life. The title is of course an obvious reference to the music of Stevie Wonder, notably his career-defining opus *Song in the Key of Life* (1976). Though Marvin Gaye's *What's Going On* could be regarded as the quintessential black protest recording, Wonder more consistently provided a window into a wide-ranging and dynamic African-American humanity.

Though I have to give props to my editor, Matt Byrnie, for coming up with the book's title, I must admit that conceptually the title owes something to the work of fellow social critic and novelist Norman Kelley, who published a groundbreaking essay on the political economy of the music industry a few years ago. Originally published online and subsequently published in *Black Renaissance/Renaissance Noire*, another version of Kelley's essay "Rhythm Nation: The Political Economy of Black Music" appears in the introduction of a collection that Kelley edited titled *Rhythm and Business: The Political Economy of Black Music*. According to Kelley, "At the bottom of this $14-billion domestic music industry is a disrespected pool of black talent: America's colonized Rhythm Nation."[4] Though I am less concerned here with the issues of colonization that Kelley brilliantly explores in his essay, I share his notion that there does exist such a thing as a "music" nation—a nation of folks whose passions, gripes, joys, and tears are conveyed via the music that we call rhythm and blues.

The first section of the book, "Rhythm," primarily focuses on a range of contemporary neo-soul performers, with a particular emphasis on how the music of these contemporary artists is indebted to earlier generations of "Soul Providers." This is witnessed in the fascinating digital duet between hip-hop artist Erick Sermon and the late Marvin Gaye, but also in a group of "grown-ass women"—Angie Stone, Jill Scott, and especially Jaguar Wright—who reach back to neo-soul's past, drawing some inspiration from the profane (and gleefully so) music of Millie Jackson, whose "Phuck U Symphony" from her live recording *Live and Uncensored* (1981) would make Jay Z blush. If Jackson was deemed "outside the box" in a 1970s pop arena that survived the clothing styles of Bootsy Collins, Verdine White (of Earth, Wind, and Fire), and LaBelle's *Battlestar Gallatica* look, then spoken-word artist Camille Yarbrough could only be described as obscured. Yet, Yarbrough and her underground classic *The Iron Pot Cooker* (1975) has also been recovered, directly in the music of Fatboy Slim (who sampled Yarbrough's "Take Yo' Praise" on his own "Praise You") and spiritually in the music of Macy Gray, Res, and Ursula Rucker, who are decidedly on "Some otha shit"—well outside the proverbial box.

LaBelle is directly recalled in "Bellbottoms, Bluebelles, and the Funky-Ass White Girl," a chapter that explores the significance of a chance collaboration between the trio and the anti-chanteuse Laura Nyro. The product of their collaboration was the brilliant and largely forgotten *Gonna Take a Miracle* (1971). It's my belief that that disc represented a brave new world of feminist conversation across race, one that has rarely occurred within pop music, save in forced dialogues between Eve and Gwen Stefani ("Let Me Blow Your Mind") and the likes of Lil' Kim, Christina Aguilera, Mya, Pink, and Missy Elliot, who remade LaBelle's classic "Lady Marmalade" (1974) for the soundtrack of *Moulin Rouge*. In this regard, it is very much my intention to use these artists and their music as guideposts to the contemporary African-American (black) cultural anxieties related to issues such as gender, feminist politics, political activism, black masculinity, celebrity, and the fluidity of racial and sexual identity. Of note are the ways in which Bilal articulates a distinct black masculinity informed by a "pimp aesthetic," and the controversy over Tweet's (Charlene Keys) rather open discussion of masturbation (we think).

Many of the chapters in the book are inspired by an aesthetic conception that Audre Lorde biographer Masani Alexis De Veaux has referred to as "newblackness." Taking some liberties with De Veaux's concept, "newblackness" embodies a radical fluidity within "blackness" that crosses genders, sexualities, generations, religions, ethnicities, and whatever attributes individual "black people" claim as being part of the blackness they possess.[5] Perhaps no contemporary artist captures this era of "newblackness" better than Me'Shell Ndegéocello. Such fluidity is powerfully articulated in her most recent work, *Cookie: The Anthropological Mixtape*, in which Ndegéocello challenges rigid perceptions of black identity and homosexuality. In Ndegéocello's world, the mix tape is the literal embodiment of the praxis of fluidity, as the disc flows seamlessly into different themes, textures, and voices. On one strident track, Ndegéocello brings together the disparate voices of Claude McKay, Etheridge Knight, and the late June Jordan. Taking some inspiration from Ndegéocello, I try to bring pop queen Alicia Keys into a conversation with German philosopher Jürgen Habermas.

The second part of the book, "And Blues," uses the improvisational rhythms of black music as a metaphor to examine current events in black life, including the public dispute between former Harvard University professor Cornel West and Harvard president Lawrence Summers, the firing of former Black Entertainment Television (BET) talk-show host Tavis Smiley, and the controversy surrounding Sarah Jones's poem "Your

Revolution." In many regards, many of this book's chapters push further some of the arguments that I make in *Soul Babies: Black Popular Culture and the Post-Soul Aesthetic*, though this book is also a reflection of my concerted efforts to create a critical language that is as "fly, funky, and out tha box" as the very music and events that I scrutinize.

RHYTHM

CHAPTER ONE

●●●●●●●●●●●●●●●●●●●●●

REVOLUTIONARY MIX TAPE

And I'm sorry, I just—I don't even do hip-hop. We're just all some watered-down derivative, you know. There's some neophytes in the vibe, but basically, hip-hop being counterculture, underground culture, that's sorta dead. That's not going down. And it's all mainstream. It's just a bunch of pop music. . . . No one's striving to be Miles Davis. And, you know, I wanna be like Miles Davis.
                    —Me'Shell Ndegéocello, *OneWorld*, February 3, 2002

Commercial images of the sexualized allure to or aversion for black females eclipse images of black female political agency in conventional culture: As the political outlaw is transformed into the sexual outlaw, the activist becomes a commodity consumed in the hunt, imprisonment, or rehabilitation.
                    —Joy James, *Shadowboxing: Representations of Black Feminist Politics*

Everybody knows who Marvin Gaye is, but don't nobody know who Eugene McDaniels (a.k.a. the left rev. mc. D.) is. Gaye's *What's Going On* and McDaniels's *Headless Heroes of the Apocalypse* were both released in 1971, but whereas one recording has become the artistic benchmark of protest music, the other has existed in relative obscurity. Though McDaniels has always maintained that *Headless Heroes* was largely satire, it was and still is a stinging indictment of American imperialism and race politics. Born and raised in Kansas City, Missouri, McDaniels had a relatively successful pop career in the early 1960s recording for the Liberty Record label. Profoundly affected by the tenor of American race politics and the assassination of Martin Luther King, Jr., in 1968, McDaniels left the country for a few years. It was during this period that McDaniels penned "Compared to What," which was recorded by Roberta Flack on her debut, *First Take* (1969), and became an international hit for Eddie Harris and Les McCann, who recorded a live version of the song on *Swiss Movement*, their Montreaux recording that was released in 1970. The song was one of the first political songs that McDaniels wrote, and it opened the door for his two Atlantic releases.

Headless Heroes contained critiques of blue-eyed soul ("Jagger the Dagger") and the good Right Reverends ("Lovin' Man"), and offered examples of the "shopping while black" phenomemon ("Supermarket Blues") and the futility of race hatred ("Headless Heroes"). On the latter track, McDaniels suggest that "Jews and Arabs" and "nigguhs and crackers" were "Semitic" and "racial" pawns in the "mastergame" in which the "player who controls the board" sees them as little more than "cannon fodder." In the album's most stinging critique, McDaniels gets at the root of American imperialism and its relationship to the genocide of America's native population. On the track "The Parasite," McDaniels describes some of the early settlers as "ex-hoodlums" and "jailbirds" who used "forked tongues" in their drive to pollute the water and defile the air. Referencing America's ideology of "Manifest Destiny," McDaniels sang that as "agents" of some god-figure, they did "damned well what they pleased," including murdering and pillaging the "native" population.

Like his contemporary, cartoonist Ollie Harrington (Aaron McGruder is his critical progeny), McDaniels was not afraid to provide America with a satirical, though thoroughly critical, view of itself. But shortly after the release of *Headless Heroes*, McDaniels was "dropped" from his label. Though there is much myth and rumor that surrounds McDaniels's break with the Atlantic label, it was a line from "The Parasite" that probably facilitated the demise of McDaniels's commercial career, as the artist dropped a thinly veiled reference to the Nixon administration ("promote law and order / let justice go to hell"). As

Eugene McDaniels, Headless Heroes of the Apocalypse

myth would have it, then–vice president Sprio Agnew gave a quick holla to Armet and Nesuhi Ertegun, the founders of the Atlantic label. According to McDaniels, "They fired me on the spot and killed the record."[1] Trying to provide some context to the experience, McDaniels recently related that "it was a black man in the open . . . at last I had a chance to say what I believed in my deepest heart about politics, slavery, and the genocide of the Indians. Music was the only forum I had to express myself. Who is going to listen to me talk on the street corner."[2]

After the debacle, McDaniels went back into the songwriting groove, eventually penning old friend Roberta Flack's "Feel like Makin' Love" (1974), which according to McDaniels has been recorded 478 times.[3] McDaniels knows how many times the song has been recorded because he maintains the publishing rights to it. His decision to retain rights to the song was a direct product of his experience with Atlantic: the label dropped him, but retains control of the masters. Echoing one of his artistic progeny ("if the you don't own the masters the Master owns you"), he bitterly asserts that "we are in a slavery business . . . record companies are slave owners. Artists have next to no rights to their own material."[4] In recent years, McDaniels's music has been resurrected via hip-hop recordings by A Tribe Called Quest, Organized Konfusion, the Beastie Boys, and Pete Rock and CL Smooth. Out of print for more than a decade, the album became a collectible, often going for a hundred dollars a copy. (Coming correct, I "liberated" my own copy from a college radio station I held it down at for a few years.) In a reversal of fortune that only the logic of hip-hop can allow—as Russell Potter puts it, hip-hop "constitutes a reversal of the traditional modes of production and consumption"—the album was widely bootlegged in the early 1990s as hip-hop "spiritually" recovered what McDaniels lost two decades earlier.[5] Thus a revolutionary recording from the early 1970s was thrust into the unique culture of mix tapes, which despite the hypercommodification of hip-hop, including the consumption of "sanctioned" major-label "mix tapes," remains the site where hip-hop skills are organically authenticated.

Thirty-one years after the release of *Headless Heroes*, Me'Shell Ndegéocello issued her own "revolutionary mixtape," which may be the most stridently political "soul" recording since *Headless Heroes*. The title of Ndegéocello's disc, *Cookie: The Anthropological Mixtape* (2001), gets at a street-level relevancy—the place where DJs and unsigned hype earn their reputations via a mix-tape culture that helps validate skills *before* the record deal. The same street level where bootlegging (all together now, "h to the Izzo . . . ") conveys a ghetto authenticity that moving 3 million units to little white kids in Kansas ain't never gonna translate into. But even as Ndegéocello tries to get at a notion of an "authentic" blackness (the kind that anthropology supposedly helps validate), that remains beyond any real definitions (what Greg Tate calls an "anti-essentialist essentialism"), her privileging of the very concept of a mix tape deals with real-time concepts like flow, fluidity, and hybridity as means to construct sound, ideas, and, most important, black identity.

Cookie: The Anthropological Mixtape is the first major pop recording that speaks to the era of "newblackness," a term coined by Mama Soul (Masani Alexis De Veaux). "Newblackness" is a "blackness" that is defined by a radical fluidity that allows powerful existential "conversations" within "blackness" across genders, sexualities, ethnicities, generations, socioeconomic positions, and socially constructed performances of "black" identity (like Dunbar said so long ago, "We Wear the Mask"). In effect, it is the "language" of a blackness that many black folks had been afraid to embrace for fear that somehow it was a reduction or erosion of blackness. Ndegéocello's comfort with this concept of fluidity, and the fears that such fluidity elicits in those who want to hold on to an essential blackness, has been witnessed throughout her career with tracks such as "If That's Your Boyfriend (He Wasn't Last Night)" (*Plantation Lullabies*, 1993), "Leviticus: Faggot," and "Mary Magalene" (both from *Peace beyond Passion*, 1996). Ndegéocello has never felt a need to defend or explain the supposed ambiguity that is so crucial to her music, because the "spaces and places" that she claims and cultivates are never in competition with themselves, but rather an admittedly complex and creative articulation of what it means to be "blackwomanbisexualbassplayersentientbeingGramscianintellectualand revolutionarysoulsinger." As Ndegéocello reflected very early in her career, "I'm not gay enough? I'm not black enough? I don't care. Meet me and make your assessment."[6]

And this is how Me'Shell Ndegéocello had always been stepping, beginning with her debut, *Plantation Lullabies*, where she began to talk about the walking black dead on urban plantations across America— what we now call siege mentalities, in response to the ways that folks self-medicate ("inhale now feel the rush, hold it I'm losing touch") on celebrity, playa-hatin', material desires, and the usual suspects like "bling, bling and booty" and the consumption of "bling, bling and booty" (courtesy of our good friends at Viacom). Wasn't nobody diggin' Me'Shell Ndegéocello (okay, you can say it out loud: "nuh-day-gay-o-cello") when she was trying to holla at her peeps in the hood, so sis stepped on to get her art on. The cerebral-bending *Peace beyond Passion* and the slow-motion, sketchy brilliance of *Bitter* (1999), which both drop nods to Bill Withers, Marvin Gaye, and Jimi Hendrix, were lost on R&B and neo-soul audiences, while Me'Shell, like that cat Lenny Kravitz, pushed the "boundaries of blackness" (quick shout to Cathy Cohen) beyond market segmentation and voter demographics (a subtle reminder that all black folks ain't got to choose between Jesse Jackson and JC Watts or Maxine Waters and Condi Rice). With the brilliant *Cookie: The Anthropological Mixtape*, Me'Shell Ndegéocello is back on "Nigga Blvd.," selling fly-ass wolf tickets and holding the critical eye up to the folks with the soul (holla back, W. E. B.), who ain't never been tryin' to deal with her in the first place.

Many of the core themes of *Cookie: The Anthropological Mixtape* are contained in the opening track, "Dead Nigga Blvd. (pt. 1)," which is a sly (even derisive) homage to the ghetto streets that get renamed in memoriam to "great black leaders." The intersection of 125th Street and Lenox Avenue in Harlem, for example, is where black nationalism (Malcolm X Boulevard) and radical democracy (Martin Luther King, Jr., Boulevard) meet—along with Magic Johnson's Starbucks and more than a few crack-heads. Ndegéocello uses the song to highlight the bankruptcy of symbolic campaigns to recognize "great black men" (Buggin' Out: "Sal, when you get some black folk up on the wall?") and the ungrateful attitudes of the hip-hop generation. Built around her signature poppin' bass (she claims she hadn't heard Larry Graham until after she learned to play the instrument), Ndegéocello takes on lay Afrocentrisms, in which folks hold on to an "Africa of the past" (often forgetting the fact that there were some "Africans" who got paid in the transatlantic slave trade), health issues (like how come humans feed their kids "cow milk" and "Simi-milk"), and the inability for many blacks folks to see sexuality as something that is fluid ("I can't even tell my brothers and sisters that they're fine").

Ndegéocello's not so subtle swipe at the "romancing of Africa" at the heart of Afrocentric thought is a likely product of the widespread belief (propagated by some of its most popular ideologues—namely Molefi Asante and Maluana Karenga, the father of Kwanzaa) among its followers that "queerness" is a "white man's disease" and that black queers are a measure of just how effectively white supremacy has "infected" authentic blackness. Whatever. In a recent interview, Ndegéocello suggests that "gay life, the whole gay lifestyle [meaning how it is perceived in the mainstream], is patterned off a white gay male aesthetic. Now, that ain't my vibe. . . . I love my brothers. I love my sisters. I am sexually functional with both."[7] Challenging the "in the box" thinking within the gay and black communities, she adds, "If you're gonna assess my shit [acknowledging her queerness] like it's a marketing scheme, no. If you fine, you fine . . . worse thing you could be is a closed-minded gay person. And worst thing you can be is a judgmental black person."[8]

Throughout "Dead Nigga Blvd. (pt. 1)" Ndegéocello raises questions about the real meaning of "freedom" (you can't hate on the white folks if "niggas" holdin' each other down; so where's the freedom fighters for that?), finally admitting that perhaps freedom is about the freedom to love those who hate you and to die a "beautiful" death and make "pretty brown babies." Ndegéocello's lyrics here are a reminder that her inward gaze is about strengthening black community and reproducing the beauty of the "race" both physically and aesthetically. It is this plaintive and thoughtful Ndegéocello that is present on "Dead Nigga Blvd. (pt. 2)," which appears near the end of Cookie. The song opens with Ndegéocello repeating a refrain about gaining the world and losing "your soul, worrying about what you ain't got." But it is a solo by "Kid Funkadelic," legendary P-Funk guitarist Michael Hampton, which gets at the raw passion of Ndegéocello's desires to build and maintain community. Toward the middle of the song, Ndegéocello chants "lift me up" (a shout-out to the tradition of "lifting as we climb" as personified by the black women's club movement of the late nineteenth and early twentieth centuries).

While part one of "Dead Nigga Blvd." derisively caricatures the hip-hop generation, Ndegéocello offers them an olive branch on part two by sampling dialogue from the HBO special Thug Life in DC (1999), which was directed by Marc Levin (Brooklyn Babylon and Slam). Ndegéocello's sampling of voices from various sources throughout Cookie is a form of what I call "mix tape praxis." Like the best hip-hop DJs and producers who bring various sounds, beats, and musical genres into conversation with each other without sacrificing the groove (fluidity), Ndegéocello samples a wide range of black voices, including Dick Gregory, whose speech "Human Rights and Property Rights" from *Dick Gregory at Kent State*, is tagged at the end of "Dead Nigga Blvd. (pt. 1); Countee Cullen; and Angela Davis. On two occasions in *Cookie*, Ndegéocello builds whole songs around weighty spoken-word samples.

"Akel Dama (Field of Blood)" is a tribute to Ndegéocello's "word-smith warrior" forefathers. Gil Scott-Heron's "Comment # 1 (Small Talk at 125th Street and Lenox, 1970)" opens the track discussing the "blacker than thou" mentality that has often afflicted progressive movements within the black community. Written at the height of the Black Power and black arts movements, Scott-Heron's comments give a historical grounding to Ndegéocello's attempt to counter widespread perceptions within some black communities that "queer" black bodies (and those queered because their politics, sexualities, class positions, and genders are not in sync with the "black is, black ain't" gatekeeping society) are not black enough—or black at all, for that matter. Later in the song, it is the voice of Countee Cullen (the Harlem Renaissance poet who personifies a black modernist version of the "DL" identity) that Ndegéocello recovers via his poem "Heritage." The poem's title allows Ndegéocello to claim the legacy of one of the most celebrated poets in the tradition, but also places the "queer" Cullen into the same space that is shared by stridently heterosexual wordsmiths ranging from Etheridge Knight and Scott-Heron to rabid homophobes such as hip-hop artists Common and Ice Cube. In other words, all of these men share a common heritage.

It is, in fact, Etheridge Knight, the tragically obscure "prison poet," who makes the most powerful "cameo" on "Akel Dama (Field of Blood)," with his poem "The Idea of Ancestry" (in *The Essential Etheridge Knight*, 1986). In the poem, Knight, who died in 1991, builds a complex definition of black fluidity via the forty-seven pictures of his family that adorn his cell wall; Knight states, "I am all of them, they are all me."[9] Ndegéocello uses "The Idea of Ancestry" and Knight's voice (the poet struggled with drug addiction throughout much of his life) to reinforce an idea that black community is strengthened by its diversity—in other words, a nigga is "my nigga." In the preface to *Poems from Prison* (published by Broadside Press in 1968—shout to the late Dudley Randall), in which "The Idea of Ancestry" was initially published, Gwendolyn Brooks writes of Knight that he represented "blackness, inclusive, possessed and given; freed and terrible and beautiful"; it's exactly that ethos that *Cookie* consistently forces listeners to consider.[10]

Knight is also aurally present on Ndegéocello's "6 Legged Griot (Weariness)," which conceptually is one of the strongest tracks on *Cookie*. The song, which features the voices of Knight, the Jamaican-bred poet Claude McKay, and the late June Jordan, brings a myriad of perspectives into conversation with each other. In his brilliant (and *brilliant* is not too strong a term) collection of essays, *Flyboy in the Buttermilk: Essays on Contemporary America*, Greg Tate writes of the Griot, "To read the tribe astutely you sometimes have to leave the tribe ambitiously, and should you come home again, it's not always to sing hosannas or a song the tribe necessarily has any desire to hear . . . these messengers are guaranteed freedom of speech in exchange for a marginality that extends to the grave."[11] One can only imagine what kind of truth can be articulated when the voices of Claude McKay (from his classic "If We Must Die"), June Jordan ("In Memoriam: Martin Luther King, Jr.," in *Naming Our Destiny*, 1989) and Etheridge Knight ("Hard Rock Returns to Prison from the Hospital for the Criminally Insane") are all sharing the body of such a messenger. But yet the song, which is bottomed by one of Ndegéocello's best bass grooves on the disc and a resonant solo by saxophonist Jacques Schwarz-Bart, finds its "voice" in the parenthetical title—the weariness that comes with struggle in general, but more so when so many of those struggles are fought against those who look just like you.

It is the voice of Angela Davis ("we love you Ms. Davis, whoooo, we are fo' real . . .") that is first heard on "Hot Night" (from Davis's *The Prison Industrial Complex*, 1999) with a salsa horn line (courtesy of Hector Lavoe's "La Fama"). The salsa backdrop (produced by Supa Dave West, who laced De La lovely on *Bionix*'s "Watch Out") helps to capture the kinds of shared spaces where Latino and black folks have struggled with each other and created bridges to each other's cultures. It is the aesthetic of *casitas*, stoops, block parties, bodegas, and sweaty local clubs, which in their casualness (the serious pursuit of leisure on a hot summer night) are often the basis for free-form commentaries on shared realities. In the song's chorus, Ndegéocello ebulliently sings about heading down club and drinking piña coladas "without the al-kahol." Describing herself (and perhaps Davis) throughout the song as a "revolutionary soul singer," Ndegéocello places herself in a tradition of soul singers (Wonder, Aretha, Marvin Gaye, Sam Cooke, Curtis Mayfield, and Roberta Flack, among others) who speak "truth to power."

Much has been made of the neo-soul young-uns, who Ndegéocello reached out to, but who didn't reach back (Jill Scott and Erykah Badu are the most bandied-about examples). One of the cats who did hit Me'Shell back was Talib Kweli, whose cameo on "Hot Night" (we're eavesdropping on a cross-generational conversation between Ms. Davis and Kweli) is some scorched-earth brilliance, as he simply seizes the song from Ndegéocello. In his lyric, Kweli, who is on a small list of folks who I refer to as hip-hop's Celebrity Gramscians (Dead Prez, Common, and Mos *Top Dog/Underdog* Def), acknowledges the ways in which even politically trenchant music becomes a cog in globalization ("I tell the truth, now I'm a target in their market"). Ndegéocello hits hard at this theme herself on the kick-ass "GOD.FEAR.MONEY." Dropping another nod to classic "soul" Gramscian Gil Scott-Heron, Ndegéocello sings about being "way down with the revolution" until she peeped the joint needed "corporate" sponsorship—a quick rejoinder to those who think that political hip-hop (and other forms of insurgent political pop) is somehow not implicated in the economic exploitation that such forms of music ostensibly aim to undermine.

In a rather poignant moment during an interview, Ndegéocello admits her own complicity in such exploitation as she visited the plant of a company whose basses she endorses. In the interview, Ndegéocello explains, "I knew I'd be their only black endorser, and when I went down to the plant there were all these older black women painting. I know I seem like I'm a fist-in-the-air activist, but it was hard for me."[12] On "GOD.FEAR.MONEY" Ndegéocello also gets at the ways in which celebrity undermines the work of those in the trenches as she wonders aloud if Jesus would be incarcerated and the devil a "guest VJ" on *TRL*. It's another reminder of the role that global conglomerates like Viacom and AOL-Time Warner (the parent company of Ndegéocello's label, Maverick) play in defining reality, normalcy, and morality—all attributes ultimately undercut by the ebb and flow of celebrity. A subtle reminder, also, that Ndegéocello was offered regular access to the mainstream video outlets only when she collaborated with John Mellencamp on the Van Morrison cover "Hot Night"—the same Mellencamp who helped India.Arie (the exoticized natural black woman) cross over to mainstream audiences (damn, is that "Video" they playin' on the Starbucks sound system?).

While "Dead Nigga Blvd. (pt. 1)" and "Hot Night" represent Ndegéocello's politics at their most virulent, so many of her political passions are expressed in a distinctly reflective demeanor that borders on remorse. The moving "Jabril," which is dedicated to Tupac Shakur and Biggie, is written from the perspective of someone praying to God shortly before death ("forgive me lord as I die in vain"). The song achieves a mystical and ethereal quality courtesy of Marcus Miller's angular bass clarinet (and fretless bass) lines and by an extended vocal cameo by Lalah Hathaway, whose father, Donny Hathaway, recorded one of the great mournful songs in all of black pop with "Thank You Master for My Soul" (on *Everything Is Everything*, 1969). Lalah Hathaway also appears on the beautiful ballad "Earth," which like the equally beautiful "Priorities 1–6" is in the tradition of fine and sexy Ndegéocello ballads such as "Outside Your Window" (on *Plantation Lullaby*) and the haunting "Fool of Me" from *Bitter*.

On the real, while there are real-time implications to Ndegéocello's politics throughout *Cookie*, sista-girl is also straight-up horny, embracing a sexual politics that is as wide open as her social commentary. The best example is on the cleverly titled "Barry Farms." Barry Farms is the name of a housing project in Ndegéocello's native Washington, D.C. While the song is about some serious carnal same-sex fantasies, it also highlights how even lesbian sex does not necessarily translate into a feminist politics that rejects the objectification of black female sexuality or resist a heterosexist paradigm. The song, which features percussionist Kiggo Wellman, is built around a shuffle-16th groove (known in D.C. as go-go), harking back to Ndegéocello's earliest days as a musician in D.C., and thus the song is really a coming-of-age tale about her sexuality. The song centers on a "young and fine" seventeen-year-old baby-girl who is drawn to "Ndegéocello" (presumably when she too was that age, lest we get another spin on this R. Kelly shit), but who got the "shivers" when she was around her peeps. When word gets out that she and shortie were on a more complicated tip, shortie of course stopped coming around. When she gets pressed as to why she's been on the DL (no pun intended) but still wants to get back to their groove, shortie hits back that nobody can "eat my pussy" the way Shell-shell could (mouths open and agape). In one of the great retorts in contemporary black pop, Ndegéocello hits back in the song's chorus that she should teach her "boy" how to do that.

Reminding folks that it ain't all drama, "Barry Farms" is followed with "Trust" ("make me wet"). Of course, ambiguous lyrics like "you're so hard . . . so deep" play off Ndegéocello's belief that sexuality is indeed fluid. The track also features beautiful backing vocals by Caron Wheeler (Ndegéocello appeared on Wheeler's *Beach of the War Goddess* in 1993 and cowrote "Land of Life" with her). Wheeler also provides vocals on Ndegéocello's remake of Funkadelic's "Better by the Pound" (on *Let's Take It to the Stage*, 1975) and "Criterion." The latter is easily the most musical of all of the *Cookie* tracks, with Ndegéocello playing the upright bass opposite drummer Oliver Gene Lake, pianist Federico Gonzalez Peña and Schwarz-Bart. The song highlights Ndegéocello's more traditional jazz sensibilities, but clocking in at only 4:27 it is both *Cookie*'s most accomplished musical statement and the most disappointing: the track will leave listeners yearning.

Cookie was the most eagerly awaited of all of Ndegéocello's recordings. Originally slated for an October 2001 release, the disc finally dropped in June 2002. Ndegéocello's label, Maverick (Madonna's AOL-Time Warner imprint), consciously worked to get her heard by the kinds of urban audiences to whom the project should be most relevant. To these ends they have enlisted the service of the blunted one (Red Man) and Tweet (the fluid one) on the Rockwilder—Missy Elliot–produced remix of the lead single, "Pocketbook." Upon its release to radio, the track was added to the playlist of more than sixty "urban" stations in a few weeks' time. But by mid-July the disc was all but forgotten. One can only hope that we won't have to wait thirty more years for bootlegs of *Cookie* to appear before this "revolutionary mixtape" and the "revolutionary soul singa" who inspired it get their deserved props.

CHAPTER TWO

Yeah I'm black and I wear braids sometimes. I'm more neo-soul than Blu
Cantrell or Faith Evans or Usher! Those motherfuckers sing R&B—they
don't sing soul music.

—Jaguar Wright[1]

my crew don't mind it thick, every woman ain't a video chick

—De La Soul[2]

A lot of folks pointed to a conspiracy. It was days after the 2002
Grammy Awards ceremony, and India.Arie, the Nubian-natural exotic,
went home trinketless, while the postmillennial mulatto, Alicia Keys,
went home with arms full of grammaphoned statuettes. Interpretations
of the disparity between Ms. Arie and Ms. Keys, whether emanating
from *The Tom Joyner Morning Show*, the students in my hip-hop course,
or the various listservs I belong to, was pretty consistent: Ms. Keys won
because she was "light-skin-ded." And thus the 2002 Grammy Awards
were thrown into the mix of a two-century-old debate about a color-
caste meritocracy within the black community. Truth be told, both
Keys's *Songs in A Minor* and Arie's *Acoustic Soul* were solid, but hardly
spectacular, debuts. Both were well positioned in the pop-music market
by influential mogul-like industry insiders. Early in his career, Motown

head Kedar Massenberg, broke the likes of D'Angelo, Erykah Badu, and Chico Debarge. It was in fact his work at Kedar Entertainment that positioned him to take over the legendary label that Berry Gordy founded more than forty years ago. Massenberg's exploits were every bit as impressive as those of Clive Davis, who early in his career helped launch the careers of Laura Nyro, Earth, Wind, and Fire, and Carlos Santana. Davis is widely regarded as one of the most influential people in the music industry, an aging white mack-daddy who could legitimately be called the "head nigga in charge," and in an awards process that is all about industry politics and who's the "bigga nigga," it was not surprising that Clive's shortie won out over Kedar's. Alicia versus India? It was a non-issue. The reality is that both Keys and Arie are postmillennial exotics—Keys playing off a "post-race" America and Arie a naturalized Afro-essentialism. True indeed, Keys is always gonna sell more records 'cause she the "light" one, but that is hardly the point.

I said as much to a rather large gathering of undergraduate students who had invited me to speak on the subject of "Alicia vs. India." The talk was supposed to be about gender and sexuality in music videos. Those who know how I usually flow were tripping at the title, but I had to remind them that had I called the talk "Gender and Sexuality in Music Videos," wouldn't nobody be up in the room, and the room was standing-room-only on this night, as folks left the step exhibition in the lobby to get their words in on Alicia and India. And folks got their digs in about Alicia being "lite" and how India.Arie helped celebrate dark-skinned women—and I was feelin' them on that point. As the father of a four-year-old "god-blessed dark brown child," India.Arie (like Erika Alexander and N'Bushe Wright and Vanessa Bell Calloway and Bethann Hardison, and Victoria Dillard, and—good lawd!—Suzanne Douglass, but I digress) ain't a bad role model for dark-brown baby-girls looking to see their images up on the screen and in the video. But dark skin or not, India.Arie rocking the same size 6/8 that Alicia be rockin'. It took this brotha Chris Johnson—the only true Gramscian intellectual that I know—to put the discussion in some perspective, as he momentarily put his walking copy of Fanon down and reminded folks that as a thirtysomethin' adult black male, he needs somebody that he "can hold on to," not some "video chick." On that point I had to concur. Now I ain't about objectifying black female sexuality regardless of size, shape, and color, but can some of them "thick" women get some love? I'm •talkin' 'bout some grown-ass women, the kind of women who know a little somethin' about size 14 and 18, ain't ashamed to be seen in Lane Bryant (anybody seen Kim Coles lately?), women that ain't never been afraid of some fried chicken, grits, and white gravy for breakfast, them women Duke Ellington described as "so pretty and fine" in his "love song" for the people, "Heritage." In a world where size-4 "video hoes" and "video chicks" abound like caramel macchiatos at Starbucks, it would be nice to see some women with a little more substance. I like 'em grown, and Angie Stone, Jill Scott, and Jaguar Wright ain't nothin' if they ain't the epitome of the "grown-ass woman."

/TONED /OUL

Brown-skinned black. Pleasingly thick, by all measure of contemporary standards, ghetto-fab or otherwise. The voice recalling Betty Wright in her prime. "Tonight is that night that you made me a W-O-M-A-N"—uh-huh, Angie, you all woman (quick shout to the white chocolate Brit soul of Lisa Stansfield). Yes, brown-skinned black, like (that honey) Gladys Knight in her prime (my bad—Gladys still in her prime). "My Sunshine has come . . ." and we take a trip back on that midnight train to Georgia—"Neither one of us . . . wants to be the first to say . . ."—and it is that Stone sista (let the congregation say "Sista Stone!"), with some Stone soul—"surray down, that stone soul . . ." (somebody say "Amen!"). Soul from that sista Angie ("when they come is the morning, Ms. Davis"), Angie Stone who makes it all relevant—connected—for real, like them painkillers during those first days of that monthly transition . . . (holla at me if you feeling her on this). Real music—soul music—for what my homie–mentor–scholarly mama Masani Alexis De Veaux calls "Newmerica." Or in other words, music for those for which "tragedy" and "misery" was a real taste in their mouths well before September 11, 2001, and who ain't got no joy 'cept for that brown-black woman, with the big-ass 'fro, sassing and shaying with some Mahogany Soul.

Angie Stone has been in the "game" since 1979, when she completed a trio of hip-hop-ettes known as Sequence. A decade later she was fronting the groundbreaking trio Vertical Hold, having already served as a saxophonist in Lenny Kravitz's touring band and as a writer for Jill Jones. By 1999, Stone was perhaps best known as the muse and "baby-mama" of D'Angelo. But Stone's obscurity would end with the release of her platinum-selling debut, *Black Diamond*, and its infectious lead single, "No More Rain (in This Cloud)." Driven by a loop of the percolating Fender Rhodes from the Gladys Knight and the Pips classic "Neither One of Us (Wants to Be the First to Say Goodbye)," "No More Rain" is arguably the most recognizable single from the quartet of post-soul divas—Stone, Erykah Badu, Jill Scott, and India.Arie. While the popularity of the original song helped introduce "No More Rain" to older audiences, the recording is less an appropriation of as a legitimate and distinct remake of "Neither One of Us," as Stone's bold "Soul Mama'" vocals soar. Unfortunately, despite the single's success Stone was not granted the overall acceptance experienced by the aforementioned divas. It was perhaps Stone's good fortune that she was one of the bargaining chips that BMG Entertainment used to entice Clive (Mr.) Davis to accept his own label after he was deposed from Arista. Backed by a mogul who has for more than thirty years defined the term *record-industry maverick*, *Mahogany Soul* is a stunning follow-up to *Black Diamond*.

With *Mahogany Soul*'s opening track, Stone appears more fully confident in her skills, as "Soul Insurance" offers a challenge to so-called neo-soul fakers. Borrowing the opening from LaBelle's "Lady Marmalade" ("Hey sista, soul sista"), Stone openly addresses her peers, accusing some of not really being "true to this." According to Stone, the song was inspired by a real-life experience of folks trying to steal her ideas. In publicity notes, Stone specifically suggests that "Soul Insurance" is "dedicated to all those folks try to do what I call 'commercial soul,'" adding that for her "it's not about watering down but using the roots of gospel and R&B."[3] The objects of Stone's scorn are not simply those who have "bit" her style but those she derisively describes as imitators and beat stealers. With her later "naming" of legends such as Marvin Gaye, Donny Hathaway, "my mellow" Curtis Mayfield, and

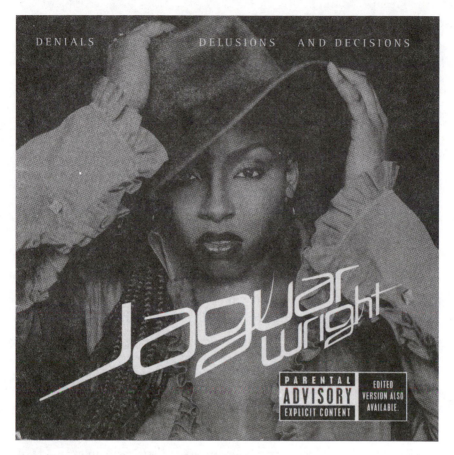

Jaguar Wright, Denials, Delusions, and Decisions

Betty Wright, who Stone describes as the "true pioneers of Soul music," "Soul Insurance" serves as a sort of neo-soul manifesto.

While Stone has been coy as to the identities of those she targets in "Soul Insurance," it is perhaps useful to note that at least two tracks on *Mahogany Soul* bear a strong resemblance to a track on Mary J. Blige's *No More Drama*. Stone and Blige recorded competing PMS songs: Blige's "PMS" and Stone's "bonus" track "Time of the Month." More telling, though, is that both Blige's "PMS" and Stone's "20 Dollars" sample one of Al Green's most underrated performances, "Simply

Beautiful." At the core of Stone's "20 Dollars" is an examination of the exploitive nature of "ghetto" dependents. The song's lyrics deal rather explicitly with the kind of trifling "round the way" behavior where folks try to make a "dollar out 15 cents" by borrowing the missing eighty-five cents from their neighbors—folks who borrow and then spend beyond their means. In the context of Stone's lyrics, "borrowing" becomes a broad metaphor for stealing, suggesting that Blige may be one of those Stone addresses when she sings, "bite somebody's shit and they gonna bite you back" on "Soul Insurance." Additionally, Stone ends the song with a reference to "Gerald." The latter reference is to the song's producer, Gerald Isaac, who, incidentally, wrote and produced Stone's "Time of the Month," making even more explicit the connections between the Blige and Stone PMS songs.

"Brotha," the lead single from *Mahogany Soul*, was "hailed" as a necessary corrective to the "brotha-hate" found in a range of popular R&B songs, including TLC's "Scrubs," Blu Cantrell's "Hit Em Up," and of course songs from those budding theoretical feminists Destiny's Child ("Bills, Bills, Bills" and "Bugaboo")—as if any of these songs have damaged black masculinity with the kind of malice with which songs like Dave Hollister's "Baby Mama Drama," or Guy/Aaron Hall's "Why You Wanna Keep Me from My Kid" have portrayed young black mothers. Produced by Raphael Saadiq (one of his best efforts), Stone's "Brotha" is one of the most wide-ranging celebrations (uncritical, I might add) of black masculinity since Tashan's brilliant "Black Man" (1989). The video for "Brotha" features still shots of notable black men (Nelson Mandela, Marvin Gaye, Jay Z, Arthur Ashe, Jim Brown, Ali, Ray Charles, and Steve Harvey among them) and cameos by Will Smith, comedian Sinbad, actor Larenz Tate (the legendary O-Dog from *Menace II Society*), and singers Luther Vandross, Calvin Richardson, and Raphael Saadiq among images of those Stone refers to as the "down for whatever" and "chillin'"-on-the-corner kind of "brotha."

The video even manages to explore black homosexuality, albeit on a lower frequency. Directed by Chris Robinson, the video could have included black men previously "marked" for "suspicion of homosexuality" (the intense speculation about Vandross's sexuality notwithstanding), but given the level of homophobia in some segments of the black community (where homosexuality is at times seen as an erosion of black masculinity) the director wisely chose not to "out" anyone notable. Instead the video features footage of actor Matthew St. Patrick in a classroom with young children. St. Patrick portrays the character of gay police officer Keith Charles on the acclaimed HBO drama *Six Feet Under*. St. Patrick's Keith Charles is one of a few black gay characters that have recently appeared on television, including those portrayed by Michael Boatman (*Spin City*) and Sonja Sohn and Michael K. Williams, who portray a lesbian cop and "homo thug," respectively, on HBO's *The Wire*. While St. Patrick's presence in Stone's "Brotha" video conveys no sense of his sexuality, the only cachet that he would have among black audiences would be as the gay cop from *Six Feet Under*. The inclusion of St. Patrick was a deft and thoughtful strategy that acknowledges the real fluidity of black masculinity, while remaining cognizant of homophobic fears among black audiences. Additionally, St. Patrick possessed a level of visibility and notoriety not afforded to real-world black queers such as the late Essex Hemphill or Bill T. Jones, who are not well-known figures among the "drunk on Viacom" audiences that Stone's video would be primarily consumed by.

However celebratory and protective Stone may be of "brothas" on the track "Brotha," in the tight spaces of relationships Stone's critique of the men in women's lives is brutally trenchant. "Pissed Off," for example, deals with the reality of women in relationships with "damaged" black men. In the context of this relationship, Stone sings, "you need an enemy," highlighting the ways that domestic violence is often predicated on the damage done to black men in the "real" world as opposed to the "home" spaces they share with the women/men they love (see Rahsann Patterson's "Treat You like Queen" for a more gender-ambivalent example). The possibility of such violence is made clear in the lyric "you got me packing, trying to get out," as the dual meaning of the word *packing* suggests that she may have to face that crossroad of violent "self-defense"—that is, sista "packing" just in case she gonna have to shoot his ass—if she doesn't "pack" her "shit" fast enough to get out of the house. In one of the song's most brilliant moments, Stone sings, "I can't allow you to live rent free in my heart." The lyric drops a nod to Gwen Guthrie's classic "Ain't Nothing Going on But the Rent" (1983), which is generally regarded as one of the most effective examples of "brotha-hate" in R&B, while making clear that the matter is not just that the "brotha" is financially bankrupt, but that, more importantly, he is emotionally and mentally bankrupt. Stone is even more explicit about such "bankruptcy" on tracks such as "Mad Issues" ("you got mad issues / and you tend to misuse") and "I Wish I Didn't Miss You." The latter song features a smart sample of the O'Jays' "Backstabber"—the 1972 single that announced that the emerging production team of Kenneth Gamble and Leon Huff were ready to take R&B to some next-level shit.

Stone's emotions with regards to the men in her life are perhaps most pronounced on the simply brilliant "More Than a Woman." The song is a duet with Calvin Richardson, whose 1999 debut, *Country Boy*, can only be described as a rebirth Muscle Shoals. The disc contains a remake of Bobby Womack's "Trust Me so Much" (Richardson sounds like Womack is his daddy!) and a host of songs that sample tracks like Al Green's version of "For the Good Times," Paul Simon's "50 Ways to Leave Your Lover," and William Bell's "I Forgot to Be Your Lover." (See Dilated Peoples's "Worst Comes to Worst" for another smart "I Forgot to Be Your Lover" sample.) With "More Than a Woman," Stone allows Richardson the kind of forum that he lacked with his first release: she can be heard cooing at the song's opening, "baby I believe it's your time . . ." The song is a passionate tribute to "black love" and the possession of "faith and patience" when things aren't going well. Throughout the song, Stone and Richardson sweetly exchange caramel-coated lyrics, as in the second verse, in which Stone sings about their marriage plans. But the passion and camaraderie (love maybe?) between the two are most powerful during the song's chorus featuring "love lyrics" that may be the best written in R&B in the past decade. The joyous, playful, and loving exchanges between the two in the song's lyrics are reminiscent of a "grown-up" version of Clint Holmes's "Playground in My Mind" ("My girl is Cindy, when we get married, we're gonna have a baby or two"). No doubt on the strength of his duet with Stone, Richardson was signed to Davis's J Records.

Mahogany Soul also includes Stone's remake of "The Makings of You." Though the song is generally associated with Gladys Knight, who recorded a version of the song with the Pips for the soundtrack to the film *Claudine* (1974), the song was originally written and recorded by the late Curtis Mayfield on his first "solo" recording, *Curtis* (1970). Stone's version of the song, which features stunning harmonies with the assistance of background vocalists Tenita Dreher, Stephanie Bolton, and Sherina Wynn, is both a tribute to one of Mayfield's most beautiful melodies and another reminder of Stone's affinity with Knight. Like Knight's and Mayfield's versions of the song, its scant two minutes can leave listeners groping for more. With Stone's attention to fine lyrics, *Mahogany Soul* is an accomplished piece of R&B music. Additionally, her smart samples allow her to legitimately add to the original versions, which, combined with a casual down-home sass, suggest that Stone may be the first of this generation of so-called neo-soul artists who really understands "Real . . . Soul Music."

PHILLY THICK

There have been stories about this. Breaking off a little live sumpthin' during *Divas Live* (2001). A barefoot, woman-loosed rendition of "He Loves Me (Lyzel in E-flat)" at the *Lady of Soul Awards*. And then the talk, often in hushed, stern tones, about that poem, where "Jilly from Philly" puts that brown-girl (sometimes caramel) grown-woman "thick-ness" in perspective. It was a live follow-up that made Badu real again (so call "Tyrone"), though her brilliant *Mama's Gun* was lost on those same audiences. Jilly had been made "real" from the start—fried pork rind, Chic-o-Stick, Philly cheese steak, pink rollers, braiding hair on the stoop (like Robert said, "c'mon and braid my hair"), dukey chain, egg and grits real. Positive noncomplicated sistuh-girl talk for bright-eyed cornrowed baby-girls in the hood . . . grown-woman talk for the beauty parlor and the kitchen, while the men, the brothas, triflin' and otherwise, be watchin' the game . . . careless whispers on long walks in the rain ("love rain down on me"). This was Jilly from the git-go, so the promise that she would be captured live—mfers still talking 'bout the Essence

Festival in 2000—was indeed a wonderful thought in an hour of mourning, terror, anger, and recovery. *Experience: Jill Scott 826+* was a clever commercial move, providing Scott with a live forum to get at that grits-and-greasy groove (look, you can't eat a Philly cheese steak without getting your hands dirty, so you gotta lick away) that *Who Is Jill Scott? Vol. One* only hinted at and the chance to get "new" material to savagely hungry audiences needing a new dose of what Angie Stone calls "Real Soul Music."

Live performances are where a litany of black performers from Mahailia Jackson to Joe Tex to Luther Vandross have made their money and staked their legacies. Artists such as Aretha Franklin (*Amazing Grace*), Earth, Wind, and Fire (*Gratitude*), and Bob Marley (*Bob Marley Live*) produced career-defining recordings in live contexts. In this regard, *Experience: Jill Scott 826+* helps counter any thought that "Jilly from Philly" is some one-dimensional "video" pinup girl for VH-1-styled positivism (not mentioning any names here). Naw, Jill Scott is about grown-woman "thangs," as in "I'll whup your ass next time if you throw some rhythm at my man again"—grown as loving hard and passionate, like sucking on that last chicken bone at the bottom of the Buffalo wing bucket. Scott speaks directly to this aspect of her music as she addresses the audience after her rendition of "Gettin' in the Way," the song that initially brought her to the attention of urban radio and video programmers. As brilliant as Scott's debut was, in the real world where videos on MTV and BET read like ethnographic surveys and forms of cross-cultural ghetto surveillance (do they really do that?), ain't nothing more appealing than a "girl fight," and the video for "Gettin' in the Way" was just that—you can almost hear the thoughts of some of the folks in the video asking, "Whose ass that big girl about to whup?" as Scott is seen walking down the way heading over to "sista girl's" house in the video.

On the live disc, Scott recalls promotional radio appearances where listeners would call in and ask why she would make a song about fighting "anotha sista." Parodying one listener's high-pitched shrill of a comment that "Jill Scott's supposed to be such a positive person," Scott responds, "First off, I never said that. We have this thinking that soon as we see somebody with a natural they automatically positive . . . some days I am, some days I'm not." Scott reminds audiences that the "song ain't even about whupping ass, it's not even about tearing a weave off for that matter . . . what the song's always been about is *principle*," adding that "sometimes in life for principle, you gonna have to kick some ass." This side of Scott, which is often missing in "People's 50 Most Beautiful" photo ops and sanitized bourgeois neo-soul documentaries, plays a starring role on the "live" disc that was recorded in August 2001 at the D.A.R. Constitution Hall (that would be Daughters of the American Revolution, right? Holla back, Marian Anderson) in Washington, D.C. Backed by her band Fatback Taffy (like chewing on bacon-flavored Now-and-Laters, I guess), Scott gives sassy, confident live spins to nine of seventeen of the *Who Is Jill Scott?* tracks, including a nine-minute version of "He Loves Me (Lyzel in E-flat)"and an original playful ditty called "Fatback Taffy."

Scott gives early indication of her desires to take her flow somewhere else on the opening track, "A Long Walk (Groove)." If the original studio version was a breezy swing groove –like eating passion fruit and listening to the Roots—the live version backed by Fatback Taffy's dirty-ass funky (damn, I feel sticky) groove is more like a long slow drag than a long walk. (Scott gives the song an even stickier slow drag groove on the Red Star Sounds compilation.) For the live version of "Love Rain," which was easily the "nastiest" track on her studio debut ("like bowels after collard greens"), Scott lays claim to the remixed version of the song (a hidden track), which originally featured Mos Def. Where the original song is a lament about falling too deeply, too quickly, too emphatically in infatuation, the live version, with scat-jazz flourishes, is transformed into a "suite" of recovery and resistance. The phrase "you broke me but I'm healing," which Scott alternately chants, shouts, and defiantly coos, becomes the new thematic basis for the song.

Scott gives a nod to her D.C. crowd with a rendition of the slap-happy "It's Love," which borrows from the legendary D.C.-based go-go traditions of Trouble Funk, Chuck Brown and the Soul Searchers ("gimmie the bridge now, gimmie the bridge now, now") and EU, who marked go-go's commercial breakthrough with "Da Butt," which was featured in

Spike Lee's *School Daze*. Whereas the studio version of the track would make Chuck Brown proud, the live version fails to impress the D.C. audience despite Scott's energetic efforts. But it is the plaintive slow grooves in which the D.C. audience really connects with Scott. The introduction to "Do You Remember" is greeted by audience members singing Scott's "ooh, ooh, ooh, ooh" even before she can. Given a dark "sippi' delta" drag, the live version is all about Scott's rather formidable phrasing. Audience members can barely contain themselves as Scott breaks into the opening lines, "Oooooh Honeeeeey, Whyyyyy you got to be so mean." Taking her time through the first stanza, Scott simply oozes phrasing borrowed from Dinah and Billie (I shouldn't have to put the last names in here, right?), relishing in her own signature voice by the time she sings "daughter of the Diaspora," reinforcing her link to the tradition of "sanger's sangers." The crowd is with her every step of the way, often finishing her lyrics when she slyly holds back—"Converse I think. . . ." By the time Dave Lidell is plunging his 'bone, Scott engages the crowd in a traditional call and response ("sistas in the house, it's time for ya'll to open your big mouths and sing"). Wasn't no religion happening, but it was fo' sho' church up in there.

Such powerful evidence of the community of live performance (see Cannonball's live "Mercy, Mercy, Mercy," Donny Hathaway's "Young, Gifted, and Black," and Sister Ree's *Amazing Grace* for some of the most powerful examples of this within the tradition), is also on display on Scott's version of "The Way." At times the audience, singing in unison, can be heard above Scott's own voice, including a requisite scream during the wonderful moment when Scott sings "grits" like it's the sexiest word in the language. Scott graciously shares aural space not only with the crowd, but with fellow Hidden Beach artist, saxophonist Mike Phillips. Scott and Phillips's musical banter is reminiscent of the wonderful live recording of Earth, Wind, and Fire's "Reasons," where Phillip Bailey's stirring falsetto matches wits with the late saxophonist Larry Myricks.

But if disc one is a living memory stroll thru "revolution Jilly," the second disc doesn't give a hint at anything that appeared on *Who Is Jill Scott?* Again, drawing largely on the talents of the Touch of Jazz production collective (4Hero contributes one song), Vidal Davis (who laced Jilly tracks like "Love Rain" and "Getting' in the Way"), and "new-comers" Darren Henson and Ivan Barias, gives Scott a harder and more cerebral edge that in few a cases, most notably "High Post Brotha," will actually make Scott more accessible to the ever influential "urban" audiences that *Who Is Jill Scott?* worked hard, if incidentally, to distance itself from.

Tracks like "Gimme" and "Be Ready" capture best the sensibilities of the "+" side of *Experience: Jill Scott*. Sampling Brass Construction's "Changing," the Ivan Barias–produced "Gimme" is a high-octane (Jill aplenty!) romp as she sings, "if you want it in the morning, just call my name." Scott gets playful at one point in the second verse, slowing down the song's insistent pace by singing, "if you want me to super freak you, s-l-o-w m-y r-o-l-l a-n-d t-e-a-c-h y-a." With the Ted Thomas–produced "Be Ready," Scott gives a nod to the stylings of Blu Cantrell's "Hit Em up Style" and Lina's *Stranger on Earth*, which both try to give 1940s- and '50s-styled scatting a contemporary (urban, that is) update. Whereas as Cantrell style often misses the point and Lina struggles to find the right balance (excepting the single "It's Alright," which has the aesthetic down), Scott's "Be Ready" reads like a twentieth-century survey of black popular music with nods to drill and step teams (it's all in the rhythm), Ella Fitzgerald, Josephine Baker, the atomic-era disco of Dr. Buzzard's Original Savannah Band ("Tommy Motolla, lives down the road . . ." unless of course Michael Jackson gets to him first), and those ghastly, ghostly backup vocals of early Funkadelic ("Can You Get to That?").

In his pimp-Gramscian mode, hip-hop artist Common collaborates with Scott on the dark, sinister, and cautionary "High Post Brotha"—about the kind of "superstar" who got the "cars and ice." Both Common's and Scott's vocals are given that tinny AM-radio texture, which metaphorically functions as that voice in the ghetto girl's ear. The song features a filtered sample of 24–Carat Black's obscure "crate digger's" special "In the Ghetto," which was earlier sampled by Eric B. and Rakim (Allah) on their brilliant "The Ghetto." The 4Hero-produced "Gotta Get up (Another Day)" breezily recalls the slice-of-life themes of "A Long Walk" and "The Way." The song is a nod to the "running in place" realities of working-class and lower-middle-class life, in which folks simply work to pay bills ("working for nothing") but still have to find meaning in their lives. Scott is joined by (presumably) Eric Roberson on "One Time" (Roberson is not given credit as the co-lead, but is listed as the cowriter and backup vocalist). Matching the playful romance of Angie Stone and Calvin Richardson's "More Than My Way" (both are currently on the mix tape), "One Time" is like that first s-w-e-e-t taste of watermelon on that first hot-sticky day in July—a mouthful of sweetness, pleasure, and satisfaction. The song brilliantly taps into the notions of bourgeois romance and ghetto love that come together and make joints like Musiq Soulchild's "Girl Next Door" so attractive to a wide range of "urban" audiences. While "One Time" is as pleasing a tune as any that Scott has recorded, ultimately the songs that make Scott's reputation on the disc are those in which she allows herself to push beyond the allowable boundaries and perceptions of her music and talents.

Such was the case in 2001 when Scott acquiesced to the Grammy Awards' regular desire to bring disparate artists together for a performance, and appeared with Moby and the performance artists Blue Man Group. I have vivid memories of Herbie Hancock, Stevie Wonder, Thomas Dolby, and Howard Johnson coming together in such a genre-obliterating performance nearly twenty years ago. While their surreal performance of Moby's "Natural Blues" was overshadowed by the over-hyped Elton John and Eminem "duet," the performance established Scott's willingness and ability to transcend the industry-imposed R&B/neo-soul box. It is in this spirit that Scott records "Sweet Justice." Scott draws on her upper register, recalling the artistry of the late "song-bird" Minnie Riperton and Deniece Williams. In the past, Scott has only used her high register—on "I Think It's Better" and "Said Enough" (*Who Is Jill Scott?*), and her stirring duet with Ronald Isley on the Isley's *Eternal.* Like "Said Enough," Scott and Vidal Davis cowrote "Sweet Justice," which samples Manheim Steamroller's "The Sky," creating a jagged, tinny, and "cold" landscape that Scott, as she does in her performance with Moby and them blue men, manages to humanize in the process, creating a song of struggle and redemption. Scott's warbled lyric "fight, fight, fight, never surrender" filters through the ear like some soul-digitized battle hymn.

While the lyrics to "Sweet Justice" resist concrete interpretations, Scott makes clear her intentions on the spoken-word piece "The Thickness," which was recorded live at the Tower, in Philadelphia. Harking back to her days on the spoken-word circuit in spaces like the October Gallery in Philly, which was prominently featured in the video for Scott's "The Way." I've made the point elsewhere that one of the significant features of Scott's commercial success has been her ability to privilege distinct "brown-girl" spaces within the music industry—would India.Arie's "Video" have hit as it did without Jilly's success the year before?—and to create a space for "big girls" to be seen as meaningful and beautiful to audiences as the more familiar tight, bright brown bodies that usually adorn "urban" music videos.[4] With "The Thickness," Scott address these dynamics in powerful and passionate ways that make the performance one of her most important.

Scott carefully prepares her audience for the "realness" of her piece, by telling them that "this is for grown folks" as she begins her narrative about a Similac-blessed honey (shout out to Black Sheep) whose "big ole legs" and "big ole tits" contradict her youth—baby-girl is all of fourteen years old. Scott informs the audience that, baby-girl so big that bruhs ain't even trying to "reach her mind." Scott's piece speaks to the ways that black female physicality is often reduced to a "thing" to be named and tamed, a process that objectifies black women and their sexualities. Within "ghetto publics" like those described in Scott's poem, it is black masculine privilege (and the black men who embrace it) that has the power to "name" black women. Along with the naming of these "bodies" comes the silencing of their voices, as Scott observes that these men like "her quiet and eager" and "sweet and meager," often telling baby-girl to "shhh," in response to her queries about their other women. Scott suggests that the young girl's inability to challenge and counter her sexual objectification is the natural product of a generation of young black girls being "degraded, exploited" and not "celebrated." Scott finds fault with music videos (on a Viacom channel near you!) in which young

brown and black girls often see "Big ole booty" that has little if anything
to do with the song. In Scott's view, a generation of Similac-blessed
beauties have accepted these images as the definition of beauty.

Taking on the role of the ghetto griot (itself a role often assigned
to black men), Scott moans, "Oh, Lord, Oh Lord, Oh Lord," asking the
"Lord" to help baby-girl understand the "magnificence" that was created in her. Later she asks that the "Lord" lift baby-girl, "lift her, lift her
. . . Let her be elevated." The lyric at once references the "lifting as we
climb" theme that was the foundation of the black women's club movement of the late nineteenth and early twentieth centuries and the social
pedestal where white feminine beauty standards are projected as the
most desired. At the end of the performance, Scott poignantly tells the
crowd that young folks such as the one in "The Thickness" are "still
children, although they're built like women. They're still boys although
they act like men." She puts the onus to "save" these children on the
"community," insisting to the audience that "if we do not stop to tell
them, snatch them up like they used to do, when we would act up down
the block. If we don't keep those traditions alive, it is our fault." Like
the stunning Chris Robinson–directed video for Alicia Keys's "A
Woman's Worth," Scott's "The Thickness" aims to counter the sexist,
misogynistic, and racist narratives about black women that often go
unchallenged within various black publics, including entities such as
BET that willingly trade in the distortion of black feminine identity
with programs like *Cita's World*, she the noted cyberhoochie host, and
Oh Drama, a "ghetto-fab" talk show hosted by Kim Whitley and veteran actress Vanessa Bell Calloway (who is still the beautiful brown
child that she was for more than twenty years as a regular on *All My
Children*).

With *Experience: Jill Scott 826+*, Scott presents a fuller sense of her
artistry and her passions. In an industry that is seemingly fixated on
youth and some of youth culture's attendant banalities—as if banging
grooves from Pink or Gwen Stefani and No Doubt are really all that
more serious than being a "slave" to Britney—Scott steps up with some
"grown-woman" music that is sure to further solidify her position as one
of the most accomplished purveyors of "Real Soul Music."

ɾHE ɾAID A BAD WORD

As always there's buzz, and since the debut of the Okayplayer.com site in early 2000 everything remotely connected to the site and its flagship artists the Roots generates its own self-contained promotional campaign. The critical success of Common's *Like Water for Chocolate* (2000) and the debuts of both Jill Scott and Bilal are the best testaments to the site's influence. And such was the case with *Denials, Delusions, and Decisions*, the oft-delayed debut by Jaguar Wright. But Wright acquired buzz in ways never expected, due to a "controversial" collaboration with Jay Z for MTV's long-running *Unplugged* series. For his *Unplugged* performance, Jay Z was backed by the Roots, who are generally acknowledged as the most accomplished *musicians* in hip-hop, and featured Wright singing backing vocals. Jay Z performs the opening verses of "Heart of the City (Ain't No Love)" much the same way it appears on his *Blueprint* (2001) disc—the song was a remake of Bobby "Blue" Bland's classic "Ain't No Love in the City" (1974)—but Wright's deep vocals, particularly on the second chorus, take the song to another level. As she sings the chorus, Jay Z can be heard in the background, "Okay ma, I feel ya," suggesting that he was intent on matching her energy as he instructs the band to "take it to church," reproducing the breakdown section that appears on the studio version. It is not until the improvised section after the third chorus that Jay Z's suggestion is fully realized as the Roots strip down to a go-go beat and Jay Z and Wright engage in a classic call-and-response exchange. It was a "church" moment that is rarely exhibited in hip-hop culture (save efforts by Kirk Franklin or Hezekiah Walker) and clearly not usually associated with a rapper with Jay Z's notoriety. That moment helped transform the listening studio into the "church of Hova" and Jaguar into the High Priestess of Ghetto Funk. Even Mary J. Blige, the so-called Queen of Hip-hop Soul, had to up her game when she joined Jay on stage for a rendition of their classic "Can't Knock the Hustle."

While Jay Z, Nas, and The Roots were exchanging crossfire—instigated by New York's HOT 97 (*Vibe* magazine style)—over whether Nas or Jay Z was the legitimate heir to the Notorious B.I.G.'s mythical throne and whether or not The Roots looked like "porch monkeys" (per Nas's commentary on their cameo appearance in Spike Lee's *Bamboozled* Jaguar Wright took the opportunity to come up in the world. The day after the performance debuted on MTV 2, everybody was asking, Who was that "chick" with Jigga? The twenty-four-year-old Wright has been in the game for about a decade; she'd gotten an early start as an MC in the group Philly Blunts. But her real opportunity came in 1999 at a Black Lily performance (a browned-skinned and Philly-Blunted Lillith Fair) where she was the opening act for a set that included the Jazzy Fatnastees, Res, and Jill Scott, all backed by the Roots. Months later, Wright was writing and singing hooks for the Roots, including the hook to "What Ya Want" (a song initially intended for Blige), the lead single from the soundtrack for *The Best Man*. When Wright joined the Roots for a performance of the song on Chris Rock's show in late 1999, it was clear that she was gonna be a "fo' real" deal.

With *Denials, Delusions, and Decisions*, Wright delivered a "fo' real" joint with a style liberally informed by "fo' real" soul (mack) divas like Millie Jackson, Betty Wright, Etta James, and Patti LaBelle. Wright's style is like one of them defiant, smack-talking twelve-year-old shorties whose hell-raising in the playground changes the world and challenges perspectives in the real time of the grown world, and if Jaguar Wright is anything, she is a grown woman. As she notes in the *City Paper* piece quoted in the epigraph, "I make cussin' sound natural. I'm not vulgar. I make grown-folks music; I don't make music for kids. It's grown language, talking 'bout grown shit for grown people."[5] Wright is, in fact, pictured inside the CD booklet wearing open-toe heels, a full-length suede coat, and "I will pimp-slap your ass" cornrows, looking like what could only be described as "Lady Shaft" (or "Lady Priest" for the real blaxploitation playas).

It is this kind of energy that informs the two tracks that make up the artistic soil of *Denials, Delusions, and Decisions*. "Same Sh*t Different Day" (parts 1 and 2) recall the brilliantly surreal and mischievous themes of D'Angelo's "Shit, Damn, Motherfucker" (*Brown Sugar*) or Common's "A Film Called Pimp." "Same Shit Different Day" (part 1), coproduced by the Soulquarian's maestro keyboardist James Poyser, drops a melodic

nod to old-school Philly "blue eyes" Hall and Oates and their unforgettable "Sarah Smile." The title is a reference to one of those tried-and-
true ghetto folkisms—don't matter the day, shit's still the same. In this
context Wright is fretting about the love trio that she wants no part of,
adding that she feels "divorce" on her anniversary. It's still the same
"shit" on part 2, but quite a different day as Wright gets her rapid flow
all up in the other woman's ass, asking why she has to be the understanding kind when "these bitches know they got that shit coming,"
adding that she's "fuckin' up this bitch tonight." Like Jill Scott's spoken
introduction to "Getting in the Way" on her live disc, Wright counters
the general perception that neo-soul is inherently peaceful and "positive." As the background vocalists insist that Wright has to think about
what other folks are gonna say, Wright defiantly asserts that she "ain't
takin' this shit no more." However defiant Wright is in either version of
the song, she is forced to accept the feeling that her life "ain't shit" without her man.

The themes of infidelity and the "other woman" also frame the brilliant "What If," which was one of the songs that Wright performed during her first appearance at Black Lily in 1999. Produced by Scott Storch,
"What If" is a smoothed-out diatribe that places the blame for her condition firmly on her wandering man: she laments that she's got all the
"right questions" and all the "sadness," while homie keeps givin' all the
"wrong answers." Trying to bring some meaning to her situation, she
admits that she can't blame her situation on "love" or her man and not
even that "other bitch" (who "can't be that smart"). Ultimately she
admits that bruh ain't the "nigga she fell in love with." Though Wright
is only twenty-four, her fixation on infidelity (other tracks like "2 Too
Many," "I Don't Know," and "I Can't Wait" also deal explicitly with the
theme) taps into broader concerns for a generation of "grown women."
Wright's anxieties reflect those among older black women, who are in
competition not just with "mythical" other women, but with real-time
images of the light and tight black and brown women who adorn music
videos and ghetto-fab comedy series and films.

Actresses such as Angela Bassett, Vanessa Williams, Ella Joyce
(*Roc*), Arnetia Walker (*Nurses*), Debbie Morgan (*All My Children*),

Sheryl Lee Ralph (*Moesha*), Victoria Dillard (*Spin City*), Suzanne Douglass (*The Parenthood*), and Vanessa Bell Calloway, as well as vocalists such as Regina Belle, Miki Howard, Chante Moore, and Faith Evans, have been hard pressed to "compete" in the markets of popular consumption without trading on some of the style and inclinations of young girls that in some cases are half their age. The recent examples of vocalists Tamia, Moore, and Evans playing to the Ja Rule and Nelly crowds are but tragic examples of this. Not yet thirty years of age, the trio is now competing with Ashanti (I'll reserve comment for another time) and the 3LWs of the world. The fact that the music of brilliant and accomplished vocalist like Belle, Howard, and Moore can't get played on "MTV Radio" (not a real entity, but an acknowledgment of the MTV-ing of commercial radio) is another disheartening example. In this regard, Angie Stone, Jill Scott, and Jaguar Wright have managed to find and maintain niches within popular music that allow them to relish in their full femininity, as full-bodied, grown-ass women.

CHAPTER THREE

● ●

DIGGIN' THE SCENE
(WITH THE GANGSTA LEAN)

One way to comprehend Miles is to view him not simply as an isolated mad genius but also a product of a distinctive aspect of African-American culture—what we might call the pimp aesthetic. . . . I'm not suggesting that he needed to be a real pimp to embrace the aesthetic. Rather, he was the product of a masculine culture that aspired to be like a pimp, that embraced the cool performative styles of the players (pronounced "playa"), the "macks," the hustlers, who not only circulated in the jazz world but whose walk and talk also drew from the well of black music.

—Robin D. G. Kelley[1]

As a matter of fact I'm the dopest nigga you ever wanted to fuck with.

—Bilal

The title of Bilal Sayeed Oliver's stunning debut, *1st Born Second*, is derived from the concept that he was the "first born prodigal son of the second generation of contemporary soul stirrers."[2] We all know the usual suspects: Badu, D'Angelo, L-Boogie (Lauryn Hill), Jilly from Philly, Mos Def, Ndegéocello, Maxwell, and the original new-schooler Lenny "How come black radio don't support me?" Kravitz. But Bilal could be the second coming of the playa, playa, pimp—pimping like Marvin (the original Soul O.G.), big pimping like Rev. Al (before that grit incident), "diamond in the back, sunroof top, digging the scene with the gangsta lean" pimping like Miles Dewey. Bilal, the playa, playa, pimp for the new millennium. By pimping, I mean the ability to "pimp" from the deepness of a black masculinity that is alternately virile, vibrant, visceral, viscous, and vicarious. Like that pimp-scholar Too Short reminded us some time ago, "Pimpin' ain't easy."

In his "controversial" *New York Times* piece on Miles Davis, Robin D. G. Kelley writes that "Pimps in African-American culture and folk-lore are more than violent exploiters of women. They are masters of style, from the language and the stroll to the clothes and the wheels," adding that pimps have also been recognized for their "storytelling abil-ity." Bilal claims as much with his intro boast, that he is like "warm lotion on your back." There is no doubt that the image of Miles Davis flowing lovely in those Hickey Freeman suits became a template for 1950s cool and that Marvin Gaye remains the quintessential Soul Mack ("you know how it is Mack come in the club") for almost two genera-tions of vocalists ranging from Spandau Ballet ("listening to Marvin . . . all night long") to Rafael Saadiq. With *1st Born Second*, Bilal aims to draw upon the richness of black masculine expression, in the process creating one of the most provocative and wide-ranging expressions of black masculinity in popular music since Prince's 1982 classic *Controversy*.

Ever since Bilal "dry humped" the stage at BAM (the Brooklyn Academy of Music) at a 1999 tribute to Prince, references to his Prince-like qualities have flourished. But these references do not do justice to an artist whose music and style draws upon a wide range of artists including Bob Marley, Marvin Gaye, the enigmatic Sly Stone, Pete Rock and CL Smooth ("When they reminisce over you!"), King Pleasure, Langston Hughes, pre-pop Kool and the Gang, Dr. Dre, Miles Davis, and of course Prince. At so many points during *1st Born Second* Bilal sounds like a contortionist trying to squeeze every ounce of Philly (Blunt) soul out of his scrawny little body, a body that contradicts the immensity of Bilal's talent and heart. As one of my boys put it when he first glimpsed Bilal's "Soul Sista" video, he thought that Musiq Soulchild had been in the gym and lost some weight. No offense to Bilal's Philly soul brother, but the comparisons end, empathically, there. So do those that align Bilal with D'Angelo. Comparisons of Bilal to D'Angelo are natural, given the artists' proximity to Ahmir "?uestlove" Thompson's Soulquarian universe. Like D'Angelo's *Voodoo*, *1st Born Second* may have been the most anticipated and oft-delayed release in recent R&B history. At one point the online vendor CDNOW jokingly listed the release date of *1st Born Second* as the year 2025.

Jokie-jokes aside, Bilal's debut was challenged by consumer apathy, not in the sense that folks weren't interested in the project's lead singles, "Soul Sista" and "Love It," but in the sense that audiences for the most part were unable or, more likely, unwilling to distinguish Bilal from the likes of Musiq, D'Angelo, and others. As Bilal suggested in an interview with Jim Farber, "people don't have a lot of common sense when it comes to music. They don't know the history and they don't listen."[3] While Bilal's comments may suggest some derision and condescension toward the audience that was ostensibly supposed to help him achieve that "platinum, baby" level he desired, they are also the comments of an artist who put a great deal of himself into his art and was forced to watch the release of that art delayed because of his label's sensitivity to consumer laziness. Case in point: *1st Born Second* was pushed back from a late June 2001 release to accommodate the promotion of the B-side of "Love It," the Dr. Dre–produced "Fast Lane." It was the mark of Dre that pushed Bilal beyond the neo-soul promised land and (back) onto the plantation of urban radio. A new version of the song was remixed featuring a cameo by Jadakiss.

In 1998, Bilal was attending the Mannes Conservatory of Music in New York City and singing jazz once a week at the Sidewalk Café, where Aaron Combs of the Spin Doctors was the house drummer. A tape of tracks that Bilal recorded at Combs's home studio was passed on to Ali Shaheed Muhammad (A Tribe Called Quest), with copies eventually touching the hands of Q-Tip (then of A Tribe Called Quest), ?uestlove, and Common. A year later, Bilal was singing backup for D'Angelo, and after he made Prince's "International Lover" a Bilal song at the BAM tribute, the vocalist was signed to Moyamusic, an imprint of Jimmy Iovine's Interscope label. The imprint label was founded by

Damu and Fa Mtume, who are the male progeny of the musician and trenchant social critic James Mtume, who fronted the seminal 1980s R&B group Mtume and was a member of the Miles Davis Band in the mid-1970s.

Most audiences were first made aware of Bilal courtesy of his breathtaking backing vocals on Common's *Like Water for Chocolate*, most notably on "Funky for You," where he and Jill Scott tag an two-minute old-school soul shout at the close of the track. Later in the spring of 2000, an early version of "Soul Sista" appeared on the soundtrack of the Gina Prince-Bythewood film *Love and Basketball*. Cowritten with daddy Mtume, who also orchestrated KC Hailey's remake of Bobby Womack's "If You Think You're Lonely Now" a few years ago, and produced by Rafael Saadiq, "Soul Sista" is a slow gospel march that would have caught the attention of listeners in any era, if only because Bilal's layered falsettos recall the spasmic energy of Joe Cocker at Woodstock.

A more finished version of the song with additional backing vocals was released with a provocative black-and-white video in the fall of 2000. In an industry that increasingly finds value in accessibility, "Soul Sista" took a backseat to Musiq's quaint "Just Friends (Sunny)". While Musiq's debut, *Aijuswanaseing*, was lauded as the rebirth of Philly soul, Bilal awaited the release of a second single. It was the second single, "Love It," that heightened anticipation for *1st Born Second*, with a video that ironically borrowed some flavor from Musiq's "Sunny." The track was produced by Mike City, who has produced a string of quality releases with Carl Thomas ("I Wish"), Dave Hollister ("One Woman Man"), and of course the round-tha-way baby-girl, Sunshine Anderson. "Love It" again highlights Bilal's striking falsetto, especially in the song's chorus.

According to critic Raquel Cepeda, the ever so masculine Sisqo ("Thong, th, th, thong, thong") purportedly claimed that Bilal sounded "like a woman" on the track. Someone should sit the masculine one down with a stack of vocals by Eddie Kendricks, Phillip Bailey (he of the three elements, Earth, Wind, and Fire), Ted Mills (Blue Magic), and of course (Little) Jimmy Scott. Whereas "falsetto" vocalists have been perceived as being "soft"—think of Tico Wells's "Choir Boy" in the

Robert Townsend film *The Five Heartbeats*, in reality the falsetto voice is the product of hypermasculine performance, be it derived from the regular Reverend Mack-Daddy infomercial circuit—inspired no doubt by the original "playa-revs" like Ike, Father Devine, and "sweet" Daddy Grace—or the brothers flexing for real in HBO's *Pimps Up, Hoes Down*. Like Russell Simmons puts it in his autobiography, *Life and Def: Sex, Drugs, Money, and God*, "People don't understand this now but the high-pitched falsetto, crying singers were the most ghetto. . . . For all their talk of love there was something very pimp-like, manipulative and fly about that sound."[4]

In other words, you got to be mackin' fo' real if you gonna step to some honey in one of them high-pitched voices that send the roaches scurrying when the lights come on. Again recalling the pimpery that my man R. Kelley (that's Robin, not Robert) associated with the music of "Dewey," the falsetto voice was part of an elaborate black oral form known as toasting. According to Kelley, "Toasts, like sermons, are judged by delivery, phrasing, pacing and a sense of dynamics, which often includes the use of falsetto voice, whispering and artfully placed pauses to elicit 'call and response' with the audience."[5] And for sure there is much "big pimpin'" taking place on Sunday mornings in pulpits where the "flow" is as important as the message. Think of Arsenio Hall's performance as Reverend Brown in *Coming to America*. There are Negrotarians and members of the neo-soul bourgeoisie that take offense to such performative antics. Nevertheless, the cream—cash and lubricant—flows, as Bilal reminds us throughout *1st Born Second*. And it is about flow, the kinds of social flow that lead to social and cultural capital, the kind of flow that allows Jay Z into various social arenas as "Hova," Jigga, and Shawn Carter (it's big pimpin', baby!). Flow like Eddie Cain, Jr.'s (Michael Wright) quip (straight gangsta style) to a rival pretty boy, "How does it feel to be me?"—a line that remains the most memorable from the Five Heartbeats. Thus, it is not surprising that the two cuts in which Bilal's pimp flow (falsetto) is most prominent are the Dr. Dre–produced "Fast Lane" and the project's opening track, "For You."

Written by Bilal, "For You" is like a dreamy stuttered pimp stroll through south Philly, replete with the kind of sinister bass (bassoon) lines that Marcus Miller used so effectively on Miles Davis's *Tutu* and later on the soundtrack for the film *Siesta*. Midway through the second verse, Bilal disarms listeners with a double-speed falsetto, racing through the lyrics with an urgency that implies the passion with which he repudiates the pimp life on the real (this might sound like some "pimp shit" but it ain't), while wholly recognizing its power—game recognizing game. In the song's bridge, Bilal literally pleads—more preacher than pimp—for honey to "come into the light" because she could be a "star," suggesting that as a lover, he would dote on his boo like a pimp dotes on his "hoes." On "Fast Lane," which was written with the Mtume brothers and Mike City, Bilal examines the underside of the pimp life, however "so fresh and so clean" it may be. In what is a regular occurrence throughout *1st Born Second*, Bilal's vocals literally explode and splatter across Dre's soundscape, particularly on the track's chorus, where he sings of living in "fast lanes" where folks "get caught up" and "shot up." With a minor nod to P-Funk—later a straight-up jack on the Dre–produced track "Sally"—"Fast Lane" is one of the most effective thematic tributes to Curtis Mayfield's cautionary "Freddie's Dead," which was first released nearly thirty years ago and has yet to lose any of its power.

Like his narrative interpolation of Curtis Mayfield, Bilal throws a nod or two to some of his musical influences throughout *1st Born Second*. As he lamented to Jim Farber, "There's not many skilled musicians in the field anymore," adding that "Rock bands know how to play but not R&B [acts]. I want to see black bands again—like Earth, Wind, and Fire."[6] He celebrates a broad tradition of those bands throughout *1st Born Second*. On "Reminisce," which was produced by J-dilla (that Detroit "nigga" Jay Dee, whose *Welcome to Detroit* is some next-level hip-hop production) and features Mos Def and Common, Bilal reflows Pete Rock and CL Smooth's "T.R.O.Y. (They Reminisce over You)." Common's first foray into writing love songs, "Reminisce" is an infectious slice of ghetto love recalled—a time of "hallways and sliding doors" (ain't nothin' like elevator lovin'). Bilal throws some "luv" toward Robert Nesta Marley and the original "ghetto" poet Langston Hughes on "Home," which is one of two tracks that was wholly written and produced by Bilal himself. Recalling Marley's "One Love" and "One Drop,"

Al Green, Let's Stay Together

Bilal's own sluggish production is rescued by his exquisite vocals. Bilal even manages to replicate the way Marley often playfully self-answered questions with a raspy growl ("Will I see heaven again? I don't even know, I don't even know . . ."). The brilliance of the song's lyrics, which animate a mythical African homeland with "streets . . . paved with gold," lies in Bilal's subtle revision of Langston Hughes's signature poem "The Negro Speaks of Rivers." Whereas Hughes wrote that his "soul runs deep like rivers," Bilal sings, "It's all too deep my soul," at once referencing Hughes's legendary tome and acknowledging that such a vision remains just that for the generation of "first born seconds."[7]

As rivers go, listeners are baptized in the "church of Bilal" on the track "Slyde," a clever spin on what the church folks call "backslidin'," which begins with a reference to Kool and the Gang's "Jungle Boogie" and intimates the music of Sly Stone ("Everyday People"). Recalling Prince's struggles with naming his emotions on the track "Adore" ("love is too weak to describe how much I adore you"), itself a spin on Stevie Wonder's "As" ("Loving you / Until the day that you are me and I am you / Now ain't that lovin' you?"), Bilal can ultimately only admit to his boo that he is "just so fuckin' in love" with her and that he can't "verberate that shit into words." Though Bilal's purported attempt to remake "Adore" never materialized, "Slyde" allows Bilal to comment on a musical trajectory that begins with Sly Stone, passes through Stevie Wonder, Bootsy Collins ("Bootzilla, baby"), the pre–JT Taylorized Kool and the Gang, and Prince.

Some of the most original tracks of *1st Born Second* are those that feature Bilal's classically trained jazz vocal sensibilities. As Bilal reflected in an interview with *USA Today*, "Most things I do are either instrumental or I'm thinking of some jazz cats."[8] On "All That I Am (Something for the People)," cowritten with Common, Bilal's vocals are equal parts Eddie Jefferson ("Filthy McNasty"), King Pleasure ("Moody's Mood for Love"), the Pharcyde ("she keeps on passing me by"), and Bilal himself, mixed in with name drops of ghetto realists Donald Goines and Iceberg Slim. Again, Bilal's focus on the "pimp life" and the violence and misogyny inherent in it—Goines and Slim were largely responsible for making the pimp life "nationally known, and internationally respected" in the early 1970s—is not simply a celebration of that life, but given his jazz training is an acknowledgment of the ways that hustling is deeply connected to the improvisatory spirit found in many jazz performances. Though "Love Poems" is solidly within the tradition of Philly's current spoken-word movement, with a hint of the Earth, Wind, and Fire–Ramsey Lewis collaboration "Sun Goddess," the song is taken to another level with Bilal's Ornette Coleman–ish scatting behind the poetry of Keisha Whatley, in an uncredited performance.

Bilal's jazz skills are particularly evident on the tracks "When Will You Call" and the mind-bending "Sometimes," which both allow Bilal to examine improvisation within the context of the breezy jarring uncertainties that often accompany romantic relationships. Written by Bilal, "When Will You Call" begins with a cheesy blues intro in which Bilal laments that his woman hasn't called him in three days. What begins as a camp blues number is shortly transformed into a spacious, mature jazz vocal. "When Will You Call" recalls the "Days of Wine and Roses"–style pop-jazz of the 1960s done by artists such as Johnny Hartman, Nancy Wilson, and Barbra Streisand, but with a harder edge as he sings, on the song's bridge, she just packed her "shit and left." By the song's end—like Luther Vandross, Bilal is a finisher—what had been an in-joke about the "miserable blues" has become a vibrant performance of recovery and resistance ("gotta start a new life without you").

While Jay Dee's production (for the SoulQuarians) on "Reminisce" is firmly within the best traditions of hip-hop production, fellow SoulQuarian James Poyser, buoyed by "?uestlove"'s stuttering stop-and-start rhythms, imbues "Sometimes" with a fertile musical landscape to fully realize Bilal's stream-of-consciousness lyrics. The track begins with an introduction reminiscent of Mos Def's brilliant "Umi Says," abruptly shifting gears as Bilal addresses his personal demons and contradictions, wishing that he was "drug-free" and that he could know "truth without searching" as he complains about the one-sided nature of his relationship. Bilal's quest for life-affirming answers is derailed by his "selfish" girlfriend. In a darkly comical moment, Bilal grudgingly admits that she makes him wish he did have "home training," later lamenting that it hurts him when he thinks of knocking her on her "ass" and visualizes putting a "foot up" her ass. As Bilal purges himself of his romantic frustration, he begins to refocus on larger issues like hoping to "live to see 25" or that he could "be like Moses" and move his peeps out of the "hood" in search of a "better life." The shifting focus of the "political" and the "personal" in the song collapses into a gospel-driven frenzy that urgently resists the kind of "holy ghost" climax that finds the "converted" possessed by the spirits. It is at this point that the listener understands that Bilal sees his dysfunctional relationship as an impediment to his spiritual goals as he exhorts himself to move at his "own pace," listen to his "own mind," and do his "own thing." Bilal tells his lover that he was brutally honest with her (earlier in the song), because he "loves" her and he wants to "grow" with her, but she wants to "run in the other direction," so he has to "stay" on his own "path" until he "wins." It is with Bilal's acknowledgment that he is "gonna win" that the songs flattens out and evokes the spiritual focus that Bilal desires throughout the song. The song ends with Bilal singing "I have no doubt. I have no fear," punctuated with a minute-long (wah wah) scat that suggests a harmonious reality.

The conceptual immensity of Bilal's "Sometimes" is matched only by the project's closing track, "Second Child" (a nod to Hughes's "Genius Child"?). The track, which was written during a time when the artist was deeply immersed in the music of Jimi Hendrix and Miles Davis (*On the Corner*), strips away the romantic prestige of the pimp/hustler lifestyle, evoking a gritty, tragic, and surreal urban landscape. The grating discord and dissonance of the song are deliberately meant to alarm and provoke listeners. The song begins with an autobiographical narrative from a "second child" who was "born in the closet" to a mother who had "her clothes still on"—a child literally born "smothered" in his mother's pants. According to the "second child," all he got was "hand-me-downs." In an interview, Bilal admits that the song was his reaction to "watching the news everyday and seeing all the injustice that's still happening to blacks."[9] Whereas the song is an explicit critique of social injustice and poverty in America's inner cities, the "second child" theme of the song implicitly suggests a failure on the part of previous generations to "provide" for its generational children. In his book *The Hip-Hop Generation*, Bakari Kitwana notes that "it is difficult to find instances where Black baby boomers in mainstream leadership are collectively making a difference in the lives of young Blacks, who constitute a significant portion of Black America," adding that organizations like the NAACP are "often out of synch with the hip-hop generation."[10] Bilal's suggestion that the "second child" was a "second class citizen spawned by kings" highlights the irony that while previous generations have provided a fertile artistic legacy, there continues to be those who are subjected to misery and squalor despite the efforts of those generations. Bilal's generation openly asks, "Who can spot that nation now?"—placing some of the blame firmly on the generation of "nation builders" that were the most outspoken and visible purveyors of black nationalist thought in the 1960s and 1970s. The explosive cacophony of the song's latter half correlates to the "accumulation of anger . . . built up inside" the artist.

"Second Child" suggests that there is a significant upside to being a twentysomethin' artist. No doubt Bilal has only scratched the surface of his talents. More accomplished than Prince's *For You* and D'Angelo's *Brown Sugar* and on par with Terence Trent Darby's *Introducing the Hardline*, Dionne Farris's *Wild Seed Wild Flower*, and the Notorious B.I.G.'s *Ready to Die*, in my mind *1st Born Second* is one of the most significant debuts in black pop of the past twenty-five years—all done with a pimp's flair.

CHAPTER FOUR

HABERMAS IN THE HOOD

In the aftermath of Jill Scott's surprising breakthrough in 2000, there have been several remarkable female debuts in R&B. Besides the perpetually overhyped India.Arie, vocalists such as Syleena Johnson and Sunshine Anderson have also emerged as solid singer-songwriters running the gamut of neo-soul exotic, postmodern chitlin'-circuit chanteuse, and round-the-way baby-girl. While I suspect that much of India.Arie's debut project was cautiously manufactured somewhere in Kedar-world (I believe there's a Dionne Farris somewhere up in her spirit that needs to be loosed), all three of these artists, with various degrees of difference, were allowed to be active agents in the music they produced. Such autonomy has been practically nonexistent within R&B. Even as Beyonce coyly tries to get us to believe that she is an "independent" woman and a "survivor" who is gonna "work it out," the reality is that outside of the neo/alternative/organic-soul universe, a great many R&B songstresses wear sequinned dresses, long black boots, halter tops (or too-tight T-shirts) and sing songs written and produced by men.

And such were the plans at Columbia Records for a seventeen-year-old musical prodigy named Alicia Keys. Unfortunately for the label, Keys had other plans, and after an amicable spilt from Jermaine Dupree's So So Def camp, Keys was signed to Arista by Clive Davis, who bought out her contract at Columbia. Among this generation of

MTV divas, Alicia Keys is one of the few who has consistently captured the fancy of the critical mainstream. Blessed with "millennial exotic" good looks (read: light, bright, and racially ambiguous), a mature artistic demeanor that belied her twenty years, and the full attention of the dominant record mogul of the past thirty years in Clive Davis, it was not surprising that *Songs in A Minor* and the single "Fallin'" would dominate music and video charts throughout the year. Perhaps lost among all the hype—legitimate or manufactured—were the critically sophisticated videos directed by Chris Robinson of Squeak Pictures that accompanied the singles "Fallin'" and "A Woman's Worth."

The song "Fallin'" combines Keys's natural blues register with a subtle (brilliantly so) sample of James Brown's "It's a Man's, Man's, Man's World." Keys opens the track a capella with the lyrics "I keep on falling in love with you," drawing out the phrase "in love" for several seconds before squeezing the phrase "with you" into the last bar of the intro as she begins her piano line. The intro at once attempts to draw the audience into the "deep blue" spaces of forbidden love that the song documents and invokes the gospel tradition, made famous in classic soul recordings, of singing behind the beat. The full weight of the James Brown sample is made clear in the video for "Fallin'," which opens with Keys sitting at a piano and closes with Keys visiting her incarcerated boyfriend.

While jailhouse visits have become an all too common occurrence in black popular culture, the video deepens the significance of these visits as a busload of mothers, girlfriends, wives, and baby-mamas travel from an urban center to the kind of rural community—think of the north country in New York State—where new prisons, along with the compulsory Kmarts and Home Depots, have been constructed at alarming rates. While the primary discourse about the prison industrial complex centers on the unprecedented incarceration rates of black and Latino men, the video flips the script to highlight the equally unprecedented incarceration rates of women of all colors and black women in particular. According to Angela Davis, "most debates addressing the crisis resulting from overcrowding in prisons and jails focus on male institutions. Meanwhile, women's institutions are proportionally proliferating at an even more astounding rate than men's."[1] Footage in the music video of the women and children traveling on the bus explicitly evokes the temporary "imagined communities"—to use Benedict Anderson's term—of families "torn apart" by the absence of a patriarchal figure.[2] Thus the pastoral images in the video of "men" working in the field, which conjures the image of southern chain gangs and the presumable emasculation of black masculinity that the realities of chattel slavery and Jim Crow segregation heightened, are meant to reinforce the oppressive nature of prison labor. Ironically, the video reveals that it was in fact a group of women who were working in the fields. This becomes dramatically clear when the women in the field raise their heads and sing along with Keys, "I keep on fallin' in love with you," suggesting the ways that female incarceration rates are deeply imbricated in the efforts of these women to protect men who are likely involved in illicit activities.

Incorporating what I've dubbed the "Kemba Smith Aesthetic" the video for "Fallin'," which earned a MTV Music Video Award for Best New Artist, puts a distinctly womanist spin on the prison industrial complex. Kemba Smith was sentenced in 1995 to twenty-four and a half years in prison for drug trafficking conspiracy, money laundering, and making false statements to federal officers. Despite the severity of her conviction, Smith in fact never sold or consumed drugs. Rather, Smith was guilty of "protecting" her "boyfriend" Peter Hall, who was the point person in an East Coast crack cocaine drug ring that extended from New York City to Hampton, Virginia, where, at the beginning of the 1990s, Smith was an undergraduate student at Hampton University. In the "name of love," Smith often carried Hall's gun in her purse, carried bag money, and bailed him out of jail. Unwilling to help federal authorities locate Hall, Smith was herself indicted and convicted. At the moment that Smith was finally willing to give up Hall, he was found murdered in a Seattle, Washington, apartment. Smith became a cause célèbre for the shortcoming of the criminal justice system—how can someone who never sold or took drugs face such a harsh sentence?—after her story was featured in the now defunct *Emerge* magazine in 1996. Under the leadership of its editor, George Curry, the magazine regularly chronicled Smith's story and, no doubt, given Curry's ties to the Black Congressional Caucus, hugely influenced Bill Clinton's decision to commute her sentence in December 2000 (though Big-Willie Slick somehow managed to forget about Leonard Peltier).[3]

With Kemba Smith as an undercurrent, the "Fallin'" video's director, Chris Robinson, gives a real feminist "voice" to the increasing incarceration of women in the United States by forcing viewers to engage the images of incarcerated women working in the fields. The video's ability to make these claims is buttressed by the use of James Brown's "It's a Man's, Man's, Man's World" sample, countering the general misconceptions about the rates at which black and Latina women are incarcerated and subjected to hard labor. The video offers one of the rare occasions when an artist and video director are in sync aesthetically, creating a new objet d'art that stands beyond the original track, bringing a new depth of meaning and passion to the original song. This "message" is likely the product of Robinson's collaborative style, which openly embraces the input of artists and producers, like JayZ ("I'll Do Anything"), Kelly Price ("As We Lay"), Snoop Dogg ("Snoop Dogg"), and a virtual all-star cast for Big Pun's posthumous tribute, "It's So Hard."

The follow-up video, for Keys's "A Woman's Worth," examines "a woman's worth" within the public sphere, highlighting the divide between the public and the private domains of black femininity within the context of the ghetto public. The video opens with shot of Keys's feet as she walks across a ghetto intersection, while singing the song "Fallin'" as it plays on her headset. The audio of the song serves to create narrative continuity between the video for "Fallin'" and that of "A Woman's Worth." In the first video, Keys plays a character lamenting her proclivity for falling in love with the wrong men. In this case the object of her affection is one of them "chocolate boy wonders" (shout to Pete Rock) whose time in the drug game translated into real time spent in prison. A significant portion of the "A Woman's Worth" video is spent detailing his struggles to find work on his return and the way that Keys's character comforts him in his frustration.

But the attention to Keys's "feet to the ground" also serves as a visual subtext to her sexuality—heightened by her attire, a cut-off lace shirt and form-fitting jeans—and the tradition of "streetwalking women" that LaBelle ("Lady Marmalade") and Marlena Shaw ("Street Walkin'

Woman") gave voice to twenty-five years ago. Both songs obviously focus on the choices that some women are forced to make as "women of the street." They also show how these women make these choices with full knowledge of the implications of their chosen professions (can we accept that they are laborers on the real and not just freaks?), with a sense of empowerment and even dignity in a world that offers women, particularly black women, very few substantive choices for economic empowerment save marriage, menial labor, or traditional low-paying jobs as nurturers (teachers, nurses, day-care providers, and so on). In other words, we talking about "proud" walkin' women. Such choices echo Hattie McDaniel's classic quip that she would rather play a maid in film than be a maid in real life. Given the choice of being a domestic—considering the ways that black domestics were often the targets of sexual harassment in the houses where they cooked, cleaned, and suckled (see Tera Hunter's bomb-ass book *To 'Joy My Freedom*)—there was a certain power involved in attaining some control of their economic resources and sexuality as "street women."

Shaw describes her brilliant "Street Walkin' Woman" (*Who Is That Bitch, Anyway?*, 1975) as "almost a documentary of some of the scenes I've lived through as a woman out there in show business unescorted and unprotected. This causing me a surface shell of hardness."[4] Shaw's comments are instructive to "A Woman's Worth": in the frames immediately following the opening scene, Keys's character is confronted—harassed, really—by a thirteen-year-old-ish "shortie" who yells at her, "Ay yo shortie! What's up? Ya lookin' good today. Ya gonna give me some time or what?" Though the scene is not unlike the "good-natured" (at least in the mind of the offender) harassment that women regularly attract on urban streets, the confidence with which the teenager steps to the older, adult Keys suggests that he sees such activity as some measurement of his maturing masculinity.

And behind this moment is the knowledge that the public abuse faced by black and Latina women is often dramatically different than that faced by white women, and even more so in poor and working-class "minority" communities that don't benefit from the police presence and protection afforded women of all races and ethnicities in major urban areas. These differences can be extended to the portrayals of these women in urban and hip-hop videos. Whereas white women dominate in the pornography industry, it is primarily black and Latina women who appear most often in pornographic-style music videos, such as Mr. Cheeks's "Lights, Camera, Action" or the hugely influential "Rump Shaker" video from the mid-1990s. These pornographic images of black and Latina women are openly distributed on a "free" basis throughout the day on MTV and BET and widely consumed by young men of all races, while such images of white women are "protected" within the "pay" pornographic industry. In other words, young men are introduced to particularly sexualized images of black and brown women in the absence of a significant presence of white women being portrayed in the same manner.

This practice heightens the contrast between the sexuality of black and brown women and that of white women: white women are assigned a privileged status in this context, while black and brown women are treated differently as sexual objects, and thus are subject to forms of harassment that some white women would never be subject to, specifically harassment by black and brown men. Given the history of black masculinity in this country, one wonders if the young shortie in Keys's video would have been emboldened to step to a young white woman in the same way, in a world where, less than fifty years ago, Emmett Till became the most powerful footnote to the practice of "reckless eye-balling." (For the uninitiated, the fourteen-year-old Till was lynched "cotton-gin engine around his neck" style—think of the implications of this tool of destruction at the dawn of the Civil Rights movement—for "flirting" with a white woman.)

This early sequence with the young shortie and Keys's character is sharply juxtaposed with images of Keys's beau heading back to his cell after she visits him (footage from the "Fallin'" video), and then his own "streetwalking" in search of productive work. The quick shift between the image of the shortie stepping to Keys's character and her beau in the pen is important because it builds a narrative link to the kinds of questionable and illegal activities (street pharmacy) that would have a thirteen-year-old boy hanging on street corners and the inevitability of black male incarceration for those activities. Not so ironically, when Keys's beau returns to those street corners himself, confronted by his former peers, he is effectively "queered," dismissed for wearing the uniform of "legitimate" labor: the white dress shirt and tie. This scene speaks to the power of masculine urban spaces like street corners, where "boys-to-men" are granted very little room to resist the pack mentality that defines so much of black gang culture without some kind of repercussions. Keys's beau can here resist these spaces and ignore the derision of those who inhabit those spaces because he has paid a significant price—incarceration—for investing in the culture of those spaces. And his survival has been realized in part because of the intervention of a caring, loving woman like Keys's character. Similarly, the trajectory of the shortie's street life and his views on women may also be altered because of the intervention of Keys's character as nurturer/mentor. The rest of the video focuses on the duality of her role, as domestic nurturer of her beau and his "damaged" masculinity (remember, bruh ain't got a job), and social nurturer to a young man trying to better understand his own masculinity in relation to women.

Popular notions of men being sensitive to the "issues" of women have usually invoked chivalrous acts of kindness, such as holding doors and footing the dinner bill. Director Robinson gives a nod to such chivalry in a scene in which an older woman who is struggling with several bags of groceries is helped by an adult male. This scene serves to heighten the generational differences in the social fabric of ghetto publics. While some commentators may be given to romanticizing the quality of black urban life in the 1940s and 1950s, it was not unusual for the "thugs" in the community to show intense respect for their elders. One of the defining marks of black urban life during the past twenty years—coinciding, incidentally, with the emergence of a formal hip-hop industry and culture—has been the proclivity of black youth to disregard the value and safety of elders within their communities, or what Michael Eric Dyson has called a "Juvenocracy," where some black communities are literally held under siege by black youth run amok.[5] This idea of "black youth rule" is, of course, another nuance of the contemporary black urban world, one that, given the regular demonization of black youth and the cultures of survival that they construct (including hip-hop), is often overstated, or at least undercontextualized.

But Robinson's subtle point in the video is well taken; fifty years ago, a black woman about Keys's age would not likely have been harassed as she is in the video by a thirteen-year-old male hanging on the corner. The point here is not that such vulgarities did not occur in the past, but rather that they were less likely to be played out so publicly. One feature of the contemporary moment, in this regard, is the very powerful conflation—collapse, really—of the private onto the public. Now, distinctly private modes of address appeal to mass-consuming audiences, whether it is R. Kelly's "Feelin' on Your Booty," the ghastly lyrics and video for the Nas/Queensbridge's Finest collaboration "Oochie Wally," or the vulgar and misogynistic behavior of some men at the Puerto Rican Day Parade in New York in 2000. But the kind of vocal harassment that Robinson depicts at the video's opening is just one aspect of "A Woman's Worth." He also directs an eye toward how women are valued and devalued within domestic spaces. Keys's character is depicted throughout the video at home, trying to comfort her man, likely providing some affirmation that he has made the right decision to get out of the drug game, despite the difficulties he is having in finding regular work. You can imagine her character echoing labelmate Angie Stone's line "Never mind them hatin' niggas."

Some of the most intimate scenes in the video come when Keys's character braids her man's hair, highlighting the ways in which she is valued nonsexually, and vice versa. This particular evidence of nurturing is dramatically countered by scenes from the domestic space of the young shortie Keys confronts earlier in the video. The audience witnesses the drama in shortie's home life, as his father verbally abuses his mother and abruptly tosses food and dishes from the dining table onto the floor as he storms off in a rage. Suddenly, there is a very visible connection between the boy's views on women and the seeming lack of regard or possibly disdain that his father has for his mother. Unspoken in this scene are the connections between domestic abuse and the lack of self-esteem that many men possess because of their inability to feel empowered in their work-related activities.

If the video is to serve as some kind of inspiration for men to better understand the "damage they do," logically the young shortie witnesses his mother crying alone in her bedroom, creating a kind of epiphany, as he begins to make concrete connections between his conversations with Keys's character and what he has just witnessed in his own home. Fittingly, while aimlessly walking at night in the rain (to get away from the drama in the house), the boy finds Keys in a phone booth: she offers him "shelter" and some interpretations of the events he has just witnessed. Keys's character thus represents the ways that women are often integral in men's generating any sensitivity with regard to their own sexism and misogyny. Both Keys the character and Keys the artist can be seen as legitimate, if limited, social agents. Whether or not the men depicted here became anti-sexist agents in their own right is beyond the scope of a four-minute music video intended for the audiences of MTV's *TRL* (*Total Request Live*) or BET's *106th and Park*. Robinson and Keys's goals are much more attainable; they create visual narratives suggesting that (black) women are worthy of care, respect, and protection because of their creation of nurturing spaces for their men and their families.

This, of course, falls well short of a concrete feminist stance. Instead, the video echoes the very popular response among men accused of sexism that at least they haven't "beat" their woman or "called her a bitch." It also reflects the even more popular belief among those same men, and way too many in the general public, that simple demands from women that they be "respected" and "acknowledged" are some form of "radical feminism." It is this belief that has led a wide range of popular artists like Kelis, Eve, Lil' Kim, and Keys to be perceived as "feminist" artists and those who do offer succinct critiques of sexism and misogyny (Sarah Jones and Ursula Rucker come immediately to mind) as "man-haters."

Unwittingly, though, the video for "A Woman's Worth" suggests otherwise. Throughout the video, Keys the artist appears in all black, performing on a Fender Rhodes in the commons of the Walt Whitman housing projects in Brooklyn, New York. Historically, the commons were where "community" came together to exchange ideas and concerns—a public extension of the "tavern" and "salon" spaces that Habermas (he of the hugely influential and problematic *The Structural Transformation of the Public Sphere*) thought were so integral to democratic societies. There has been a rich tradition of creating, maintaining, and defending such spaces among folks of African descent in the United States and the Caribbean.

And, very often, music (think juke joints, speakeasies, dance halls, house parties, and "two turntables and a microphone" in the park) formed an important dynamic in the success of those spaces. Speaking about the Walt Whitman Houses, Robinson confirms this tradition to some extent when he states that there was "great beauty in this environment."[6]

Interestingly, Keys appears alone in the commons. Perhaps this resulted from the production crew's desire to protect the shoot from being disrupted by what was described, also in the pages of *In Style*, as "locals who waved and hollered from nearby sidewalks and windows."[7] But the image of Keys performing to an "empty" commons is useful to understanding the limits of the video and of Keys as a feminist agent. (There's no small irony in the fact that the *In Style* article was a "style" piece about clothing ensembles and braids.) If such public spaces are crucial to developing some kind of anti-sexist and anti-racist consensus within the communities in which they exist, the video suggests that they are also, still, spaces unreceptive to messages that counter sexism, misogyny, and patriarchy. Only twenty years ago, such public spaces were overrun by ghetto denizens open to the powerful performances of black and brown masculinity for which hip-hop has provided the context. Twenty years later, Alicia Keys—whose aesthetic sensibilities would have been impossible without the influence of hip-hop—sits alone in those same commons, with a message that critiques and counters some of the negative excesses of hip-hop's masculinist influences.

In their essay "Native Daughters in the Promised Land: Gender, Race, and the Questions of Separate Spheres," You-me Park and Gayle Wald argue that racial-ethnic women's identity within the public sphere is "compromised by the demand that they maintain their 'private' identities even in the 'public' sphere."[8] "Alicia Keys the nurturing character in the videos for "A Woman's Worth" and "Fallin'" is widely circulated and celebrated for her "progressive" views on black men—think of the triumvirate of Keys, Eve, and Angie Stone on the remix of Stone's "Brotha"—while Alicia Keys the artist sits alone, in the commons of the Walt Whitman Houses, giving voice to the travails of young black women who cannot resist the allure of those same men or the demons (patriarchy, poverty, phallocentrism, materialism: take your pick) that possess them.

CHAPTER FIVE

OH MY!
(THE SEXUAL HEALING INTERLUDE)

There probably wasn't anyone who even casually listened to urban radio in the early months of 2002 that had not been drawn into the gyration-inducing, mystical sound that was Tweet's song "Oops (Oh My)." The song topped the *Billboard* urban music chart and peaked at number eight on the *Billboard* Hot 100 chart. The song appears on Tweet's debut project, *Southern Hummingbird*. Produced by Tim (call me Timbaland) Moseley, who has laced the likes of Missy Elliot, Ginuwine, Jay Z, and the late Aaliyah, the song ranks among Moseley's best productions. But beyond the groove, the song has generated attention because of its unbridled expressions of sexuality. It is easily one of the most explicitly sexual songs in pop music since George Michael laid waste to his glam-pop Wham image with his first solo release, "I Want Your Sex." To say the least the song is controversial. As parent Nicole Cardwell opined, "I thought it was disgusting. . . . I just don't think kids should be told how to do those things."[1] Another mother said that her seven-year-old daughter was singing the song around the house before she was able to fully understand what her daughter was singing. The woman admits that the "song is hot and stuff, but I think it needs to be a little bit cleaned up."[2] While young children may pick up on the theme of the song (holla back, Jocelyn Elders), there are more important issues about black female sexuality that are at the heart of the song.

Taking a page out of Britney's "sex games as pop hit formulas," the thirtysomething Charlene "Tweet" Keys is literally in the act of sexual discovery as she coyly sings in the song's chorus about her shirt going over her head and her skirt dropping to her feet, casually uttering, "oops . . . oh my" with every sensual discovery. Conventional wisdom suggests that baby-girl is discovering the act of self-pleasuring, which, given our society's general squeamishness about self-actualized female sexuality (meaning there ain't got to be a phallus in the room), is actually a bit of a progressive concept. And of course references to "self-pleasuring" is nothing new in the tradition of black music, whether it was Chuck Berry singing about his "Ding-a-Ling" or Marvin whispering, that "it's not good to masturbate" during the closing fade of "Sexual Healing." But at a particular moment when black woman regularly appear in music videos and films as the sexual props of a wide range of men (as if Billy Bob's character treated Halle's any worse than a host of brothas have treated sistas in films like *The Best Man* or *The Player's Club*), there was something significant about the voice and image of a black woman who was firmly in control of her sexuality, especially at the stage of discovery (who can forget Shug Avery helping Celie "discover" her spot in *The Color Purple?*).

But in a culture in which self-actualized women are seen as threats to the "strong black man," and black patriarchal privilege masquerades in the bedroom, the pulpit, and the street corner as anointment, the fact that baby-girl might get her swerve on without the presence of black testosterone raises questions, for some, about homegirl's sexual preferences. Given the kind of homophobia that flows through some black communities, it is perhaps not so ironic that the "spectacle of possibility" that *some* black body might be a *queer* black body has significant commercial value. Luther Vandross and Whitney Houston, for example, are historically linked because they both have been the unfortunate victims of rampant rumors within the black community that they were dead. These rumors are in no small way connected to ongoing speculation about their sexualities, though rumors about Houston's drug addiction perhaps better explain how the rumor of her death carried more value in some black circles than the 9/11 terror attacks that occurred on the same day that the Houston death rumors began to circulate.

Tweet doesn't shrink from the "spectacle of possibility" as the song regularly trades sex-pleasuring innuendo for lesbian innuendo. At one point in the song, Tweet sings about how she felt a body just like hers and looked over to see a reflection of herself, raising the distinct possibility that there is somebody else in the room that looks and feels like her—in other words, another sista. Later in the song, as Tweet openly asks, "Who can this be?" and looks over to the left, it is Missy Elliot who responds with ditties about how she was "lookin' so good" that she couldn't reject herself and how she was "eyeing" my thighs, but a "pea can't grind" (I guess we could call this the birth of "clitoral rap"). This section of the song plays off public speculation about Elliot's own sexuality. In many black circles, "Oh My" has been simply referred to as the "Lesbo" song. The otherwise forgettable video for the song even plays off this tension as Elliot's disembodied head performs her section of the song from a phone booth. Phone booths share the same spatial dynamics as "closets." Unlike a "closet," though, which can function as a hiding place, a phone booth is also a site of communication and transformation (thinking about that Clark Kent–Superman thing here), thus one could speculate that in the video Missy Elliot is either affirming or simply feeding into audience curiosity about her own sexual fluidity.

In the "Sexual Healing (Oops Pt. 2)" remix that appears at the end of Tweet's *Southern Hummingbird*, she sings that this "feeling" that baby-girl's been feeling is more than "sexual healing" but rather about "loving" herself. This suggests that for baby-girl, self-pleasuring is more about coming to terms with her own sexuality and developing a sense of self-love. The term *sexual healing* is of historical importance in black popular music because of Marvin Gaye's recording of the same title. Tweet's referencing of the song shifts the song from one in which black female sexuality is utilized solely for the purpose of black male sexual pleasure (however bomb-ass Marvin's song is, it's clear the from the lyrics and the video that Gaye saw women as tools to heal his sexual madness) to one in which black female sexual pleasure is at the center of the narrative with little regard for the proverbial patriarchal orgasm (two minute style or otherwise). Tweet later affirms this idea, flipping the lyrics of Luther Ingram's classic "If Loving You Is Wrong (I Don't Want to Be Right)," urging "Every woman" to say in unison, "If loving me is wrong, I don't want to be right." In interviews, Tweet explains that *Southern Hummingbird* is a "therapy album," as many of the songs were written as she dealt suicidal depression and deep personal insecurities. She adds that "a lot of people think ["Oops"]" is "sexual . . . but it's about self-love and appreciation."[3] Thus "Oops (Oh My)" is a part of Tweet's recovery process.

In either case, whether "Oops (Oh My)" is about the act of masturbation or a same-sex sexual encounter, the song is a powerful articulation of self-defined black female sexuality. In this regard, Tweet represents something distinct from other figures like Lil' Kim and Foxy Brown, who may push the envelope on self-defined sexuality, but do so in a context that is stridently heterosexual (which self-pleasuring is not) and one that easily slips into a space where they still remain little more than sexual objects (see Lil' Kim's disturbing "How Many Licks" from her *Notorious K.I.M.* for a reference). Given the discomfort in black communities with both frank discussions about masturbation and sexuality in general and homosexuality in particular, it is not surprising that versions of the song made available to radio and clubs featured what I call the "heterosexual" mix. Employing the services of Fabolous (the second coming of Mase), the "heterosexual" version attempts to recenter "Oops" in a distinctly heterosexual context. But most disturbing in Fabolous's verse in the remix is the line "Oops, there goes my kids on your face" (what they call "facials" in the industry). With one simple shift, the song is transformed from a celebration of autonomous female sexuality into a vulgar, demeaning moment of black female objectification. Unfortunately, for far too many people this is more acceptable than the possibility that black women could satisfy their sexual desires without the presence of men.

CHAPTER SIX

● ● ● ● ● ● ● ● ● ● ● ● ● ● ● ● ● ● ● ●

THE E-DOUBLE AND THE TROUBLE MAN

Dating back to Natalie Cole's eerie duet with her late father, Nat King Cole, on "Unforgettable" a decade ago, recording technology has facilitated the possibility of digitized duets from the grave. These songs are reminiscent of the Dirt Devil commercials with Fred Astaire or the recent Alcatel commercials in which a digitized Martin Luther King, Jr., speaks to an empty mall at the site where the 1963 March on Washington was held. Many audiences have been disturbed by such gimmicky attempts at selling vacuum cleaners and potted distortions of historical events. In an editorial, Julianne Malveaux, who was unfamiliar with Alcatel, wrote, "Whatever they are, I am appalled, even as I learned that King's heirs were paid well."[1] Echoing Malveaux's concerns, Michael Eric Dyson asserted that "it's not simply that we have to ask Alcatel the question, we have to ask the people who allow that message to go forward. That's the King family."[2] The controversy surrounding King's Alcatel commercial is of course part of an attempt by black pundits and others to protect a significant black icon from crass commercialism. According to one of King's former lieutenants Reverend Joseph Lowery, "if the company would use Dr. King's image to deliver a message that was Dr. King's message like world peace and [the] end of violence, I think it would be perfectly appropriate and a good use of . . . new technology to deliver an old message."[3]

And it's not just black folks who are all up in arms about the commercial defilement of black icons. Jazz guitarist Pat Metheny (who is white), for instance, was quite frank in his disgust with Kenny G for recording a "digital duet" with Louis Armstrong (kind of like a dinner of Swanson's frozen chicken with "Krissy"). In response to Kenny G's version of "What a Beautiful World," Metheny published a damn-near-nine-thousand-word diatribe on his web site that accused Kenny G of among other things, creating a "new low point in modern culture."[4] Fellow guitarist Richard Thompson (who is also white) affirmed Metheny's critique with his own song, titled "I Agree with Pat Metheny."

The fact of the matter is that since the success of Cole's duet with her father, which resuscitated her then dormant career, many artists and labels have attempted to craft pop hits by coalescing disparate audiences. One of the best recent examples was the attempt to bring the hip-hop generation closer to the legacy of legendary reggae artist Bob Marley. *Bob Marley: Chant Down Babylon* featured Marley dueting with Erykah Badu, Lauryn Hill, Guru and his sons, Ziggy and Stephen Marley. In some respects this was natural, as hip-hop has often attempts to collapse the generation gap, via its sampling practices, which is how, for instance, a new generation of listeners were generated for the music of Lou Donaldson and David Axelrod. Hip-hop's sampling practices have been heavily scrutinized by many, including record companies aiming to have artists and other labels pay up for "stolen beats" and those who think that sampling is not a "pure" form of musical expression. Whatever. The reality is that the best sampling in hip-hop has often furthered the influence and aesthetic quality of the art form, as was the case with the brilliant sonic bricolage of Public Enemy or the cascading horn lines, often heisted from Tom Scott and Eddie Harris, that formed the basis of so many Pete Rock productions (see "They Reminisce over You" for an example). Perhaps one of the most fascinating recent examples of hip-hop sampling is Erick Sermon's collaboration with the late Marvin Gaye on the song "Music."

"Music" was initially released as the lead single from the soundtrack of the forgettable film, *What's the Worst That Could Happen?*, which features Martin Lawrence and Danny DeVito. The song was later included in Sermon's debut for the J label, *Music*. The soundtrack to *What's the Worst That Could Happen?* also includes a digitized duet with Craig Mack ("Here comes the brand new flava . . .") and the late Frank Sinatra singing "High Hopes" of all things. While the Mack-Sinatra collaboration comes off as cheesy and camp and will do little to introduce the classic vocalist to younger audiences, the Sermon-Gaye track is a brilliant reworking of an alternative version of an obscure (at least among casual Gaye fans) Marvin Gaye track from his 1982 *Midnight Love* recording. The Sermon-Gaye collaboration will genuinely have the effect of introducing Gaye, in a more significant way, to the hip-hop generation. *Midnight Love* was the last full-length recording that Gaye completed before his untimely death and it garnered him the only Grammy Awards in his celebrated and important musical career.

Marvin Gaye had been in a state of exile, first in Hawaii, then England, and later in Ostend, Belgium, for roughly two years when he completed the *Midnight Love* sessions in the spring of 1982. Gaye had left his Los Angeles after the IRS repossessed his house and home studio because he owed back income taxes. Gaye was a notorious procrastinator who liked to work at his own pace despite the high demand for Marvin Gaye "product." Gaye's home studio allowed him to work through the artistic and philosophical contradictions that marked the best of his music, notably on projects such as *What's Going On* (1971), *Let's Get It On* (1973), and the critically disparaged *Here, My Dear* (1978). The latter recording, which in retrospect may be one of his most brilliant, was largely inspired by a court-ordered settlement in which Gaye's royalties from the recording would be used as alimony payments for his ex-wife Anna Gordy Gaye, the sister of Motown founder Berry Gordy. (Gaye recorded for Motown for much of his career.) At the time his studio was seized, Gaye had been tinkering with a recording of big-band standards, originally charted a decade earlier by Bobby Scott, called *Vulnerable*, and a project called *Love Man* that was conceived as a return to the classic '70s Gaye. *Love Man* was eventually scrapped, though the musical tracks became the basis for Gaye's final Motown recording, *In Our Lifetime* (1981), which captured the self-contained psychological thriller that was Gaye's life and mind. Recorded while Gaye was in

Marvin Gaye, In Our Lifetime

Hawaii, *In Our Lifetime* instigated Gaye's break with Motown—the label released the recording before Gaye was "finished" with it.

In heavy debt to the IRS, in the throes of a second divorce, and addicted to weed, cocaine, and crack (according to Gaye biographer David Ritz), Gaye was grasping for life, at least in the philosophical sense, when then CBS VP Larkin Arnold reached out to the singer to plot his return to the music charts. The product of Arnold's outreach program for CBS was *Midnight Love*, which was released in November 1982. The lead single from the project, "Sexual Healing," became Gaye's first major pop hit in almost a decade and earned him his first and only Grammy Awards for Best R&B Single and Best R&B Instrumental (for the B-side of "Sexual Healing") in early 1983. Although not one of Gaye's best recordings—"Sexual Healing" was the project's only hit single—*Midnight Love* nevertheless remains inextricably connected to his body of great work, because of the infectious "Sexual Healing" and the fact that it was the last recording released in his lifetime.

Gaye was purportedly working with Barry White for the follow-up to *Midnight Love* at the time of his death in 1984. A year after his death, CBS released *Dream of a Lifetime*, which included unfinished and raw tracks that Gaye had been working on at the time of his death, including "Savage in the Sack," "Masochistic Beauty," and "Sanctified Lady," which was originally recorded as "Sanctified Pussy." A relative flood of previously unreleased Gaye material became available after his death, including *Romantically Yours* (1985), which featured the earliest versions of the Bobby Scott *Vulnerable* charts and "Piece of Clay," which was included on the soundtrack for the John Travolta film *Phenomenon*. In 1997, the full *Vulnerable* sessions were released, exposing Gaye's luscious and layered approach to standards. Had he survived, these recordings would have garnered Gaye newfound artistic appreciation. According to Bobby Scott, Gaye, along with Aretha Franklin, "sculpted and improved any song they sang. They each came out of that holy place in black music that breeds genius."[5] In 1998, Sony released the Midnight *Love and Sexual Healing Sessions* with little fanfare and not much promotion. Apparently, Erick Sermon was one of the few people in the industry who paid attention.

Sermon has had a solid decade-plus career as half of the stellar "East Coast gangstas" EPMD, who emerged in 1988 with their Sleeping Bag debut, *Strictly Business*, which was filled with certified East Coast classics like the title track and "You Gots to Chill." On the strength of their first two projects, EPMD were signed to Def Jam in 1990. Sermon, affectionately known as the "E-double," and his partner PMD (Parrish Smith) later formed the Def Squad, an artistic collective that at various times included K-Solo, Das EFX, the most "beautifullest" Keith Murray, and the indefatigable and blunted on the "regla" Redman. After the breakup of Sermon and Smith's partnership in the mid-'90s (they later reunited for the underwhelming *Back in Business* and *Out of Business*), Sermon established himself as an in-demand producer working with his regular Def Squad crew and folks such as Bounty Killer, LL Cool J, Method Man, and vocalist Dave Hollister. As witnessed by the crates he dug in for Redman's debut, *Whut? Thee Album*, where he helped reinvigorate the career of the late Johnny "Guitar" Watson with his recasting of Watson's "Superman Lover" on Redman's "Soopaman Lover," Sermon is a legitimate sound archivist.

Sermon's use of Gaye is also not surprising given the hip-hop generation's fascination with Gaye. The youngest members of the hip-hop generation were likely introduced to Gaye's music via the very popular California raisins ad campaign in the early 1980s, which featured dancing raisins singing Gaye's "I Heard It Through the Grapevine." Both the raisins and Gaye's song were recently brought out of retirement for new ad campaigns for the Hardee's restaurant chain and the Brach's candy company. But for the oldest wing of the hip-hop generation—the post-soul generation—Gaye's music was a direct link to the social instabilities of childhood. As Tai Moses relates, Gaye's *What's Going On*, for example, "conjures up a newsreel of my childhood, the events of a decade oddly compressed."[6] Logically, when the hip-hop and post-hip-hop generations were faced with the generation-defining crisis of the 9/11 terror attacks, they turned to Marvin Gaye and "What's Going On" to find the words to express their anger, fears, and grief. The recent all-star version of Gaye's song, which featured the likes of Ja Rule, Nelly, *NSYNC, Alicia Keys, Wyclef Jean, and Britney Spears, was recorded as a benefit for the Global AIDS Alliance (pre-9/11) and the September 11 Fund.

While Gaye's vocal style has been consistently recalled by R&B vocalists like El Debarge, Christopher Williams, Kenny Lattimore, Bilal, and D'Angelo—all of these men tapping into Gaye's hypersexuality—it has not had an obvious presence within the world of hip-hop, the notable exception being Brand Nubian's use of Gaye's *Trouble Man* (1972) soundtrack on their damn-near-brilliant *In God We Trust* (1993). Ironically, *Trouble Man*, a largely instrumental recording written for the Robert Hooks film of the same title, really portends that kind of urban malaise that hip-hop has so effectively referenced. A dark, murky recording, with brooding, introspective melodies, that reeks of late-1950s hard bop sensibilities (it's definitely a Detroit thing), *Trouble Man* evoked the kind of sinister urban landscape that *What's Going On*'s "Inner City Blues" only hinted at. That landscape would later be refigured in a host of cultural products ranging from the Batman film franchise to Wu-Tang's *36 Chambers* (1993). Though the late Tupac Shakur consistently recalled Gaye in the way that he chose to layer his vocals (Gaye's *Let's Get it On* and *Vulnerable* are the best examples of Gaye's extraordinary talents in this regard), Sermon's production on "Music" may be one of the first successful attempts to make Gaye's artistry—not just his political and sexual messages—relevant to contemporary hip-hop and mainstream urban audiences.

Sermon, whose slow drawl-lisp is reminiscent of the novelty Rapping Duke recording of the mid-1980s, wisely gets out of the way, making Gaye the centerpiece of "Music." The song begins with a bass line that deepens and embellishes the bass track of the Gaye original(s). The first voice heard on the song is that of Gaye singing, "Just like music," a refrain that gets repeated throughout the song. Sermon's lyrics are meant as a tribute to music and its importance in his life. For Sermon, music creates an alternative sphere where he can retreat from the world and find some semblance of catharsis. In the first stanza, Sermon relates the power of music, stating that he uses it to "relax" his mind so that he can be "free" and "absorb sound that keep me 'round." He adds that he needs the "music" to keep him "flowin'," to keep him "growin'," and finally to keep "E" from knowing "what happens out there." At one point Sermon says, "without my music . . ."—at which point Gaye is heard singing in his signature yowl, "Oww! I'll go crazy." That moment is one of many where Sermon and Gaye interplay with each other. At another point later in the song, Sermon suggests that whatever his problem may be, "music'll be right there," and "together" he and his music make a "perfect match." After making this statement Sermon queries, "Is that true, Marvin?" to which Gaye responds, "Yeahhhhh!" in his classic falsetto. The song's chorus features Gaye singing the refrain, "Turn on some music, I got my music." Not simply a gimmick—though I wouldn't put that past the NYLA label and its distributor, Interscope, or Sermon for that matter—the song allows Sermon and Gaye to "bond" with the "music" that was so important in both their lives, across time and consciousness, in ways rarely realized by most digital gravediggers.

"Music" is loosely based on a Gaye composition called "Turn on Some Music," which originally appeared on the *Midnight Love* recording. One of the most affecting tracks on the recording, "Turn on Some Music" is largely a song about Gaye asking his lover to "put three albums" while they make love "long, long, long." In its own right it is an interesting spin on the relationship between romance—sex, really—and music. Gaye biographer David Ritz recalls how the singer read him lyrics of a song called "I've Got My Music," which was a "treatise on music's ability to heal the wounded heart. The story was intensely and unmistakably personal."[7] "I've Got My Music" was an early incarnation of what would become the album cut "Turn on Some Music." Ritz notes that the "gist of the song changed completely; the song was no longer about healing the heart. Marvin was taken by the struggle for sexual strength and the pressures of long-lasting lovemaking."[8] In this regard the song was part of a natural progression in a project that Gaye hoped would be commercial. As Gaye said to Ritz, "I'm worried that I'm getting introspective . . . no one will listen. I can't afford to miss this time. I need a hit."[9] *Midnight Love*, of course, provided him a hit with "Sexual Healing," highlighting the sexual fixations that would dog Gaye in his final years (hence the later track "Sanctified Pussy").

Gaye in fact recorded earlier versions of "Turn on Some Music" that became available to the public with the release of the *Midnight Love and Sexual Healing Sessions* in 1998. The double-CD includes two alternative versions of "Turn on Some Music," including the aforementioned "I've Got My Music" and an earlier vocal-only version of "Turn on Some Music," which is where the Gaye vocals on "Music" are drawn from. The only constant in all three versions of the song is an opening section, which differs in minor ways. Gaye's lyric about music being his "therapy" that takes "pain" from his "anatomy" is consistent on all three versions. The basic sentiment of this lyric is of course represented in

Sermon's own original lyrics on "Music." On the "Turn on Some Music" track that appeared on *Midnight Love*, the later verses of the song explicitly document Gaye's lovemaking event with references to his sexual stamina even after the "second jam" falls down an hour later. Gaye's lyrics recall an earlier technology: continuous play meant sticking three or four albums on the six-inch stem of an automatic turntable instead of putting a CD on shuffle.

On both of the earlier versions of the song, the lyrics in the second half are dramatically different from those that appear on the "Turn on Some Music" that was released in 1982. In the vocal version of "Turn on Some Music" that was made available on the *Midnight Love Sessions*, the section that would later begin with the "second jam" falling down instead begins with references to music being the "soul of the man" and how music makes "happy days," makes the "clouds flow," and is "more precious than gold." This section of the song is laid intact on top of Sermon's bass line beginning the section of "Music" where the track ceases to be a Sermon-Gaye collaboration and essentially becomes a "new" Marvin Gaye track. The song continues through an improvised section that is present on all three versions of the original Gaye track where the late singer sings "la-da-da-da-daaa-dah-dah-dah . . . doo-doo, doo, doo, doo" as the song fades. The closing is reminiscent of the closing of Gaye's "Please Stay (Once You Go Away)" on his landmark sexual "treatise" *Let's Get It On*.

The *Midnight Love and Sexual Healing Sessions* offer a unique insight to the creative process of one of the twentieth century's most affecting and provocative artists. Gaye would often improvise lyrics as he worked through different melodic strategies—lyrics that were often important in their own right. Listening to Gaye's creative process also captures emotional states that are often missing from the finished product. Thus there is something very powerful listening to Gaye moan "aw shit" on the alternative vocal version of *Midnight Love*'s "Till Tomorrow." Gaye's original label Motown, would also take advantage of Gaye's creative process by releasing work-in-progress versions of Gaye's achievements *What's Going On* and *Let's Get It On*, which both featured stunning alternative versions of well-known tracks from both recordings—the different versions of

"Just to Keep You Satisfied" recorded by Gaye, the Originals (1970), and the Monitors (1968) are worth the price of admission alone—as well as unreleased "transitional" recordings that marked the state of Gaye's creativity as he traveled from "protest to climax." According to Harry Weinger, who oversaw the releases of the deluxe editions of *What's Going On* (2001) and *Let's Get It On* (2001), Gaye's "experiments on this journey deserve to be heard. Connecting the dots would not be easy. But for someone like Marvin Gaye, I knew it would be worth it."[10]

Further evidence of Gaye's popularity and commercial potential was realized in late 2000, when the Marvin Gaye estate became the first estate to sign on to a Pullman Bond securitization deal.[11] The Pullman Bonds are named after David Pullman, founder of the Pullman Group, which specializes in creating bonds out of intellectual properties. The bonds are often referred to as the Bowie bonds, as David Bowie was the first artist to take advantage of the bonds, securing $55 million against future royalties for his songwriting catalog. To date, legendary Motown producers Holland-Dozier-Holland ($30 million), husband-and-wife creative team Nick Ashford and Valerie Simpson ($10 million), who wrote the classic "Ain't No Mountain High Enough," which was recently featured in the film *Remember the Titans* (2000), and James Brown ($30 million), whose "I Got the Feeling" seems to be in just about every romantic-comedy film trailer, have signed on with the Pullman Group.

For Erick Sermon's part, he was faced with the daunting task of bringing to "life" one of the grand icons of African-American life and American music. Sermon succeeded because he adhered to some of the best principles of hip-hop. Whereas hip-hop samples have often blatantly distorted the intent and integrity of the original versions, Sermon's "Music" remains true to the basic premise of Gaye's original composition—one that Gaye, ironically, had himself distorted in an effort to be more commercial. Thus Sermon's "Music" serves to preserve Gaye's legacy as an "introspective" artist. Lastly, Sermon's "Music" highlights the best aspect of hip-hop: its ability to appropriate, refigure, deconstruct, and reanimate existing texts ("Marvin Gaye" being a major late-twentieth-century text) to create something that is new and distinct that only adds to the brilliance of the original.

CHAPTER SEVEN

BELLBOTTOMS, BLUEBELLES, AND THE FUNKY-ASS WHITE GIRL

Nights in New York, running down steps, into the echoes of the train
station to sing

— Laura Nyro, liner notes, *Gonna Take a Miracle*

As I used to tell Laura all the time, she is a black woman in a white
girl's body.

— Patti LaBelle, *Don't Block the Blessings: Revelations of a Lifetime*

At one point in Danzy Senna's novel *Caucasia*, the primary character,
fifteen-year-old Birdie Lee, is derisively described as "Queer." Such a term
would have likely been a fitting description of Laura Nyro. As a toddler,
Nyro sat at the feet of her piano-tuning, trumpet-playing father and
"composed" little melodies, effectively honing the songwriting and vocal
skills that would mark her 1966 debut, *More Than a New Discovery*
(Verve, later reissued by Columbia as *The First Songs* in 1973). "Queer"
indeed was this teenaged white-girl, who could be seen standing on the
corner of the High School of the Performing Arts singing doo-wop,
challenging our romantic sensibilities that somehow these corners were
solely the provinces of masculine fantasies. Like Birdie Lee, who with
her sister Cole created a mystical language called "Elemeno" and devel-

oped an affinity for passing, Nyro found some comfort in crossing borders and challenging conventions. (Nyro regularly created words in her
songwriting, the term *surry* from the chorus to "Stone Soul Picnic"
being a prime example.) Never formally trained as a pianist, Nyro developed her own unique style. According to her father, Nyro "didn't even
have a knowledge of chords; she'd figure them on her own and memo-
rize them."[1] The shifting, sliding textures of Nyro's 1968 recording, *Eli
and the Thirteenth Confession*, are apt metaphors for those comforts. As
the Bronx-born bohemian girl who helped define the female singer-
songwriter a few years before Carole King's *Tapestry*, Nyro could claim
a long line of progeny including Suzanne Vega, Tori Amos, Rickie Lee
Jones, Teena Marie, Kate Bush, and Patti LaBelle. It was with LaBelle
and her "soul sisters" Nona Hendrix ("I Sweat . . . ") and Sarah Dash that
Nyro recorded her groundbreaking 1971 album *Gonna Take a Miracle*.
Released over thirty years ago, the recording encapsulates the risk-
taking, note-bending, genre-bounding style that made Nyro one of the
most fascinating and evocative pop vocalists of the late 1960s and early
1970s.

Many critics have suggested that Nyro was initially little more than
a "blue-eyed" soul singer, though it is an insult to Nyro's art and legacy
to ever align her with the kind of novelty genre (white folks singing like
black folks) that has produced the likes of the Righteous Brothers,
Michael Bolton, or Mitch Ryder. Ryder, at least, can claim that he was
from "D-Troit" (holla back, Kid Rock and Eminem). Nyro, like vocalists
Teena Marie, George Michael, and Brit Lewis Taylor (who in my mind
may be the most important soul vocalist to debut in the last decade),
simply complicates—but doesn't repudiate—claims that there is such a
thing as "black" singing. "Blue-eyed" soul shares an affinity with what
Paul C. Taylor calls the "Elvis Effect," where "white participation in traditionally black avenues of cultural production produces feelings of
unease."[2] Whereas "blue-eyed" soul is at best discomforting parody and
genuflection and at worst sinister appropriation (see Michael Bolton),
Nyro evokes the metaphor of "white chocolate," maintaining all the
"flava" and texture that one would expect in the sweetest chunk of deep
chocolate.

Her affinity for bending blue notes notwithstanding, Nyro was quintessentially New York City, a collage of the cultural sounds and gestures that had come to define the Knickerbocker metropolis. In the lyrics to the title track of her second recording, *New York Tendaberry*, Nyro said of the city of her birth that it looked "like a city" but felt "like a religion." The Bronx-bred Nyro was a product of the kind of multiethnic working-class enclaves—of Italians, Jews, African Americans, Afro-Caribs, and Puerto Ricans—that defined New York. These enclaves were, rather ironically, dislodged by public-works projects like the Cross-Bronx Expressway and the World Trade Center. It was on these streets that she was first introduced to a capella–style doo-wop. As Nyro biographer Michele Kort describes it, these "streets became outdoor amphitheaters."[3] One indication of Nyro's wide-ranging influences—New York gumbo, if you will—is the number of distinct groups that would turn her compositions into classic 1960s pop. Tracks like Blood, Sweat, and Tears' "When I Die" (*Blood, Sweat, and Tears*, 1969), Barbra Streisand's "Stoney End" (1970), and the Fifth Dimension's "Wedding Bell Blues" (1969) were all written and recorded by Nyro on her debut, *More Than a New Discovery*. Practically the house writer for the latter group, Nyro also penned (and recorded) their crossover hits "Stoned Soul Picnic" and the political "Save the Country" (which the group, given their own white-bread blackness, dutifully neutered).

Nyro never enjoyed the kind of commercial success that other artists did with her music, though her follow-up recordings, *Eli and the Thirteenth Confession* (1968), *New York Tendaberry* (1969), and *Christmas and the Beads of Sweat* (1970), earned her legitimate critical acclaim and a solid following. After the release of *Gonna Take a Miracle* (1971), Nyro took a sabbatical, marrying David Bianchini briefly, and traveling back and forth between their home in Gloucester, Massachusetts, and her apartment in Manhattan. Nyro didn't record again until after the demise of her marriage in 1974. Nyro's mother, Gilda, died of ovarian cancer in the midst of recording sessions for Nyro's "comeback," *Smile*. Most critics suggest that Nyro's output for the remainder of her life, including *Nested* (1978), *Mother's Spiritual* (1984), and her last studio project, *Walk the Dog and Light the Light* (1993), more thoroughly reflected the so-called radical feminist and animal rights issues that were her passion.[4] In contrast to this conventional thinking, I'd like to suggest that the germs of Nyro's more radical political sensibilities were contained in the earlier *Gonna Take a Miracle*.

Released on November 17, 1971, *Gonna Take a Miracle* has been described by some critics as "a collection of covers of others' songs" and as her "tribute to the Sixties."[5] Others have suggested that the album was a product of Nyro's "writer's block."[6] At the time of her death in 1997, Stephen Holden, writing in the *New York Times*, was more on point when he suggested that the recording was a tribute to "New York street music."[7] Generally speaking, the recording, which marked the beginning of Nyro's industry sabbatical, is one of the least regarded of her first series of recordings. Writing about *Eli and the Thirteenth Confession*, critic Don Butler perhaps captured these perceptions when he wrote, "Nyro never quite scaled those heights again, though her next album, New York Tendaberry, came close. . . . I lost track of Nyro after New York Tendaberry."[8] Butler's comments legitimately speak to the displacement of Nyro's style of coffee house music in the aftermath of Carole King's more polished *Tapestry* and the work of James Taylor, but also to the fact that Nyro began to dig deeper into the style of music that was more organically connected to the political movements of the era. For example, her 1970 release *Christmas and the Beads of Sweat* was produced by classic soul producer Arif Mardin and the Rascals' Felix Cavalieri, and featured the Muscle Shoals sound that marked Aretha Franklin's 1967 breakthrough, *I Have Never Loved a Man*.

But it was with *Gonna Take a Miracle* that Nyro more fully embraced the "black" styles that had always bubbled under her music. The recording featured the legendary production team of Kenneth Gamble and Leon Huff, who only a year later would celebrate the emergence of their "new" label, the Sound of Philadelphia, courtesy of number-one hits by Billy Paul ("Mrs. Jones") and Harold Melvin and the Bluenotes ("If You Don't Know Me by Now"). The duo had produced Dusty Springfield the year before. But in the most dramatic move, Nyro collaborated with the emerging trio known as LaBelle. Featuring the soulful histrionics of lead vocalist Patti LaBelle, the trio would become the standard-bearers of sexually assertive feminist sensibilities in pop music with the release of "Lady Marmalade" in 1974. According to LaBelle in her autobiography *Don't Block the Blessings: Revelations of a Lifetime*, *Gonna Take a Miracle* was the product of a chance meeting with Nyro. LaBelle tagged along with manager Vicki Wickham (Ready, Steady, Go), who was interviewing Nyro for *Melody Maker*. After Nyro and LaBelle sat at a piano singing some of the R&B hits that Nyro had grown up singing, Nyro asked LaBelle to sing background vocals for the project.[9] I contend that Nyro and LaBelle's *Gonna Take a Miracle* not only serves as a "tribute" to the burgeoning politics of the "soul" era, but also represents the organic rubric of Nyro's later queer and feminist politics. *Gonna Take a Miracle* systematically challenged and undermined the racial and gender assumptions associated with New York–style "street singing"—the early incarnations of doo-wop and the Detroit-based soul music that Motown founder Berry Gordy would dub "the Sound of Young America."

At the time of their collaboration, the LaBelle trio was in a state of transition. In its earliest form, the group was a quartet known as the Ordettes, which included Patsy Holte, Nona Hendrix, Sarah Dash, and Sandra Tucker (Sandra was later replaced by Cindy Birdsong, who later replaced Florence Ballard in the Supremes). Upon signing with Harold Robinson's Bluebelle label in 1962, the group was renamed the Blue-Belles and its lead singer, "little" Patsy Holte, became Patti LaBelle. At the time of their signing, the Blue-Belles actually already had a song that was a hit in their native Philadelphia, "I Sold My Heart to the Junkman," though it was not a song that featured Dash, Hendrix, Birdsong, and LaBelle. The "original" Blue-Belles were in fact the Chicago-based Starlets, who signed a "six-month" contract with Robinson a month before, despite the fact they were already signed to Carl Davis's Pam Records. When the Starlets pulled out of their contract with Bluebelle, Robinson was stuck with a hit record and no group to promote it, so the Ordettes were signed to become the the Blue-Belles.[10] The Blue-Belles went on to become solid Chitlin' Circuit regulars until Wickham became their manager in 1970 and wanted to instill wholesale changes to the group, most notably changing the name of the group, then known as Patti LaBelle and the Bluebelles. According to LaBelle, Wickham saw the group, now a trio after Birdsong's defection to the Supremes in 1967, as "three black women singing about racism, sexism and eroticism."[11] Their "debut," *LaBelle*, included a cover of Nyro's "Time and Love."

The project's title track was originally recorded by the Royalettes in 1965. "It's Gonna Take a Miracle" is one of five tracks, including three that were recorded by Martha and the Vandellas, that were originally identified with "girl groups." The opening track, "I Met Him on a Sunday," is remake of the Shirelles' "I Met Him on a Sunday (Ronde, Ronde)," which helped introduce the group to mass audiences in 1958. The Shirelles are arguably the most popular of the black girl groups that were not products of the Motown assembly line. Nyro's choices here are important in that they acknowledge the influence of girl groups within a genre that has until recently been given short shrift by music critics and scholars and has contemporarily been at the core of the national romantic nostalgia for the 1950s and so-called simpler, less complicated times. (For example, the recent PBS productions, *Doo Wop 50* and *51* pass off the strident industry apartheid of the time as friendly competition.) In this regard, Nyro's renditions of the music of the Shirelles and the Royalettes—songs that open and close the project—are some of the most conventional choices on the album, as they simply pay tribute to one of the most popular and most obscure of the girl groups. But even those conventional choices go beyond the "white girl" paying tribute to the "shimmying, sequined" brown girls. Nyro's choices represented a legitimate attempt to canonize the influence of those women in a genre in which girl groups are generally seen as little more than harmonious eye candy, not to mention the disparities between the reception of mainstream eye candy and their chocolate-drop sisters—the career arcs of Ronnie Spector and Darlene Love being instructive here. In this regard, Nyro, as a figure who is regarded as being one of the most, if not the most significant female singer-songwriter in pop music (Roberta Flack, Joni Mitchell, and Carole King notwithstanding), elevates the genius and brilliance of those groups as vocalists.

"I Met Him on a Sunday" opens with Nyro trading lyrics and "coos" with the trio, against a backdrop of hand claps and snapping figures—

LaBelle's signature style, as heard on the lyric "and he didn't come Friday." The song's opening immediately connects the project to the "street sounds" that frame Nyro's memories of the late 1950s and 1960s, but also recalls the ways that young black girls often cultivated unique and alternative spheres of expression in street games such as double-dutch and hand-clapping games. In her fascinating essay "Translating Double-Dutch to Hip Hop: The Musical Vernacular of Black Girls' Play," Kyra Gaunt argues that "women are rarely represented as genera-tors of black music culture and style in spite of their actual participation. They are more often perceived as subsidiary to the 'real' players of musi-cal invention. . . . However, if one considers double-dutch and hand-clapping games as musical activity, African-American girls' and women's musical authority is evident."[12] With the chorus, the quartet's vocals are joined by Nyro's signature piano as the soaring harmonies of LaBelle take the song to an artistic complexity that the original did not achieve. The song then abruptly shifts gear in a way that is reminiscent of the kinds of "queer" shifts that marked *Eli and the Thirteenth Confession*. This particular moment on the album signals that Nyro is not simply parroting the "street music" of her youth, but attempting something more substantive.

Nyro's intentions are clearer in her renditions of "Jimmy Mack," "Nowhere to Run," and "Dancing in the Streets," which were originally recorded by Martha and the Vandellas. In comparison to the Supremes, the queens of Motown, Martha and the Vandellas, as Suzanne Smith notes, "projected a grittier, less refined, more defiant image."[13] Thus Nyro's choice to record the music of the Vandellas suggests that she wanted to more directly connect to the vitality of that sound and that model of black femininity as opposed to the crossover pop candy of the Supremes. Whereas Nyro and LaBelle play it straight on "Jimmy Mack" (a subtle reminder on Nyro's part that the "white girl" can sang!), the political undercurrents of the project are made more explicit with Nyro's renditions of "Dancing in the Street" and "Nowhere to Run," which both clock in at around five minutes, making them the longest tracks on the recording. The length of the songs represents a clear effort to recon-stitute the general perceptions of the songs.

Such interpretations of these songs are also buoyed by some of the perceptions of the recordings at the time they were originally recorded. As Marvin Gaye, who cowrote "Dancing in the Street," related in his biography *Divided Soul*, "Of all the acts back then, I thought Martha and the Vandellas came closest to really saying something. It wasn't a conscious thing, but when they sang numbers like 'Quicksand' or 'Wild One' or 'Nowhere to Run' or 'Dancing in the Street,' they captured a spirit that felt political to me."[14] Smith notes in *Dancing in the Street*, her fascinating social history of Detroit and the Motown Corporation, that "Dancing in the Street" was never just a party song. Music, particularly music created in Detroit's black community during the 1960s, could rarely, if ever, transcend the politically and racially charged environment in which it was produced.[15]

Nyro and LaBelle's version of "Dancing in the Street" is conflated with Major Lance's "Monkey Time." The Lance tune, which was written and produced by Curtis Mayfield, morphs into "Dancing in the Street" about a minute and a half into the five-minute recording. The song's lyrical themes are naturally married, as both discuss dances and parties with folks "dancing so hard" to "sweet, sweet music" and "swinging and swaying" to the grooves found in the street "way over town." Nyro sings the "Monkey Time" lyric "way over town" twice before segueing into "Dancing in the Street." This is also congruent with the opening lines of "Dancing in the Street," which name Chicago, New Orleans, and New York as cities "ready for a brand new beat." Given the political era in which the songs were originally recorded, it is not difficult to understand Gaye's assertion that a song like "Dancing in the Street" was political: these cities, along with Detroit, were likely incubators for the kind political rage that was unleashed in Watts during the summer of 1965.

More specifically, as Smith chronicles in *Dancing in the Street*, many commentators saw a link between the song and the riots that broke out in Detroit in July of 1967. One observer suggested in the Kerner Commission Report that youth were "dancing amidst the flames."[16] In this context, "Monkey Time" and "Dancing in the Street" link the insurgent politics of black youth in major urban centers. The 1967 Detroit insurrections, which came two years after the 1965 Watts rebellion, were among the many reasons why Motown founder Berry Gordy, Jr., relocated his Detroit-based company to Los Angeles in the early 1970s. Gordy's move mirrored the general migration of whites and middle-class blacks out of the city. By the mid-1970s, Detroit was in the midst of a tragic economic downturn that was largely precipitated by the collapse of the city's automobile industry.

In this regard, Nyro and LaBelle's decision to recast the original Vandellas lyric "Can't forget the motor city" as "Don't forget the motor city" seems a conscious reference to the insurrections and the social and cultural malaise that would haunt the city for some time. The lyric is performed in classic "drive" form as a refrain alternately shouted with the lyric "dancing in the street," giving this moment in the song an even more explicit political meaning. Additionally, the explicit linking of "Monkey Time" to "Dancing in the Street," given the latter's history as more than a dance song, suggests that leisure activities like dancing and partying (or what the Last Poets call "party and bullshit") and dance styles such as the Monkey or the Sophisticated Cissy, can be metaphorically linked to black political agency. It may also be worth noting that Nyro's sanctioning of "Monkey Time" highlights the political narratives that undergird the music of the song's composer, Curtis Mayfield, who at the time of the Nyro and LaBelle recording was making the transition to "serious" singer-songwriter. His groundbreaking *Superfly* soundtrack would be released just months after *Gonna Take a Miracle*.

In contrast to "Dancing in the Street," Nyro and LaBelle's performance of "Nowhere to Run" is less connected to the racial politics of 1960s urban America and more connected to the performance of feminist sensibilities. The song, which is standard tormented-lover-who-can't-break-away fare, was written by the famed Motown production trio Holland-Dozier-Holland. The song was also performed as a pre-MTV video for "Murray the K's" (Murray Kaufman) television program *It's What's Happening, Baby*. The performance was staged on the Ford Mustang assembly line with Martha and the Vandellas sitting inside an unfinished Mustang. Smith notes in *Dancing in the Street* that while the performance served as a free commercial for the Ford company and buttressed Motown's position as a legitimate corporate entity, the song also highlighted the "tedium of assembly-line work" and the fact that auto-workers had "nowhere to go if automation displaced them from their jobs."[17] As an alternative to Smith's reading and in contrast to the traditional reading of the song, I would like to suggest that the song represents the struggle of women and feminists within highly structured patriarchal and masculine spaces. In other words, women who have "nowhere to hide" from the power and influence of patriarchy ultimately have to cultivate spaces within and in spite of that patriarchy in order to articulate their feminist and womanist sensibilities.

Within these interpretative contexts, Nyro and LaBelle read the song relatively straight throughout the first two minutes. Then, in classic Nyro style, the song abruptly shifts, with Nyro first repeating the lyric "I've got nowhere to run to" in a lilting falsetto four times, briefly followed by LaBelle repeatedly shouting, "no, no, ain't got nowhere." The LaBelle performance in this instance is emphatic and defiant, suggesting the very different terrains in which white women and black women have often embraced feminist expression: Nyro's lyric is repressed and restrained in comparison to LaBelle's. LaBelle's distinction between having nowhere to "run" and nowhere to "hide" suggests the further complications of race for black women, as their brown skin will not allow them to "hide" within a racist society, even if they can "run" from patriarchy. After the LaBelle refrain is repeated four times, the trio repeats its section, this time joined by Nyro. Nyro's lyrical joining suggests the broader ways that black and white women were linked within the structures of patriarchy that dominated their lives. Musically, this moment of the song is notable because the backing musicians on the track drop out; Nyro and LaBelle sing virtually a capella, accompanied only by the sounds of hand clapping and a jangling tambourine.

Though the traditions of black gospel are undercurrents throughout the recording—LaBelle's voice would have it no other way—this moment of the song is explicitly gospel. In this regard, this section of "Nowhere to Run" recalls the improvised drive sections that often accompany live gospel performances. According to gospel historian Ray Allen, many gospel songs feature extended segments of chanted and sung improvisation known as 'drive', 'gospel' or 'working sections'. A drive section begins when the instrumentalists stall on one chord while the background singers repeat a single vocal line over and over. At this point the lead singer begins to ad-lib, switching from his or her regular singing voice into a tense, high-pitched, rhythmically repetitive chant or singing chant.[18]

Nyro's use of her falsetto voice at the beginning of the drive section fits within these improvisational conventions. The exchange between Nyro and LaBelle in this section also speaks to the practice of switching leads within gospel drives. As Allen notes, "Improvised drive sections allow lead singers to express their own personal feelings" and serve as their "final and most persuasive strategy for achieving social and spiritual union with their listeners."[19] Thus, within this moment of "Spirit-induced joy" or "gospel frenzy" Nyro and LaBelle create a space for feminist catharsis, notably within the context of black feminist or womanist spiritual practices. At the end of the a capella section of the song, Nyro repeats her earlier refrain, though she noticeably embellishes the lyrics in ways that she didn't during the earlier refrain. Nyro's second "solo" refrain suggests the ways that white women can be impacted by the feminist realities of black women.

Gonna Take a Miracle was the first project in which Nyro recorded primarily the compositions of other artists (she did cover the Drifters' "Up on the Roof" on *Christmas and the Beads of Sweat*). Kort notes that Nyro "always used her own chords and start-and-stop tempos on others' tunes, fully 'Nyro-izing' them."[20] Nyro often battled with her male producers to more fully realize her own artistic vision. Reflecting on the initial versions of Nyro's very first single, "Wedding Bell Blues," Herb Bernstein, who produced Nyro's debut, *More Than a Discovery*, says that "she had that little riff—dah bah buh DOO buh DOO—that she used a lot, but she'd stop every sixteen measures and go into another tempo. I said 'look, I'm as artistic as the next person, but you have to think about the commerciality of these things . . . you're gonna lose the average listener.'"[21] Nyro's longtime road manager Lee Housekeeper adds that Nyro was a "good target in those days because she dared to be creative

... and on top of that she was a woman. Everyone called her overindulgent." Housekeeper also notes that artists such as Simon and Garfunkel were also extravagantly creative, but they were "selling zillions of records and they were men."[22] In this context it's not surprising that Nyro would turn initially to Mardin and Cavalieri (for *Christmas and the Beads of Sweat*) and then to Gamble and Huff as producers, given their associations with R&B and soul, who would be more in sync with her fluid artistic spirit. A track like "Nowhere to Run" perfectly captures such fluidity.

Songs like "The Bells" (cowritten by Marvin Gaye), "You've Really Got a Hold on Me," "Spanish Harlem" (which Aretha Franklin recorded just months before Nyro), and "The Wind" were all originally recorded by and largely thought of as "male" songs. Though all of the songs can be interpreted as non–gender specific, the choices do reflect Nyro's ongoing efforts to place her own "feminine" voice into a tradition. According to Nyro, "The Wind," originally recorded by Nolan Strong and the Diablos, was one of the first "rock and roll" records she ever heard—"earthy, romantic music."[23] Nolan Strong was a cousin of Motown artist and producer Barrett Strong and was an early influence on Smokey Robinson, who, like Strong, was a falsetto. Nyro's recording of "The Wind" and "You've Really Got a Hold on Me" represents a thoughtful and informed tribute to Detroit-styled doo-wop and its logical excavation in the early Motown sound. But in one instance, Nyro's choice of recording a male-gendered song offers interesting insight into Nyro's sexuality.

In her obituary for Nyro, who in 1998 succumbed to ovarian cancer like her mother had, Michele Kort coyly writes, "to the shock and sadness over her premature passing (she was just 49) was thus the added take for many old fans: Laura Nyro was gay?"[24] Nyro was essentially outted as a bisexual (she preferred the term *woman identified*) in the official press release of her death, which listed Maria Desiderio as her partner. Nyro was very protective of her personal life, so there had been little public inkling that she was gay. But there were longtime fans who always viewed Nyro's music as "gay." Most point specifically to the recording "Emmie" (from *Eli and the Thirteenth Confession*), in which Nyro sings about the young woman "Emmie/Emily" who ornaments the "earth for me." For some of those fans, including Kort and songwriter Desmond Child (who penned Ricky Martin's "Livin' la Vida Loca"), it was not that Nyro was acknowledging her sexuality with the song, but rather that she "helped us realize we were gay . . . helped us acknowledge we were bent."[25] Though it has received scant attention (Kort barely mentions it in her biography), Nyro and LaBelle's version of "Desiree" also serves a "queered" aural space. While Nyro's "Emmie" was a composition of her own that was addressed to a woman, "Desiree" was originally recorded in 1957 by the Harlem-based Charts, who were all men. Given the heterosexist context of the original version, the Nyro-LaBelle version subverts the song's original intent ("why do I love you so?"), in effect celebrating same-gender romance.

Nyro and LaBelle's version of "Desiree" highlights interesting similarities in the reception of Nyro and LaBelle among male homosexual audiences. Kort suggests that for some gay men "Nyro's powerful femininity" was an inspiration to them.[26] Theater critic David Roman's comments are instructive in this regard. Reflecting on his own youth, Roman writes of Nyro, ·

> apart from Joni Mitchell, there is no other female singer whom I most associate with the formative years of my adolescence. . . . I believe listening to the music of Laura Nyro and Joni Mitchell helped me through a queer adolescence marked by fear and confusion. Both were a lifeline to something other, something outside the tight constraints of a normal world. Full of mystery and possibility, their music moved me inward so that I could eventually come out.[27]

Historically Judy Garland has often been cited as inspiring the "feminine performance" of post–World War II male homosexuals. Roman comments suggest that Nyro also inspired such a role.

Garland's relevancy to post–World War II gay men is largely the product of her proximity (and that of her defining film role) to gay men. In a humorous essay about a "gay pride" parade, comic Bruce Vilanch compares the contemporary movement to an earlier era: "there wasn't

any pride but by whillikers, there was dignity. We hid in dark bars listening to Judy Garland records. . . . We spoke in code. You weren't out,
you weren't even gay—you were a friend of Dorothy."[28] "Dorothy" is of
course a reference to Garland's character in *The Wizard of Oz*. The
phrase *a friend of Dorothy* is most directly related to the character of the
Cowardly Lion (portrayed by Bert Lahr). In a brilliant essay, Reid Davis
suggests that the character was an example of a cinematic "sissy," arguing that the movie's "stereotype of sissiness, the Cowardly Lion, operates
both as an aesthetic (the character of the Cowardly Lion) and a social
construct (a production of the sissy type)."[29] Thus, for some gay men, as
Vilanch attests, Dorothy's relationship with the Cowardly Lion became
a metaphor for their own "private" homosexuality, one that
"Dorothy"/Garland ostensibly protected. Garland's status in this regard
was further cemented by her proclivity for marrying gay/bisexual men,
as two of her husbands (Vincente Minnelli and Mark Herron) were
gay/bisexual.[30] Michael Joseph Gross notes that critics often used their
reviews of Garland's performances to derisively critique homosexual culture.[31] The general public became more familiar with Garland's relationship to gay male culture in the United States in the late 1960s after the
appearance of Mart Crowley's 1968 play *The Boys in the Band* (which
references Garland directly in the dialogue; the play's title was drawn
from dialogue in Garland's film *A Star is Born*) and the Stonewall riot in
June 1969. The riot ("Out of the closets and into the streets), which has
been romantically portrayed as a coming-out party for the gay rights
movement, occurred only a few hours after Garland's funeral in front of
a well-known gay bar in New York City's Greenwich Village.[32]

Of interest to me here is Patti LaBelle's own history with black male
homosexuals who embrace feminine modes of performance. LaBelle has
been linked to Garland's legacy on the strength of her over-the-top rendition of Garland's signature tune "Over the Rainbow." Originally
recorded by the Blue-Belles in 1966, the song remains the cornerstone
of Patti LaBelle's live performances. As Paul Outlaw writes, "for a gay
man of color, it has always been permissible to identify secretly with a
Superwoman, whose big personality or big voice expresses his yearning
for romance."[33] According to Outlaw, "if a brother get too caught up in

the image of black femininity—'Oo, I wanna be like her"—he may have to behave like the snap queens made notorious (and popular) by *In Living Color*'s Antoine and Blaine," adding that for some of these gay black men "getting in touch with that inner girl-child demands the Divas."[34] It is in this context that Patti LaBelle has become one of the primary templates for a black male performance (either as homosexuals or in comedic drag performances) of the "Diva." In his classic live recording *Living Proof*, disco star Sylvester, who for a long time was the most well known "out" black musical performer, coyly references LaBelle's stature among black male "Divas" (those who are gay, bisexual, heterosexual, and "unknown") in his stirring (and LaBelle-like) performance of the LaBelle composition "You Are My Friend." Within this context, black gay men were not a "friend of Dorothy" but rather a "friend of Patti."[35] What I am suggesting here is that the collaboration between LaBelle and Nyro created not only a space for cross-racial feminist thought, but also one that allowed the possibility for gay male performance of femininity or the "Diva."

In addition, *Gonna Take a Miracle* allows a broad conversation between alternative concepts of public spaces, spaces where the New York/San Francisco coffee house aesthetic comes in contact with the all-praised Chitlin' Circuit. Given the marginalization and even demonization of these spaces from the American mainstream of the late 1960s and the 1970s, the kind of coming together of the Haight-Ashbury crowd and the Apollo theater faithful, fully realized with Aretha Franklin's legendary *Live at the Fillmore West* recording (1971), was not as far-fetched as it might have seemed. This was a dynamic that the Black Panther Party realized very early in their development. And yet there were other examples, such as "Ms. Ree" bringing the soul to Carole King's "Natural Woman" four years before King would take the stage herself and elevate the singer-songwriter concept to the next level with *Tapestry*. In the world of early-1970s pop, there was no greater validation of your skills than to claim that the "Queen of Soul" sang your tune—made it a pop standard on the real. Even the radical multiracial chic of Miles Davis's *Bitches Brew*, or the later work of Wayne Shorter and Joe Zawinal (who was as Chiltin' Circuit as they come in the role of the Austrian-born funk master behind Cannonball Adderley classics such as "Mercy, Mercy, Mercy" and "Country Preacher") with Weather Report, spoke to the powerful ways in which artists were progressively altering the often segregated musical landscape.

I submit, though, that the collaboration between Nyro and LaBelle was the most significant of these pairings because it placed the issue of gender and sexuality in the mix, alongside traditional critical musings about race. This was an era when several women singer-songwriters were coming to the forefront with progressive and even radical concepts of themselves as musicians, women, and social agents. For every Carole King there was a Roberta Flack, whose *First Take* (1969) is one of the most exquisite debuts ever in black pop. For every Joni Mitchell there was a Valerie Simpson, who recorded two groundbreaking discs for Motown that threw the label for a promotional loop—they were clueless as to how to promote her. And tragically, for every Janis Joplin there was an Esther Phillips, whose version of Gil Scott-Heron's "Home Is Where the Hatred Is" was as stone cold as a recovering addict laying comatose on the cobblestone. Think of the musical possibilities that would have emerged if any of these women had been allowed to "speak" to each other in the way that LaBelle and Nyro did with *Gonna Take a Miracle*.

Ultimately it was the trio of LaBelle that realized so many of those possibilities. In the years between *Gonna Take a Miracle* and Nyro's "comeback" disc, *Smile* (1976), LaBelle would release four recordings, including *Moon Shadow* (1972) and *Nightbirds* (1974), the latter of which includes their classic pop crossover "Lady Marmalade." Prior to taking on the job of managing the trio, Vicki Wickham was quoted as telling the trio that they couldn't "wear those nice little frilly frocks and wigs, we've got to rethink it. You've got to make a statement, you're women, there's a lot to be said."[36] Wickham's comments were a firm reference to the tradition of girl groups like the Supremes, who donned the very pretty uniforms of pleasure and sophistication for audiences at places like the Copacabana. Everything that the trio did in that five-year period ran counter to that tradition. According to Patti LaBelle, "Our first album cover would give the world a glimpse of things to come.

Roberta Flack, First Take

Vicki wanted us to lose the empire dresses and wear jeans. *Jeans.* She
wanted us to imitate the scruffy, don't-give-a-damn look of white rock
groups. . . . I damn near died."[37] In her remarkable "Poem for Aretha,"
Nikki Giovanni speaks pointedly about the attempts of various black
female vocalists, such as Nancy Wilson, Dionne Warwick, and Diana
Ross, to fall visually in line with the Black Power aesthetics of the period
("Diana Ross had to get an Afro wig").

The three aforementioned women are notable because they were, to
varying degrees, prime examples of the crossover sensibilities of some

Laura Nyro, Gonna Take a Miracle

black artists at the time: they were more likely to be found performing in upscale supper clubs than on the Chitlin' Circuit. While there were prominent examples of new artists who fit firmly into the new black aesthetic of the early 1970s (Roberta Flack and Valerie Simpson among them), Aretha Franklin and LaBelle were among the few female artists who were legitimately able to remake themselves. Franklin's image, for example, vacillated between the soul sista in dashiki garb (see the cover art for 1972's *Young, Gifted, and Black* and *Amazing Grace,* and *Hey Now Hey (The Other Side of the Sky),* (from 1973) to the sexy Afroed mama portrayed on the covers of *Let Me in Your Life* (1973) and *With Everything in Me* (1974).

LaBelle pushed the envelope even further in this regard, drawing from a blank template of black femininity in which the only constant was a belief that black women were best positioned to challenge the essentialist nature of blackness and womaness, on some level recalling Anna Julia Cooper's classic sayings, "when and where I enter [the black woman] the black race enters with me." Although Nona Hendrix wrote many of the group's provocative tracks, including the stirring "Sunday's News" and "Touch Me All Over," both from *Moon Shadow*, like the songs from *Gonna Take a Miracle* discussed above, the trio took on tunes decidedly outside of the canon of black pop. Songs like Pete Townsend's "Won't Get Fooled Again," the Stones' "Wild Horses," and Cat Stevens's "Moon Shadow," the title track of LaBelle's second release, are given a new coat of paint. But this paint is funky, churchified, and decidedly feminist in its projection. LaBelle even managed to take on the reigning soul griot of the era with a god-fearing rendition of Gil Scott-Heron's "The Revolution Will Not Be Televised." (Note: A griot is a traditional West African poet-historian. Black Art poets such as Gil Scott-Heron and Sonia Sanchez are direct links to the tradition, as are hip-hop artists of contemporary era.) It is such risk taking, as witnessed on LaBelle covers as well as originals, that sets the stage for the group's biggest commercial success. After doing two discs for Warner and one for RCA, *Nightbirds* (1974) was their first release for the Epic label. Epic was responsible for the progressive legacy of Sly and the Family Stone, but it also managed to underpromote the late Minnie Riperton and drop Shuggie Otis the same year that *Nightbirds* was released, because Epic had no idea how to promote Otis's recovered classic, *Inspiration Information*, which was reissued recently on David Byrne's Luaka Bop label.

If Gonna Take a Miracle was a tribute to the street-corner domains of black and Latin youth, LaBelle's "Lady Marmalade" was a tribute to one of the only public spaces where women were allowed some sense of autonomous expression. Produced by the Creole funk master Allen Toussaint, who had laced the Pointer Sisters the year before with the infectious "Yes, We Can, Can," and written by Kenny Noland and Bob Crewe, "Lady Marmalade" became the trio's only million-seller. The classic chorus, with the line "Voulez-vous coucher avec moi ce soir?" ("Do you want to sleep with me tonight?"), is one of the most memorable pop music lines from the 1970s. Rather than a narrative about the illicit and illegitimate culture that supports prostitution in places like New Orleans and Hunts Point ("pimps up, hoes down"), in the hands of LaBelle the song became an anthem of sexual assertion and empowerment—themes that had been present in LaBelle's music throughout the period. Thus, a track like Marlena Shaw's "Street Talkin' Woman," when it was released a year later, could be legitimately interpreted within a feminist context to the extent that feminist discourses have argued that women should control how their sexuality is portrayed and realized.

According to LaBelle, when Nyro joined the trio on stage to perform "Lady Marmalade" in the spring of 1975, it was a high point of the group's career. By 1977, the group had disbanded, with Hendrix moving on to more fully express the soul-rock hybrid that had always been at the heart of her compositions, and Dash having some minor success performing disco music. But it was Patti LaBelle who emerged as the most significant voice of the trio, achieving mainstream success with her classic 1984 track "If Only You Knew" and "On My Own," which she recorded with Michael McDonald on her MCA debut in 1985. Though many of LaBelle's current fans are likely oblivious to the legacy of the group, and even more so about the significance of Nyro to LaBelle's career, in her autobiography *Don't Block the Blessings*, LaBelle admits that she and Nyro developed a strong personal bond even as their professional profiles went in opposite directions.

In the spring of 2001, the legacy of the group LaBelle was invoked as Lil' Kim, Missy Elliot, Christina Aguilera, Pink, and Mya came together to record "Lady Marmalade" for the soundtrack for the film, *Moulin Rouge*. Though the quintet is directly connected to the legacy of Nyro and LaBelle, the kind of sexuality the trio LaBelle flaunted in the early 1970s is little more than a marketing ploy for teeny-bopper pop. Yes, sex always sells, and that was part of the reason why LaBelle struck such a chord with the original "Lady Marmalade," but where the original held power because it challenged so many taboos surrounding black female sexuality, twenty-five years later the new version was just further evidence that the performance of sexuality remains just about the only place that women have any real influence within the music industry. Meanwhile, a host of important women artists—Sarah McLachlan, Res, Tracy Chapman, and Ursula Rucker, to name a few—will never have the kind of access to audiences and consumers that the Pinks, Eves, and Gwen Stefanis regularly have on *TRL* or *106th and Park*. And while smart tracks like the recent collaboration by Stefani and Eve, "Let Me Blow Ya Mind" are promising, the real apartheid conditions within the music industry go against the kind of groundbreaking collaboration that Nyro and LaBelle realized three decades ago with *Gonna Take a Miracle*. Somewhere, Nyro, Esther Phillips, and Janis Joplin dream of the day that Shelby Lynne walks into a studio with Jill Scott.

CHAPTER EIGHT

NUYORICAN NOSTALGIA

(*For Francisco Pabon*)

"Sweet kids in hunger slums / firecrackers break / and they cross / and they dust / and they skate / and the night comes . . .
> —Laura Nyro, "New York Tendaberry"

The duality between apparent fixity and imminent relocation may account for the special appeal of casita design among the impoverished and disenfranchised [Puerto Ricans] of the South Bronx. Under the present conditions of inner-city life, they too, like their nomadic ancestors in Puerto Rico or at some earlier time in their own lives, face constant threat of removal or having to pick up and do it somewhere else.
> —Juan Flores, *From Bomba to Hip-Hop: Puerto Rican Culture and Latino Identity*

These albums are gonna be the encyclopedia of a sound that was born in New York.

> —Little Louie Vega

The nation—the world, really—has been in a "New York State of Mind." Post-9/11 so much of the city has been memorialized, mourned, celebrated, deified, remembered. While a tattered flag is seemingly on national tour and the New York Mets and Yankees don NYPD and NYFD caps and other paraphernalia, the very core of the city—its people—are innocent bystanders in the drive toward revenge and economic recovery. While the nation rightfully mourns the municipal heroes who died on 9/11 and the captains of (financial) industry who lost their lives, there has been little attention to the folks—the everyday folks—who toiled and barely survived with barely survivable living wages working as cleaning staff, busboys, maintenance workers, and food service workers. These folks, many black and brown, with accents that recalled Santa Domingo and Kingston, more than Brooklyn and the Bronx, have given and taken so much from New York, New York. In a particularly touching NPR segment on the "Sounds of the World Trade Center" memorial project, one gentleman reflected that he missed the sounds of Salsa that emanated from the radios of the Latino workers who cleaned offices after business hours.

Kenny "Dope" Gonzalez and Little Louie Vega know these people well. For more than a decade, the duo, professionally known as Masters at Work (MAW), has been the most effective progenitor of what has come to be known as Nuyorican soul, a cultural and social mélange of the sights and sounds of the "real" New York—the place of pastrami, jerk chicken, cuchifritos, ginger beer, Now-and-Laters, piraguas, and Sunday summers at Orchard Beach or Pelham Bay Park, where the rhythms of "spanglish" and patois manage to overwhelm even the city's famed high humidity. This is the New York of the mid- to late-'60s. Lucy and Desi (the Cuban band leader who reportedly disliked Puerto Ricans) are off to Connecticut, but for those like them desiring to stay close to New York City, Robert Moses took care of everything: Jones Beach, the Cross-Bronx Expressway, the Henry Hudson Parkway—the ways that folks like Lucy and Desi got out of Dodge because *their* city was being overrun by those brown and black and all the (nonwhite) colors in between. This is the New York that was created post-1965 with an immigration act that changed the face of a nation by repealing the national origin quota that allowed for more favorable immigration opportunities for western and northern Europeans (the right kind of whites, apparently). According to census data, there were over 1 million immigrants, primarily from the Caribbean, Latin America, and Asia, who came to New York in the two decades following the 1965 Immigration Act. During that first decade, the majority of "Latino" immigrants were from the island of Puerto Rico. While significant energy was expended by Puerto Rican nationals over the issue of statehood versus nationhood, a significant portion of native Puerto Ricans created a new space for the cultivation of an "authentic" Puerto Rican sensibility in the city of New York.

Although the writer Eugene Mohr traces the roots of term *Nuyorican culture* to 1916, well-known "Nuyorican" scholar Juan Flores identifies a distinct Nuyorican vision that emerged in the 1960s with the publication of Piri Thomas's *Down These Mean Streets* in 1967 (the Nuyorican counterpart to the late Claude Brown's *Manchild in the Promised Land*) and poetry collections by Pedro Pietri (*Puerto Rican Obituary*, 1973) and Tato Laviera, whose early work is compiled in *La Carreta Made a U-Turn* (1979). In his book *Divided Borders: Essays on Puerto Rican Identity*, Flores writes that "with the Nuyoricans, the Puerto Rican community in the United States [had] arrived at a modality of literary expression corresponding to its position as a non-assimilating colonial minority. The most obvious mark of this new literature emanating from the community is the language: the switch from Spanish to English and bilingual writing."[1] But Flores is careful to caution that "this language transfer should not be mistaken for assimilation in a wide cultural sense . . . using English is a sign of being [in America], not necessarily of liking it here or of belonging."[2] The Nuyorican sensibility is probably best captured by poets Miguel Algarin and Miguel Pinero (see the recent Benjamin Bratt film *Pinero*) in the introduction to their anthology *Nuyorican Poetry: An Anthology of Words and Feelings*, where they write that "for the poor New York Puerto Rican there are three survival possibilities. The first is to labor for money and exist in eternal debt. The second is to refuse to trade hours for dollars and to live by your will and 'hustle.' The third possibility is to create alternative behavioral habits."[3] Algarin and Pinero were among the founding members of the now famous Nuyorican Poets Cafe that is part of a larger tradition of New York–based Puerto Ricans "establishing makeshift, neighborhood spaces . . . to accommodate the rising generation of bilingual and English-language writers."[4]

Whereas social spaces like the Nuyorican Poets Cafe and the New Rican Village were set up to respond to distinct literary and spoken-word concerns, both are part of a tradition of "makeshift" social spaces created by Puerto Ricans, the casita being the most prominent example. According to Flores in his most recent book *From Bomba to Hip-Hop: Puerto Rican Culture and Latino Identity*, casitas are "those little houses, modeled after the humble dwellings in rural Puerto Rico of years gone by, which have sprung up in the vacant lots of New York's impoverished Puerto Rican neighborhoods since the late 1980s . . . [their] design and atmosphere magically evocative of the rural Caribbean and now serving as a social club and cultural center for inhabitants of the surrounding tenements."[5] The genius of casita culture lies in the ways that the Puerto Rican poor in the South Bronx and El Barrio (East Harlem) have transformed the vacant lots of those boroughs into something of value and sustenance. The images of burned-out tenements and vacant lots accompanied some of the most vivid and accordingly distorted images of the black and Puerto Rican poor in New York City in the 1970s and 1980s. Then president Jimmy Carter's "celebrated" visit to Charlotte Street in the Bronx in 1977 (a calculated stab at Republican congressional leadership and former president Gerald Ford, who told NYC to "drop dead" as the city teetered at the edge of economic collapse in the mid-1970s) and the film *Fort Apache, the Bronx* went a long way in demonizing the South Bronx and its inhabitants in the public imagination. In contrast to those negative images, casitas and the music that found a home in their spaces "celebrate the blatant fact of collective occupancy."[6]

Like the Chitlin' Circuit institutions that foreground black working-class identity and cultural expression in the post–World War II era, casitas represent a conscious attempt to reconstitute community and common identity among Nuyorican immigrants. The "glue," if you will, that brings these often disparate bodies together is the music of bomba and plena, which are African-based forms of Puerto Rican popular music. In his earlier book *Divided Borders*, Flores argues that the "popular song has played a central role in the cultural life Puerto Ricans in this country."[7] Flores later suggests that in this regard the "worlds of the casita and plena are thus symbiotically related as forms of performative expression of working class Puerto Ricans, especially those of Afro-Caribbean origins from the coastal areas of the island."[8]

Flores identifies Marcial Reyes as one of the folks responsible for bringing plena to Puerto Rican communities in New York in the 1950s. The birth of plena dates back to the migration of the families of formerly enslaved Africans from the islands of St. Kitts, Nevins, Barbados, and Jamaica at the beginning of the twentieth century. While there was a distinct African presence in Puerto Rico before that era, plena was an attempt to reconstitute the "Boricuan" identity that has been celebrated contemporarily in the music of Latino hip-hop artists like the late Christopher "Big Pun" Rios (see his collaboration with Joe on "Still Not a Playa") and Fat Joe. Flores explains that the emergence of plena "coincided with the consolidation of the Puerto Rican working class; it accompanied and lent idiosyncratic musical expression to that historical process" as these populations were displaced and marginalized because of American rule (which began in 1898) and later by efforts to industrialize.[9] As Flores asserts, with the coming together of "former slaves, peasants and artisans" and the convergence of their "life experience and social interests," plena, parallel to the African-American blues, became a primary conduit for the popular expressions of the Puerto Rican working class, including their concerns about less than affirming labor conditions.[10] The working-class roots of plena is particularly important to an understanding of how plena functioned in Puerto Rican spaces in New York in the mid-twentieth century, as the form emerges in opposition to the more privileged "Afro-Cuban" forms of music that made international stars of musicians like Machito, Maria Bauza, who both collaborated with Dizzy Gillespie in the 1940s, and later Mongo Santamaria ("Watermelon Man"). The privileging of Afro-Cuban music reflected the general privileging of Cuban immigrants over Puerto Rican immigrants—hence my earlier mention of Desi Arnez's ethnic politics. While the differences in Afro-Cuban forms and music like plena and bomba cannot be simply reduced to an issue of authenticity, the latter forms did more reflect the sensibilities of the emerging Nuyorican working class.

By the mid-1950s, Puerto Rican immigrants were sharing working-class and poor urban spaces with the generation of post–World War II African-American migrants from the deep South and what was becoming a steady stream of Afro-Caribbean immigrants from Jamaica and Trinidad-Tobago. Whereas Leonard Bernstein's classic musical *West Side Story* perhaps romanticized the clashes between New York Italians and Puerto Ricans in the postwar period, the reality was that many Puerto Ricans were forced to share public space with African Americans. Because many of the communities that Puerto Ricans shared with blacks had long been identified as "black" spaces, it was often incumbent upon the newly arriving Nuyoricans to build cultural bridges between the two communities. The best example of those bridges is the emergence of the "Latin boogaloo" in the mid-1960s.

The boogaloo sound was grounded in a strong backbeat, which can be traced to the work of legendary New Orleans drummer Earl Palmer. Saxophonist Lou Donaldson had a hit jazz recording in 1963 with "Alligator Boogaloo," which featured Palmer protégé Leo Morris (Idris Muhammad) on drums. The "Boogaloo" backbeat was one of the nuanced features of what became the Motown sound, which speaks to how popular and widespread the boogaloo was at the time. The Latin boogaloo was created "accidentally" at the Palm Gardens Ballroom in New York City when musician Jimmy Sabater suggested that band leader Joe Cuba play a song he had written for the kinds of black audiences they often played for. That song would be "Bang, Bang," which very quickly became known as the birth of Latin boogaloo. For a three-year period, musicians such as the Joe Cuba Sextet, Joe Bataan, the Pete Rodriguez Orchestra ("I Like It like That"), Willie Colon, and the legendary Willie Bobo, whose *Spanish Grease* (1965) and *Uno Dos Tres 1*2*3** are some of the few Latin boogaloo recordings available on compact disc, became Chitlin' Circuit sensations. Latin boogaloo reflected the interest of Puerto Rican youth in both mambo music and doo-wop.

Willie Bobo, Uno Dos Tres 1-2-3

According to Flores, "two musical languages thus coexisted in the world of the boogaloo musician—that of his cultural and family heritage and that of life among peers in the streets and at school. The challenge was, how to bring these two worlds together and create a new language of their own."[11]

More important, Flores notes that the Latin boogaloo coincided with the later stages of the Civil Rights movement, which in New York City reflected the political sensibilities of the Black Panther Party and SNCC (Student Nonviolent Coordinating Committee) leaders H. Rap

Brown and Stokley Carmichael (Kwame Toure) more than those of
Martin Luther King, Jr., and the SCLC (Southern Christian Leadership
Convention). It also coincided with the maturation of the first generation of Puerto Rican youth born and raised as Nuyoricans. Like the generation of black youth who came of age in post–Harlem Renaissance
New York City, this generation of Puerto Rican youth were less willing
to negotiate the challenges of disenfranchisement and exploitation in
the city in the moderate terms their parents did. The radicalization of
this generation of Puerto Rican youth is best represented in the work of
that first generation of Nuyorican artists (Piri Thomas, Pedro Pietro),
organizations like the Young Lords Party (YLP), who like the Black
Panthers were often misconstructed as "gangs," and incidents like the
"Garbage Riots" of July 1969.

In the latter example, members of the Young Lords Party reacted to
community complaints that the New York City sanitation department
systematically refused to pick up garbage in East Harlem and other
communities of color. At first, members of the Young Lords heisted
brooms and bags from sanitation workers and began a clean-up themselves. Eventually they carted mounds and mounds of uncollected
garbage into main traffic thoroughfares, effectively bringing commuter
traffic to a halt. The group, founded by Cha Cha Jimenez in Chicago
using the model set by the Black Panthers, would organize a Harlem-
based satellite in early 1969 with now prominent New York City media
figures like Pablo "Yoruba" Guzman and Felipe Luciano serving as part
of the group's founding central committee. As Luciano reflected a few
years ago, "I thought [the garbage riot] was very unromantic. I couldn't
imagine myself leading a march for garbage when there was so many
other issues out there. But that's what the community wanted, and our
philosophy was to do what the community wanted."[12] Other notable
"protests" by the Young Lords included the December 1969 takeover of
First United Spanish Methodist Church, where they established a
breakfast program, health-care facility, and child-care center, and a
much publicized takeover of the notorious Lincoln Hospital on 149th
Street in the South Bronx after thirty-one-year-old Carmen Rodriguez
became the first woman to die under legalized abortion laws in New

York State. Her death fueled ongoing claims by the Young Lords and black nationalist groups like the Black Panthers and United Slaves (US) that the legalization of abortion was aimed at diminishing the black and Latino urban poor. But as Jennifer A. Nelson notes, the Lincoln Hospital takeover reflected the Young Lords Party's progressive move (via the leadership of the organization's women) toward a feminist stance that "encompassed access to voluntary birth control, safe and legal abortion," alongside broad-based community issues such as a quality health-care system, free day care, and an end to poverty."[13] Luciano, the group's founding chairman, also doubled as a member of the "Original" Last Poets (documented in the film and recording *Right On*), thus capturing the common interests of black and Latino communities at the end of the 1960s.

The Last Poets are significant in this regard as Jimmy Sabater suggests that boogaloo "was basically an early form of rap."[14] The Last Poets, along with Gil Scott-Heron and the Watts Prophets, represent one of the many direct artistic links to hip-hop. But their visibility also indicates that from its inception hip-hop was a mélange of influences and voices including the black arts movement, Jamaican dub poets (Linton Kwesi Johnson), Jamaican sound systems (which Kool Herc reconstructed in the South Bronx), the black comedic tradition (see Pigmeat Markham's "Here Comes the Judge"), and Latin boogaloo. Though the latter was quickly pushed aside by colluding salsa labels and promoters, the kinds of cultural bridges that boogaloo afforded was quickly reconstituted in the sensibilities of still younger generations of blacks and Latinos in New York via the embryonic forms of hip-hop but also within the salsa movement (the great Eddie Palmieri looms large here) and the emerging dance music (disco) culture in New York City.

It is literally on top of this fertile multicultural ground (not to sound cliché) that the Masters at Work (MAW) vibe rest. The thirty-six-year-old Little Louie Vega is a boogie-down native (that be "the Bronx") who came up with a healthy appreciation of salsa courtesy of his uncle, salsa singer Hector Lavoe, who recorded and performed for the Fania All-Stars, named after the most prominent salsa label of the 1970s. He was also exposed to the break-beat genius of Jazzy Jay, who held it down in

Vega's Bronx River neighborhood (the home of the Zulu Nation). But as a teen, Vega began to frequent some of the underground house music spots in New York City, most notably the Paradise Garage, where the late and legendary Larry Levan held it down. By the mid-1980s, Vega himself had become a house and Latin freestyle DJ of some note, regularly spinning in spots such as Devil's Nest, Roseland, the Loft, and the post-disco Studio 54. Kenny "Dope" Gonzalez, who was born in Mecca ("Straight from Brooklyn, better known as Crooklyn"), kept a distance from "Latin" music, but got hooked into the house music scene courtesy of famed house producer Todd Terry. It was Terry who brought Vega and Gonzalez together in 1989, when Vega stepped to Terry about remixing Gonzalez's "Salsa House" (Nu Groove Records, 1989). A year later, Vega asked Gonzalez to provide beats for what would eventually become the debut recording of Marc Anthony. The work with Marc Anthony was the founding collaboration of Vega and Gonzalez and began a prolific ten-year period during which they remixed (really reconstituted) folks like Debbie Gibson (who they made relevant again with their 1991 remix of "One Step Ahead"), Vanessa Williams, Deee-Lite, Janet Jackson, and Incognito and produced acts such as Luther Vandross and BeBe Winans.

But the heart of the MAW movement is a loose collective of salsa, soul, and dance music artists that the duo brought together under the guise of Nuyorican soul. During the early 1990s, some of the MAW productions were credited as "Masters at Work featuring Tito Puente and Eddie Palmieri." The willingness of Vega and Gonzalez to actively seek out and embrace the music and talents of Palmieri and Puente was notable because it brought earlier forms of Latin (Nuyorican) music, like Afro-Cuban and salsa, in direct conversation with the house, Latin freestyle, hip-hop landscape that birthed "post–(Latin) Soul" figures like Vega, Gonzalez, and others. As Vega reminisced in a recent magazine feature, "It was a tight-knit thing where you had your whole crew, everybody knew everybody . . . in a way we're tryin' to recreate our old neighborhood; in a subliminal way, we're always tryin' to bring people together."[15] This spirit was captured perfectly in the 1997 release *Nuyorican Soul* (Giant Step/Blue Thumb), which featured vocalists

Jocelyn Brown and India, George Benson, Roy Ayers, the TropiJazz all-stars, including Puente, pianists Palmieri (who contributes two originals, "Taita Caneme" and "Habriendo el Dominante") and Hilton Ruiz, and flutist Dave Valentin, and TSOP (Gamble and Huff's label the Sound of Philadelphia) arranger Vince Montana, Jr.

The recording opens with a funk-ass version of the Rotary Connection classic "I Am the Black Gold of the Sun." The song is a nod to the West African influences that undergird the *Nuyorican Soul* project but also emphasizes the cultural and musical hybrids that the collective represents—an example that Rotary Connection forged three decades ago under the influential producer Charles Stephney (who also crafted the early Earth, Wind, and Fire sound). Stephney cowrote the song with Richard Rudolph, who met his future wife, the late Minnie Riperton, while both were in the group. Their own interracial marriage would be the most lasting metaphor for the kinds of boundary shifting the Rotary Connection attempted in their music and clearly stands as an inspiration for the very kinds of community bridging that Masters at Work hope to achieve. The project then slides into "It's Alright, I Feel It!" an original cowritten by the Masters with vocalists Benny Diggs (who directed the New York Community Choir on Nikki Giovanni's brilliant *Truth Is On the Way* in 1970) and Jocelyn Brown, who is the featured soloist on the track. Brown has done background vocals for a wide range of artists over the last decade but is best known for her 1983 anthem "Somebody Else's Guy," which was a great example of the quality postdisco dance music emanating out of New York City. "It's Alright, I Feel It!" with its gospel house flourishes, provided by pianist Terry Burrus and then unknown drummer Vidal Davis (*Who Is Jill Scott? Vol. One*), harks back to those days of mid-1980s New York dance music.

But the track also sets up an example of how seamlessly Vega and Gonzalez envision their music and the communities that they embrace, as the Brown track segués into two Latin jazz pieces, both cowritten with pianist Hilton Ruiz, who was heavily influenced by McCoy Tyner and Chick Corea. The tracks were inspired by a trip Vega and Gonzalez took to a DJ festival in Southport, England, where they peeped folks getting their dance on to Pharoah Sanders's *Journey to the One*, which features the muscular hard-bop groove "You Got to Have Freedom" (quick shout to my man Maurice Bottemley). On "Maw Latin Blues" Ruiz trades in the Steinway for a Hammond B-3, giving the song an initial Chiltin' Circuit feel. But the song finds its real groove via Richie Flores's straight gangsta Conga solo, so much so that by the time Dave Valentin gets his flute on it's clear that it may be the blues, but it's a blues straight out of El Barrio as opposed to the Delta. Valentin's flute solo on "Maw Latin Blues" literally morphs into the opening lines of "Gotta New Life," which is a direct reference to "You Got to Have Freedom." Ruiz returns to the piano, this time to play the role that the underappreciated John Hicks did on the Sanders "original." The real stars on the track, though, are vocalists Lisa Fischer (longtime background vocalist for Luther Vandross) and Brown, who trades scat phrases that are, according Carol Cooper, reminiscent of the early, early work of The Pointer Sisters.[16] The seamless flow of these three tracks are important because they reflect how the DJ's attention to flow and layering (shout to Tricia Rose) can play out in extraordinary ways in the studio.

In this regard, MAW's foundation first and foremost as DJs also breeds a technical fluidity, as they are equally adept in creating the kinds of hip-hop landscapes that might seem far removed from salsa, gospel, and big band jazz. On "Nautilus (Mawtilus)" the Masters pay tribute to pianist Bob James and his song "Nautilus," which was one of the most sampled "jazz" tracks during the early days when hip-hop was still in the park and plugged in to the lamppost. Most recently Ghostface Killah sampled the song on his first solo release, *The Ironman* (1996). James's "Take Me to the Mardi Gras" (often referred to as the "Breaking Bells") was also a favorite, and it later became the basis of Run DMC's "Peter Piper" (1986). The *Nuyorican Soul* tribute also gives props to vibraphonist Roy Ayers, who does his signature "shaba dowie yow, yow . . . " on "Roy's Scat" behind a truncated sample of his classic "Everybody Loves the Sunshine." But the cornerstone of MAW's reconstruction of CTI-era soul jazz is the brilliant, nearly nine-minute "You Can Do It (Baby)," which features vocals and guitar by the legendary George Benson, whose classic recording *This Masquerade* (1976) is one of the biggest-selling "jazz" recordings of all time. "You Can Do It (Baby)" begins with

Benson scatting and grooving behind a breakneck rhythm track. By mid-song it's all about that "gee-tar," as Benson reminds the young folks, who only know him for his "sanging," why he's the artistic son of Wes Montgomery. It's those vocals, late in the song where Benson sings "Been so long . . . You know I'm back from the world," that serve as a fitting metaphor for the vision of the whole project, as Little Louie Vega and Kenny "Dope" Gonzalez musically capture Juan Flores's thought that to be Nuyorican is to find some comfort in the timeless ability to always "pick up and do it somewhere else," whether it be on the streets of the South Bronx or in a corner bodega in Alphabet City.

MAW followed *Nuyorican Soul* with the less ambitious *Our Time Is Coming* (2002). In some regards, the recording harks back to their earliest work together, though it represents MAW at its most accessible. The contributors read like headliners of a classic soul tour, showing that when some of the soul veterans of the late 1970s and 1980s are allowed to work with attentive and thoughtful producers, like Vega and Gonzalez, they can still shine. Patti Austin, who began her career almost three decades ago as a CTI artist and who forged a solid commercial career in the 1980s on Quincy Jones's Qwest label, is as spectacular as ever on the opening track, "Like a Butterfly (You Send Me)." The song was cowritten with well-regarded house producer Blaze. Austin had much of her commercial success in the 1980s courtesy of two brilliant collaborations with vocalist James Ingram ("Baby Come to Me," which was first introduced on *General Hospital*, and "How Do You Keep the Music Playing?"), who is on a short list of the most talented R&B vocalists to emerge in the last thirty years. Both Austin and Ingram were featured in Quincy Jones's groundbreaking mix of funk, jazz, R&B, dance, and hip-hop that was featured on *The Dude* (1981). In many regards *Our Time Is Coming* attempts to achieve that same kind of commercially friendly mix; it is no surprise that Ingram would be featured on the bouncy "Lean on Me" (not the Bill Withers classic). The song begins with Ingram's signature yodel, which is as stunning as it was when he was featured on Jones's "One Hundred Ways" and "Just Once." But the most pleasing old-school cameo comes courtesy of Stephanie Mills, who blows up the spot on the titilating groove of "Latin Lover." The song highlights the bankrupt politics of an industry in which someone who possesses such a fine vocal instrument as Mills's is not currently signed to a major label. Again the fact that Ayers (who provides vocals and vibes on the title track), Mills, Ingram, and Austin have a place in the MAW universe speaks to their serious appreciation of the music that helped "raise" them.

But the real political vision of MAW is most apparent on their brilliant "remake" of the late Fela Kuti's "Expensive Shit." Fela, who died of AIDS in 1997, is increasingly being recovered by a generation of young musical activists. Fela is really the contemporary template for a specific kind of "celebrity Gramscian" who finds a presence in the work of artists like Mos Def, Common, Sarah Jones, Talib Kweli, and Me'Shell Ndegéocello. MAW's "MAW Expensive" acknowledges their longtime unrealized dreams of working with Fela, but is also an acknowledgment by the duo of their commitment to teaching and building through their music. Gonzalez and Vega are among the many "young" artists, including Fela's son Femi Kuti (*Fight to Win*, 2001), who joined veteran producer and former Black Panther Nile Ridges in the making of *Red Hot and Africa*, the still unreleased "Red Hot" tribute to Fela.

Recordings like *Our Time Is Coming* and *Nuyorican Soul* emerge at a moment when black and Latino leaders in places like New York are finally coming to terms with being under a common siege, not only in America's urban centers but globally. Al Sharpton's simply brilliant political decision to embrace the cause in Vieques, Puerto Rico, where the U.S. military puts the island's citizens at risk with bombing excences may have been motivated by his long-term desires to run for president. It was one of many moves that allowed for the unprecedented support that Puerto Rican politician Fernando Ferrer received from black communities in his bid to become New York City's first Puerto Rican mayor. The perceived power of such a coalition in New York City was fully realized in the despicable and racist tactics of Mark Green and his campaign lieutenants to delegitimize the coalition during the Democratic mayoral primaries in 2002. The efforts of the Green campaign specifically aimed to heighten the discomfort that the New York Jewish community had for Sharpton; the move ultimately cost Ferrer the Democratic nomination. Green was of course trounced by Republican candidate Michael Bloomberg ("excuse me while I light my spliff") after both black and Latino voters refused to back Green.

As the post-9/11 politics of New York City threaten to force the city's "people" into small self-interested enclaves, the music of Masters at Work is a timely reminder of the common vision that the Nuyorican spirit has forged with many of New York City's inhabitants.

CHAPTER NINE

SOME OTHA SHIT

To get inside this head of mine / Would take a monkey wrench / And a lot of wine

—Res

The caged bird isn't free. . . . Choosing to be a mystery is the one way to maintain a semblance of control, to keep your inner self to yourself. This is an act of agency for the unfree.

—Farah Jasmine Griffin, *If You Can't Be Free,*
Be a Mystery: In Search of Billie Holiday

Though neo-soul and its various incarnations have helped to redefine the boundaries and contours of black pop, often the most popular of these recordings, like Maxwell's *Urban Hang Suite*, India.Arie's *Acoustic Soul*, and Musiq Soulchild's *Aijuswanaseing*, exist comfortably alongside the trite blah, blah, blah of the 112s and Destiny's Childs of the world. Just a small reminder that "difference" is often valued only when it smells, tastes, and sounds like the same old same old. And even when artists break the mold, as Maxwell did with *Urban Hang Suite* and D'Angelo did with *Brown Sugar*, they are expected to remain true to that formula lest they risk the critical backlash that Maxwell and D'Angelo faced in the aftermath of artistically compelling projects like *Embrya* (1998) and *Voodoo* (2000), respectively. The bottom line is that contemporary R&B and the radio and video programmers responsible for making that music available to listeners and viewers remain trapped in a small black box largely informed by hip-hop bottoms and Blige-like histrionics with small traces of Luther and Whitney and enough tone deafness to have Clara Ward, Mahailia Jackson, and Sam Cooke turn twice in their graves about every four and a half minutes (I could be talking about Ashanti, but let's be real: it ain't just her). With such a small margin to work with, the seminal hybrid-soul of Lenny Kravitz, the Family Stand, Seal, Corey Glover, Me'Shell Ndegéocello, Dionne Farris, Michael Franti (both the Disposable Heroes and Spearhead versions), and even Wyclef Jean has been consistently marginalized save an occasional MTV buzz clip and the hordes of "pomo-bohos" like myself who continue to crave great "black" music even if it don't sound like Marvin Gaye or Aretha Franklin. Shareese Renee Ballard (Res), Macy Gray, and Ursula Rucker are three artists who refuse to be placed in little black boxes. In other words, these are women on some "otha shit."

With *How I Do*, the Philly-born Res (pronounced "Reese") will naturally be compared to her Philly soul cohorts, but no one will ever mistake Res's sound with that of Jill Scott or anything produced by Ahmir "?uestlove" Thompson or the Soulquarians. As a postintegration baby who did the Catholic prep thing (as opposed to the Philadelphia arts academy thing that is responsible for so many in the current crop of Philly soul elite), the twenty-three-year-old Res was exposed to wide array of music ranging from the Italian arias that she began singing at age fourteen to the music of Annie Lennox, Pearl Jam, and the Roots. This is not as eclectic a brew of music as one might suspect, but is reflective of the diverse landscape of contemporary music and the ease with which audiences—if they so choose—can cross musical boundaries. The fact that Jay Z could use the music of Alana Davis for his chilling "There's Been a Murder" gives an indication that the diversity that black radio claims that "urban" audiences don't appreciate is more likely a product of programmers and Artists and Repetoire folks wanting to have better control over the tastes of those audiences. According to Res, with her project "the vision was to put everything I like—the hip-hop, the rock, the pop, the drum 'n' bass stuff—into one sound."[1] To achieve that seemingly elusive mix, Res employed the services of DOC, who was largely responsible for Esthero's *Breath from Another* (1998). It was with DOC's production that Res was able to achieve the guitar-based hip-hop vibe that she desired, one that didn't come off as cheesy.

On the lyrical tip, Res was largely assisted by her Philly homie Santi White, who is currently lead vocalist of the alternative soul band (whatever the hell that means) Stiffed. It was White, who contributed lyrics on ten of the project's eleven tracks, who was largely responsible for Res's start in the music industry. White was an Artists and Repetoire assistant at Epic when she invited Res to New York City to work on the songs that eventually comprised *How I Do*. With White's assistance, Epic offered Res the opportunity to become lead of the revamped Groove Theory, replacing fellow Philly siren Amel Larrieux in that capacity. Res turned down the offer and eventually landed a solo deal with MCA. Res's decision to rebuff Epic is in part an attempt to eschew the kind of easy "cute black girl equal R&B ingénue" equation that pervades the industry. As she relates, "I'm a black chick and I'm cute. I mean I'm not busted or anything, you know? I could sing R&B if I wanted to and it would be kinda nice, I think, but that's not me. I mean it's music, you know? Fuck R&B. Fuck alternative. Fuck the rock and roll world. Just do what makes you feel good."[2] Before releasing her debut, Res made cameo appearances on GZA's *Beneath the Surface* and Talib Kweli and Hi Tek's *Reflection Eternal*.

It is White who is responsible for *How I Do*'s bombastic opening track, "Golden Boys." Dedicated to a veritable army of "bald headed cuties" (who could be named Tyson Beckford, Tyrese, or, for the old-school, Michael Jordan), the track calls attention to the incongruency of the sanitized black masculine images that adorn fashion magazines, MTV, and ESPN and the menacing black masculinity that is assigned to those who look just like the "bald heads," but minus the celebrity. More alarming are the ways that many of these "artists" acquiesce to these photographic black (wet) dreams in order to achieve the fame and material wealth that they desire. Res peeps their game, telling the "undercover" brothas that sistas "sit appalled" at the view, since they "know the truth" despite the fact that some of these bruhs are the "prince of all the magazines." While the lyrics suggest the obvious collection of photogenic Nubian sex-lords, including P. Diddy himself, I'm gonna step out on cue and suggest that the lyrics seemingly take a swipe at one of Philly's favorite sons, Will Smith. Throughout the song Res references the word *prince* and in one lyric sings that when she was young "I saw you on TV you made life look fun," realizing now that it was a "freak show," alluding to Smith's television sitcom *The Fresh Prince of Bel Air*. The kicker for me was the lyric that begins the second verse, in which Res sings in full swagger about the brother being placed "in these robes," being told he's the "greatest man," which reads like a veiled reference to the Ali biopic that Smith starred in and eventually earned an Academy Award nomination for. At issue is not the falsity of these images but the investments that many make in the belief they reflect a reality. Res makes such a point when she laments in the song that folks need "these images . . . to be true," as audiences are not ready to accept that they are just as "insecure" as the "golden boys" are. Even more dangerous are the investments made by black female viewers in these images (and the countless strippers turned video "hos" turned singers that adorn them). Already challenged by a general disregard for a fuller presentation of black female identity in the entertainment industry and a downright stifling and damaging concept within that industry of what the quintessential black female should look like, Res's line that "Girls like me" don't appreciate a "bubblin' mind state" thrown up in their faces is a sobering disclaimer against that which is marketed as authentic black culture.

Sobering is a fitting adjective to describe two of the project's best tracks, the lead single, "Ice King," which was cowritten by Res, and "Sittin' Back." Both tracks are easily the closest things on *How I Do* to anything in the mainstream of the "urban" music universe. Both tracks were coproduced by DOC and Mr. Khaliyl, who also adds production on "If There Ain't Nothing." "Ice King" is a brilliant sojourn into the mind state of a young woman dating a local drug dealer. "Ice" is of course a reference to the diamonds and metals ("ice and bling, bling") that adorn the playas ("internationally known and locally accepted," as

Common and Bilal put it) in the industries that traffic in illicit drugs and "authentic" urban culture. Res begins the song by acknowledging that the status that she derives from her relationship with the "Ice King" makes her complicit in his "wicked" activities; she admits that everything she gets from him comes from the "destitute and the torn." But she remains mesmerized by the character, admitting that while she sees his "wickedness" his "effervescence" still got her shook as she falls in line with those women who have been drawn to despotic "ghetto" poets like Marvin Gaye, Miles Davis, Aaron Hall, and Bill Withers and the nameless ghetto overlords for whom "playa, playa, pimping" is both personal and business and never simply a performative gesture. Although the women of drug dealers are often intimately linked to the political economy of the "bizness" (as property and at times product), Res makes a break, declaring that there are some things homie "can't possess."

It is this very desire for "bling, bling and booty" ("it's platinum, baby!") that Res deconstructs on the highly ironic "Sittin' Back." In the song, she juxtaposes the kind of well-publicized school shootings that have made terms like *trench-coat mafia* part of dinnertime conversation with the "anger in the nation" (shout out to Pete Rock and CL Smooth) that smelts beneath the desires for celebrity, material wealth, and social status evidenced in the hood. Understood fully, "Sittin' Back" is a powerful indictment of the flaccidness of (commercial) hip-hop's anger and rage. Despite the fact that hip-hop has been cited in any number of incidents involving dysfunctional white youth (holla back, John Walker Lindh), Res reminds folks that hip-hop seems more fixated with the "pimped out Lex with the rims black." No matter how menacing some of these hip-hop acts come off as in their music videos and promotional photos—part of the stylized violence that looking cool while doing a drive-by implies—most of them just tryin' to "blow up." The song again reflects Res's (and Santi White's) fixation with the bluff and fluff that exists in the entertainment industry. Res's claim that she is "jaded" and "numb to the shit" speaks to the ways in which contemporary commercial hip-hop and those who embrace it as emblematic of somebody's "ghetto" reality have been not only desensitized to the faux violence and sexual objectification in hip-hop, but also, even more alarmingly, desensitized to the violence, injustice, and exploitation that mark the lives of so many of the genre's core constituency.

Like the challenge that Sarah Jones offers to hip-hop in "Your Revolution" (FCC head Michael Powell's favorite) and Ursala Rucker offers on the brilliant "What???" from her *Supa Sista*, "Sittin' Back" represents Res's desire to offer trenchant critiques of hiphop at a time when, as Tricia Rose suggests, folks aren't even allowed to ask questions about its gratuitous violence, crass materialism, and championing of sexual exploitation, without being questioned themselves about the validity of their "ghetto passes." More often than not, many of the women who raise their voices to confront the contradictions within hip-hop are marginalized within the commune of hip-hop artists, fans, and critics.

The thing about marginalization, as Phillip Brian Harper suggests in his book *Framing the Margins*, is that the folks who are forced to live on the margins often experience those things that the mainstream views as foreign and unimaginable as real, vital, and visceral. I use such decidedly esoteric language as a means of finding some legitimate footing on which to ground my interpretation of Macy Gray's *The Id*. Like the aforementioned lyric from Res's "How I Do," at the very least one would need a "monkey wrench" and some "wine" to fully decipher the full range of intents and meanings emanating from the mind of Macy Gray. Gray, a self-described manic-depressive, is apparently the sole survivor from a universe of six-foot-tall black women, with hair that can only be described as a hot comb's fantasy, and a voice that comes from the intersection in that universe where Carol Channing, Donald Duck, Janis Joplin, former Dre protégée Michell'le, and Billie Holiday (like Sinatra, it's all about the phrasing) once shared a blunt. As the title suggests, *The Id* is (hopefully) an unabridged subconscious transmission from the deep recesses of the reigning alchemist of contemporary R&B.

Gray was first thrust into the crossfire of media spectacle and surveillance after the release of "I Try" from her 1999 debut, *On How Life Is*. Although there were high expectations among the folks at Epic for Gray's commercial success—she was first introduced to audiences as the quirky "voice" singing "Winter Wonderland" in a Baby Gap commercial during the 1998 Christmas season—the lead single "Do Something" failed to garner the kind of interest that the label thought the project warranted. "I Try" was the perfect pop vehicle for Gray's distinctive voice, and with her striking and disarming beauty she shortly become the darling of MTV programmers, eventually leading to the sale of 7 million copies worldwide of *On How Life Is* and a Grammy award. For R&B audiences still hung over on Lauryn Hill, Faith Evans, Mary J. Blige, and Erykah Badu, Macy Gray was indeed a "queer" entity; thus she was among those few "R&B" acts (which is some circles only means "rhythm and black," regardless of the genre) whose "queerness" was welcomed and indeed sanctioned by mainstream radio and video outlets like MTV and VH-1. It is a tenuous position, because these acts are seen as little more than novelties.

Bobby McFerrin and Biz Markie have not had any measurable commercial success since their novelty breakthroughs more than a decade ago, "Don't Worry Be Happy" (1988) and "Just a Friend" (1989), though Biz has recently gotten props from Jay Z ("Girls, Girls, Girls") and Mario. "Alternative" MTV darlings Arrested Development ("Tennessee," 1992) and Dionne Farris ("I Know," 1994) were not able to sustain their careers. While Arrested Development was likely done in by lead vocalist Speech, whose self-righteous pretentiousness in black pop was surpassed only by that of KRS-One, Farris was undermined by "Hopeless," a brilliantly simplistic ditty featured on the *Love Jones* soundtrack (1997). In the aftermath of debuts by Badu, Maxwell and Eric Benet, and Lauryn Hill's "The Sweetest Thing," also from the *Love Jones* soundtrack, "Hopeless" resonated within urban/neo-soul audiences in ways that the guitar-driven folk-funk of Farris's *Wild Seed, Wild Flower* hadn't. When Farris failed to deliver a follow-up disc full of "Hopeless" singles, her label (Sony) dropped her.

To Gray's credit, she has managed to remain relevant to a wide range of audiences by continually trumpeting her own self-styled "queerness," which by all accounts was a feature of her personality well before she became a pop diva. Between projects, she made peace with the neo-soul bourgeoisie with a stunning "funkified" version of "I Try" at the 2000 Essence Awards show, mentored the reigning round-the-way baby-girl Sunshine Anderson (who, I might add, is "All Woman"), represented for D'Angelo on the remix of Common's "Geto Heaven Part II," spread some cheer on Fatboy Slim's *Weapons of Choice*, and was brilliantly lampooned on *Mad TV* by their resident "mad" sista Debra Wilson in a "trick-or-treat" skit. Thus no one was really surprised when Gray took the awards-show-appearance-to-promo-my-new-joint concept to the next level by wearing a full-length dress with the September 18 drop date for *The Id* on it. Therein lies the logic in *The Id*—the diva who is willing to do "any shit" is also compelled to say whatever the hell she feels, albeit to the grooves of some 1960s psychedelic funk that is apparently strung out on postmillennial psychosis, some stank-ass King Curtis–like horns, a healthy dose of Soulquarian beats, and a real respect for "original" old-school hip-hop, as witnessed by a cameo by "the Ruler" Slick Rick and the presence of Rick Rubin as executive producer.

As if attempting to prepare audiences for Macy-mayhem, *The Id* opens with "Relating to Psychopath," a song replete with tambourines and Jerry Ruzumna's wailing piano. Trying to dispel any possibility that young audiences would view her as a role model, Gray asserts in the song's chorus that she is a "psychopath," adding that her young audience's "role model" is in therapy. Gray ups the ante on Kelis "Caught out There" with the frankly disturbing "Gimmie All You Lovin' or I Will Kill You." Crazy has never been so funky as that track, which samples Rita Marley's "Jah, Jah Don't Want" and features one of several appearances by the neo-soul overlord Ahmir "ʔuestlove" Thompson—sounds like King Curtis got a demo of one of Dr. Dre's tracks about twenty-five years early. The "baby, I'm so crazy in love with you" theme is flipped to "you're so crazy how can you love me?" on "Boo," as Gray queries out loud in the chorus about those "bitches on my machine." But even Gray knows that crazy can't hold a project together: despite her very public embrace of crazy, ultimately it's about some out-the-box soul. (Like JB said, "I don't know karate, but I know k-razy.")

The sweetly simplistic lead single, "Sweet Baby," is as beautiful a piece of pop music as any released in recent years (save Five for Fighting's "Superman [Man of Steel]"). The song, which gives a subtle nod to Lou Reed's "Walk on the Wild Side" and Stanley Clarke and George Duke's recording of the same title, features backing vocals by the equally distinct and disarming Erykah Badu, particularly evident on the song's bridge. Written by Gray in 1995 and reworked numerous times by the artist, the song soars courtesy of the stunning string arrangements by Charles Veal, Jr. Gray's finely tuned soul sensibilities are powerfully present on "Don't Come Around," which features a wide range of stellar collaborators, including the legendary Billy Preston (the fifth Beatle) on Hammond B-3, Sunshine Anderson on backing vocals, and coproduction by Rafael Saadiq (also on guitar), who atones for his rather bland production efforts on the Isley's *Eternal.* The real "star" of the song is the horn arrangement by "Printz Board," which gives the song the feel of Aretha Franklin's underrated classic "It Ain't Fair" (*This Girl's in Love with You*, 1970).

The most pleasant surprise on *The Id* is Gray's remake of Slick Rick's "Hey Young World," replete with a cameo by "the Ruler" himself. The original recording was released on Slick Rick's 1988 *The Adventures of Slick Rick*, a recording that despite the general acknowledgment that it was one of the true classic recordings in all of hip-hop is still vastly underrated. In Gray's hands, the song is transformed into a quirky, off-kilter lullaby warning "the kids" against being a "dumb dummy" who disrespects "mommy" and one of those "fools" who "ditch school." Other standout tracks on The Id include the frenzied gutbucket, "My Nutmeg Phantasy"—or in other words some crazy-ass brown funk lovin'—which features Angie Stone and Mos Def in fartoo-short cameos. On the Joplin-esque "Forgiveness," Gray borrows a melody from Hoyt Axton's "Never Been to Spain." There are of course other bizarre moments, as Gray apparently drops a nod to Dr. Zhivago on "Oblivion" and reinvents Ms. Cleir and Dee-Lite (why?) on "Sexual Revolution."

Macy Gray was not going to change the (pop) world. She has never taken herself as seriously as the critics who anointed her the savior of (black) pop a few years ago did. What Gray possesses is a distinct voice and an even more distinct personality that has given her the kind of visibility she could have never imagined—the gawky brown girl with the squeaky voice has perhaps "queered" our perceptions of the "Diva." When all is said and done, Macy Gray will simply light up another blunt, and two or three million "fans" will likely light up with her—figuratively and literally.

TAKE YO PRAI∫E

No doubt jaws dropped as the poetess proceeded to document the retribution of a young woman who was gang raped. The poem, "The Unlocking," was a lurid and disturbing close to the official "debut" release of the Roots', *Do You Want More?!!!??!* The poet, Ursula Rucker, would return for two follow-up cameos with The Roots on the tracks "Adventures in Wonderland," on *Illidelph Halflife* (1997), and "Return to Innocence," from their most recent studio disc, *Things Fall Apart* (1999). If the East Coast playas thought that the acoustic jazz-funk of the Roots was too soft for their taste, Rucker's cameos proved that the group could get straight gangsta and that gangstas didn't always possess a penis (or some facsimile of one, as gangsta raptress Boss exhibited on her 1992 track "Deeper"). Gangsta, as in Rucker's single-mom drug don theorizing in the song "Adventures in Wonderland" that she was the "vixen vampire slayer" and an unsanctioned players in a "capitalist contest" to see who gets the money.

Rucker's opportunity to record with the Roots came when noted poet and playwright Ntozake Shange declined an invitation to appear on their debut recording. Fittingly, Rucker falls firmly within the tradition of black arts–era poets such as Nikki Giovanni, Camille Yarbrough, and Sonia Sanchez, who Rucker also shares a faint visual likeness to. What distinguishes Rucker, and many other contemporary spoken-word artists, such as Saul Williams, Kevin Powell, and Sarah Jones, from fore-poets such as Sanchez and Giovanni, Amiri Baraka, and Haki Madhubuti is the influence of hip-hop on their poetic sensibilities. Giving (gangsta) bitch slaps to the ice brigade (bling, bling, baby), wacked-out Internet racists, and failing educational systems while affirming distinct woman-spaces, political resistance, and progressive creativity, Rucker's "debut" *Supa Sista* was a welcome challenge to hip-hop's materialism and posturing and the increasing complacency of the so-called neo-soul revolution.

The title track, "Supa Sista," sounds like some funked-up "gangsta folk" music that invokes the flavor of Cassandra Wilson's major-label breakthrough *Blue Lights 'till Dawn* (1994). Produced by Tim Motzer, who Rucker originally worked with on legendary Philly DJ King Britt's *Sylk130*, the song begins with Rucker's slow big drum chant of how she rose and fell as "he called my name," "changed my name," and called her blackness "untamed." The song's intro speaks powerfully to the complicated web of racist and sexist oppression—what Kimberle Crenshaw calls intersectionality—from which black women have long been trying to escape. According to Crenshaw,

> Discrimination, like traffic through an intersection, may flow in one direction, and it may flow in another. If an accident happens in an intersection, it can be caused by cars traveling from any number of directions and, sometimes, from all of them. Similarly, if a Black Woman is harmed because she is in the intersection, her injury could result from sex discrimination or race discrimination.[3]

At root is a struggle over the naming and defining of black women and black femininity. Hortense Spillers acknowledges such a struggle in her groundbreaking 1977 essay "Mama's Baby, Papa's Maybe: An American Grammar Book," where she writes, "'Peaches' and 'brown sugar,' 'Sapphire' and 'Earth Mother,' . . . I describe a locus of Confounded identities, a meeting ground of investments and privations in the national treasury of rhetorical wealth."[4]

In Rucker's mind, black women, the "supa sistas," are forces of nature, angry ghetto "whirl a girls" who "swirl" and "twirl" their way through the "darkest of days." While Rucker sees the "Supa Sista" project as an effort to "deconstruct . . . preconceived misconceptions," she also espouses a black feminist worldview that transcends specific gender politics and that can be extended to efforts to emerge from within the "muck and mire" and set the masses "on fire." It is this notion of a transcendent black feminist politics that Joy James identifies in her book *Shadowboxing*, where she identifies black women such as Mary Church Terrell, Ida B Wells Barnett, and Ella Baker as political insurgents who were not solely defined by their interest in feminist concerns. According to James, "this emphasis on political militancy and radicalism differs somewhat from the emphases of contemporary black feminisms that focus on cultural politics as isolated from state power and middle-class sensibilities."[5] Rucker echoes this theme as she asserts to "supa sistas" that their "mission is clear," especially with their sons on the "frontline."

In the guise of a simple "Letter to a Sister Friend," Rucker examines a dynamic and fluid black feminine identity. Like fellow Philly-based poet Jill Scott, the track also allows Rucker to introduce listeners to her singing talents as her very capable vocals urgently create a lyrical "Sistaspace" that is malleable, shifting, nurturing, passionate, ethereal, and mystical. The lyrics reflect the multiplicity of feminine identities that black women take on in their roles as mothers, sisters, friends, and lovers. While such lyrics can be read "naturally" in a heterosexist context, Rucker suggests a more specific notion of woman-sharing, in which her sister friend is always a mother, "sometimes" a lover, and a "sister eternal." Rucker's woman-identified fluidity can also be found in the defiant "Womansong," where Rucker asserts that she was born a "slave," a "rebel," and inherently a "queen."

Rucker's hip-hop sensibilities are most expressly represented in her poison-and-brimstone assault on commercial hip-hop on the track "What???" Backed by the speedball hard-bop production of the drum 'n' bass producers 4Hero, the track seems a direct response to Jay Z's "Can I Get A . . . " Although the chorus of Jay Z's track begins "Can I get a fuck you?" it was changed for radio and video consumption, performed instead as instead as "Can I get a What? What?" Rucker gives Hova his "What?" with her straight challenge to him as she wonders aloud whether the "nigga," "playa," and "hustlers" (the apparent limits of black masculinity in contemporary commercial hip-hop) can "rhyme," "sing," or "flow" over the beats that 4Hero drops for her. Rucker provides the ground rules for the postmillennial MC battle, suggesting that participants cannot rely on current ghetto-fab staples like "Crissy" (Cristal for the uninitiated), "thongs," "platinum," "ice," "guns," and "lies" about ghetto reps. Later in the song, Rucker directly references Jigga's "Nigga What, Nigga Who" by asking what a "nigga" gonna do "Wit your rhyme, wit your flow," which is a revision of Amil's backing vocals on the track ("get your dough, wit you flow").

The brilliance of Rucker's work is in her ability to find value, meaning, and elements of resistance in common everyday practices. Such is the case on "Philadelphia Child," where Rucker examines the lives of the "ghetto girls" and "barrio boys" who look at the city's historical landmarks and wonder what role they play in the world. Rucker finds the answer to that question in the city's legendary drill teams, who are "White-booted," with Philly attitudes, and "zooted" on Schuykill Punch as they shout on top of drums and foot stomps, "We are here . . . we live, we matter." In another sweetly drawn moment in the song, Rucker provides glimpses into the worlds of "Olympic hopefuls" who compete in delicious ghetto games like mattress flipping, subway sprinting, and classics like manhunt and run, catch, and kiss. The song's power is buttressed by Robert Yancey III's nuanced production, particularly his subtle use of strings, which insistently propels the song's narrative forward.

On the track "Brown Boy," Rucker walks the fine line between feminist critique, as witnessed on tracks like "What???" and "Womansong," and the buttressing of black patriarchy. Rucker's vacillation is likely the product of being a real-life mother struggling to raise her sons Sudan and Sol in a society that views their lives as "raw sewage." Rucker makes a specific investment in the various mythologies that have accompanied the historical transition of blacks in America from premodern African natives to what Cornel West has called "new world Africans." Often this transition, as is the case on "Brown Boy," is reduced to the dichotomies of "chief to slave" and "king to cotton picker," which do nothing to engage the complexities of African survival and resistance in the Americas. Rucker's choice of language here is likely a reflex to criticisms often faced by black feminists within the mainstream black community. As Rucker admitted in an interview, "You get so many labels, I don't need more. I don't want to pigeonhole my work and say it's feminist work." Often the embrace of a lay Afrocentrism or, rather, what I'll term the myth of true African identity is a response to what Kendall Thomas has called "a crude racialist litmus test to establish true 'blackness,'" where those who embrace anti-sexist and anti-homophobic politics, often at the expense of "true identity" myths, are viewed as outside the parameters of "true" blackness and thus the black community proper.[7] In the case of Rucker's "Brown Boy," which suggests that there has been "epic" memory loss, her investment in the "myth of true African identity" and its attendant patriarchy obscures her more principled critiques of the black male condition, in which they are viewed as "blips on the screen," "strange fruits" (a shout out from Lady Day), and "experimental recruits" (both Tuskegee airmen and syphilis carriers). The lyrics speak to the forms of oppression—the practice of lynching and the syphilis experiments on black men in the 1930s—that are specific to the black male experience. Again Rucker undermines her critique here by reinforcing the U.S. Constitution's "three-fifths" definition of black bodies ("Black not beautiful . . . Diminished to 3/5 of whole") as a male construct, effectively obliterating the legitimacy of oppressions, particularly sexual violence, specific to black women.

Rucker more deftly negotiates her gender politics on the project's most affecting piece, the tragic "Song for Billy." The track gives another spin to the crack game–sex game themes found in Rucker's earlier work with The Roots on "The Unlocking" and "Adventures in Wonderland." At its core, the song is about sacrifice, namely the sacrifice of a young girl by her mother ("once goddess"), who delivers her daughter to "monsters" for a moment of prayer with the "crystalline god." In other words, baby-girl is tragically offered up so that mama can hit the pipe again. The narrative recalls songs like Paul Lawrence's "Strung Out" ("strung out, left in doubt, f-r-e-e-b-a-s-i-n-g") and Oran "Juice" Jones's "Pipe Dreams" ("inhale now feel the rush"). The tragedy is not just the mother's addiction or her insensitivity to her very young daughter, but the men who willingly defile a girl who is not yet a "toddler," let alone a woman. As Rucker more pointedly suggests the young child was an "innocent orifice." Rucker uses the track to raise more specific questions about female sexuality and male privilege. In the aftermath of the 2000 Puerto Rican Day Parade or the most recent Woodstock travesty (lest we think only black and brown men can't control their urges), her insistence that a woman's vagina is a confirmation of gender and not an "invitation to sex" is a forceful reminder. In the end, Rucker also points to a process in which a child already understands that her own sexuality and the abuse of it by others (including her cracked-out mother in this case) are of value in a world that will see no value in her own humanity. According to Rucker, she uses her work as a "platform to address the many issues that affect me, my black brothers and sisters, and my universal human family. I hope my words and music will inspire people and encourage them to think."[8]

Rucker's debut is only the latest example of a long line of black women poets and spoken-word artists who have offered trenchant and necessary critiques of American life and culture, often without the kinds of promotional support that even the most morose rappers get in the current music industry environment. Thirty years ago, Nikki Giovanni recorded *Truth Is on the Way*, the first of two spoken-word recordings in which she collaborated with the New York Community Choir (under the direction of Bennie Diggs) performing "gospelized" versions of her already published poetry. A third recording, The Way I Feel, was done for the Atlantic label in 1975 with the legendary Arif Mardin behind the boards. Giovanni's "major"-label debut was reflective of an overall trend in which major labels became interested in signing "black" acts, effectively annexing the remnants of the independent black music industry. It was during this era that Clive Davis's then burgeoning Arista label would sign the mercurial genius Gil Scott-Heron. Many of these recordings have been forgotten, save the hip-hop community's fixation with the Last Poets, who were easily the most bombastic and militant of the most well known spoken word artists/poets of the 1970s.

One of the many important (and forgotten) recordings from that era was Camille Yarbrough's *The Iron Pot Cooker*, which was released on the Vanguard label in 1975. The recording was brought into public consciousness after Fatboy Slim used Yarbrough's "Take Yo' Praise" as the basis for his own "Praise You." In the liner notes to the recording's 2000 reissue, Kevin Powell writes,

> As a hip-hop journalist, I was keenly aware of the influence of musical wordsmiths like The Last Poets, Gil Scott-Heron . . . on what is popularly called rap music. Because hip-hop has traditionally been a very

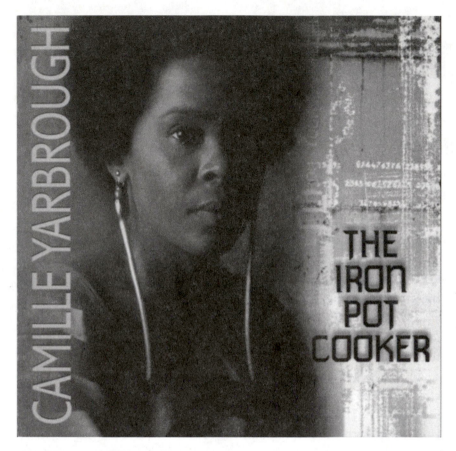

Camille Yarbrough, The Iron Pot Cooker

male-centered art form, I naively assumed that its forbears, too, had been men. This historical and cultural omission speaks volumes about the continued ignorance and oppression of woman artists in American culture.[9]

With tracks like "But It Comes out Mad," the surreal mega-poem "Dream/Panic/Sonny Boy the Rip-off Man/Little Sally the Super Sex Star/Taking Care of Business" and the brilliant "Take Yo' Praise," Yarbrough spoke insightfully to the dynamics and contradictions of black life at the culmination of the Civil Rights/black power era. The recording is legitimately, as Powell argues, the ground on which the later works of Badu, Lauryn Hill, Me'Shell Ndegéocello, Jill Scott, and Ursula Rucker stand. In the liner notes, Powell tells the story of initially finding a vinyl copy of The Iron Pot Cooker in a crate somewhere in New York's East Village. One can only hope that the music of Ursula Rucker, Macy Gray, and Res will not endure the similar fate of being obscured, ignored, and forgotten.

AND BLUES

CHAPTER TEN

RADIO FREE SOUL

Robert F. Williams was the president of the Monroe, North Carolina, branch of the NAACP in 1959, when he was thrust into the national spotlight. In his response to the acquittal of a white man who had assaulted and attempted to rape a local black woman, Williams publicly asserted to black folks that "we must be willing to kill if necessary. We cannot take these people who do us injustice to the court and it becomes necessary to punish them ourselves. In the future we are going to have to try and convict these people on the spot."[1] In classic "old-school Negro" form, the NAACP, under the leadership of Roy Wilkens (Who? as my students would say), moved to suspend Williams from his post. By the summer of 1960, Williams, by then the most radical voice within a burgeoning protest movement, was a fugitive, in flight in response to trumped-up charges of kidnapping. Seemingly "silenced," Williams and his wife, Mabel, reemerged in Cuba as the guest of Fidel Castro. It is there in Havana, Cuba, that Williams's voice would be heard every Friday night at 11:00 as the host of the "guerilla" radio broadcast *Radio Free Dixie*. Initially broadcast from a five-thousand-watt station, Williams and his wife could be heard as far away as Seattle, Washington. According to Williams, the program was "aimed at the south primarily . . . because the black people in the south didn't have any voice. This was really the first true radio where the black people could say what they want to say and didn't have to worry about sponsors, they didn't have to worry about censors."[2] Williams was supported in his efforts of resistance by friends, including poet Amiri Baraka, who sent the couple copies of new music. In one broadcast in 1966, Mabel Williams suggested that black soul singers were the "epic poets" of the black movement. Williams's *Radio Free Dixie* (also the title of Timothy Tyson's straight gangsta biography of Williams) remains one of the greatest examples of the power of black radio.

The very idea of black radio began with the pioneering efforts of Jack Cooper, who initially brokered an hour a day—aptly named the *All Negro Hour*—on WSBC, a 250–watt station in Chicago. Radio stations in major urban centers in the 1920s and 1930s brokered air time to cater to the burgeoning immigrant communities in these cities. According to William Barlow in his informative book *Voice Over: The Making of Black Radio*, "Entrepreneurs from the various ethnic enclaves in large cities like Chicago, where immigrants were a quarter of the population, bought blocks of airtime for foreign-language broadcast; they bankrolled these programs with advertising revenues raised from business operations in their respective neighborhoods."[3] By the early 1940s, white corporations that sold products to black audiences began to sponsor radio time. One of the best examples was *King Biscuit Time*, which was sponsored by the King Biscuit flour company on KFFA in Helena, Arkansas, featuring blues legend Sonny "Boy" Williamson as a cohost.

Radio became an integral medium within black communities with the emergence of so-called black-appeal radio in the late 1940s and 1950s. During this era, a generation of "personality jocks" like Al Benson, Doctor Hep Cat, and Daddy-O Daylie emerged in cities like Chicago and Austin, Texas. Both of these traditions were embodied in the figure of Nat D. Williams, who was the first African-American jockey at WDIA, a 250–watt station in Memphis. Williams began at the station in 1948, hosting a program called *Tan Town Jamboree*. The popularity of the show convinced the owners of WDIA to convert to an all-black programming format in 1949. At its peak, WDIA, which became a fifty-thousand watt station in 1954, had an audience of over 300,000 (not including the large number of whites eavesdropping on the flow), which grew to over a million listeners at night, when the signal could be heard throughout the South. Williams is significant not only because he was the brains behind WDIA's emergence as a dominant force in black radio, but because he did so in the guise of the "race man." Even before he came to WDIA, the college-educated Williams published a column ("Down on Beale Street") in the *Memphis World*. In was in the spirit of his politicized pieces in the paper that Williams debuted the public-affairs radio program *Brown America Speaks* (bruh apparently had some issues with the word *black*). According to Barlow, the show "quickly became known for candid discussions of racially charged subjects, such as segregation of the city's public facilities, job and wage discrimination in the workforce, and police brutality in the black community" (mind you, this is in the pre–Martin Luther King, Jr., South).[4]

Williams's example was no doubt an inspiration to Robert Williams and the generation of black jocks who emerged in the late 1950s and 1960s and played crucial roles during the Civil Rights movement in the 1960s. Figures like Georgie Woods, Jack "the Rapper" Gibson, Peggy Mitchell, Louise Fletcher, Hal Jackson, Herb Kent, and Martha Jean "the Queen" Steinberg all used their influence as disc jockeys to further the cause of the Civil Rights movement in cities such as Philadelphia, Birmingham, Chicago, New York, Nashville, and Detroit. According to Gibson, "we were the voice that the people listened to and if you gave us a message to say, 'There will be a meeting tonight of the SCLC [Southern Christian Leadership Convention] at the First Baptist Church' we would go ahead and elaborate all around."[5] It was not unusual for some of the major Civil Rights leaders to speak directly to the folks via the airwaves. So powerful was the medium that Los Angeles–based jock "the Magnificent" Montague was indirectly impli-cated for inciting the Watts riots of 1965.[6] Over the past three decades, black radio has continued to play a critical role in galvanizing opinion and support for issues that directly affect their core black constituencies. The best contemporary examples, of course, are the "Air Advocacy" campaigns of *The Tom Joyner Morning Show*, which despite its bourgeois trappings continues the traditions that folks like Nat D. Williams and Georgie Woods laid down two generations ago.

With today's intense consolidation of radio outlets, the relative freedom that black radio has maintained (even given the power that adver-
tisers wield over programming) is under siege. The radio industry is currently on lockdown courtesy of two companies—Clear Channel and
Infinity—that control nearly one-third of all of the ad revenue generated
from the nation's twelve-thousand-plus radio outlets.[7] Clear Channel
alone owns more than twelve hundred of those stations. This consolidation is the product of the Telecommunications Reform Act of 1996,
which lifted longstanding ownership restrictions—only forty stations
nationally and no more than four in any one market—thus allowing
radio conglomerates the freedom to buy as many stations as they desired
as long as that number did not exceed eight stations in any one market.
Clear Channel was the biggest "offender" in this regard, merging with
almost seventy different media companies and expanding Clear
Channel's empire from thirty stations in 1996 to the twelve hundred it
currently owns. The company now has radio outlets in 247 of the
nation's 250 largest radio markets. In his brilliant yearlong exposé on
"big radio," and Clear Channel in particular, Eric Boehlert suggests that
this consolidation has "cleared the way for listless, homogenized and
automated programming, along with a near abandonment of local news,
all in the name of rampant cost cutting."[8] Among their cost-cutting
strategies is something known as "cyber-jocking," where the jock records
his show for use by stations in a dozen or so different markets, which of
course allows the company to eliminate dozens of jobs at a time. Clear
Channel currently uses cyber jocks in 255 of its markets, with the exception of New York City, where stations have contracts with labor forbid-
ding their use. At the time of this writing, Clear Channel was refusing
to renew contracts at several of their New York City stations unless
cyber-jocking is allowed.[9]

If *The Tom Joyner Morning Show* represents a digitized Chitlin'
Circuit, then Clear Channel is digitized hegemony. And *hegemony* is
not too strong a word for a company that is also the largest concert promoter (Clear Channel Entertainment) in the country, owning more
than 130 concert venues and about 770,000 billboards. As Lynnley
Browning observes, few of the company's rivals could "promote a music

group on their stations, book the act in their clubs and amphitheaters, then advertise the tour on their billboards."[10] The small Denver promoter Nobody in Particular Presents (NPP), in fact, sued Clear Channel in August 2001 on the basis that "Clear Channel repeatedly has used its size and clout to coerce artists to use Clear Channel to promote their concerts or else risk losing air play and other on-air promotional support."[11] As the story goes, if acts use another company to promote their shows, Clear Channel purportedly threatens to pull those acts off their playlist, a threat that is particularly meaningful to rock music acts, since the company reaches about 60 percent of the rock-radio audience nationally.

Most folks became aware of Clear Channel's reach after the 9/11 attacks when a story circulated about a Clear Channel memo that provided program directors (PDs) with a list of songs that *shouldn't* be played in the aftermath of the attacks. The company was also responsible for those billboards that appeared shortly thereafter that feature a "waving" American flag. While such nationalism may seem like innocuous proselytizing in the name of American patriotism, it had more direct implications, according to hip-hop generation intellectual and activist Davey D (David Cook). Davey D, who hosted *Street Knowledge*, a public-affairs program, and *The LocalFlava Hip-Hop Hour* for KMEL in the San Francisco/Oakland Bay Area, was abruptly fired in a "cost-cutting" move by the Clear Channel–owned station a month after the attacks. Despite the "official" word, many Bay Area residents believed that Cook was facing retribution for his willingness to provide a "sanctuary" for Representative Barbara Lee and hip-hop artists Boots Riley (of the Coup) in the weeks after the 9/11 attacks on his show *Street Knowledge* and his indispensable web site DaveyD.com. In a historic vote, Lee was the only member of the House of Representatives to vote against a "war resolution" in the aftermath of the attacks. Though unrelated to the attacks, the Coup had already approved artwork for the cover of their CD *Party Music* that depicted an attack on the World Trade Center. The cover art was widely circulated on the Internet hours after the attack. As Tony Coleman, a local activist in Oakland, asserted, "Other deejays are not down with the streets as far as the Oakland Ghetto. The ghetto needs a political [figure] and without Davey D, they lose merit in the community whether they realize it or not."[12]

The Davey D incident is just one example of the constraints placed on black radio in the era of hyperconglomeration, but ultimately that impact is most powerfully experienced in the music that gets played—or, rather, the music that is *never* played on commercial radio stations that specialize in so-called urban formats (hip-hop, hip-hop/R&B hybrids, and to a lesser extent so-called neo-soul). Because so many of these stations are owned by conglomerates who have national interests, these stations are less-attuned to more localized musical developments. Even those stations that are "privately" owned, like New York's WBLS, which is owned by the Inner City Broadcasting Company, often have to kowtow to homogenous R&B (rhythm and bland) acts to compete for audiences—young audiences in particular—who have been feed "similac radio" for half a generation. Throughout the last decade, "big-time" black radio has been primarily producer-driven, thus a decade ago, it was not unusual to only hear acts produced by Teddy Riley, Jimmy Jam and Terry Lewis, and LaFace (Kenny "Babyface" Edmonds and Antonio "LA" Reid). By the mid-1990s, Sean (then known as "Puffy") Combs was an omnipresent force pushing an R&B/hip-hop hybrid that updated Riley's seminal "New Jack Swing" sound. Today it is difficult to listen to "big-time" urban radio without hearing blocks of recordings by Murder Inc. (Ja Rule, Ashanti), Rock-a-fella (Jay Z, Camron), or the RuffRyders (Eve, DMX). Some stations have countered by "reaching back" to "classic" soul recordings, a programming format that is largely driven by nostalgia and corporate interest in moving units of music from artists whose music has been in the can for three decades. Ironically, this "classic soul" moment, with rare exceptions (shout out to Bob Davis and "Soul-Patrol" radio), is totally disconnected from the "new" recordings of these same acts, most of which are distributed independently.

This homogeneity (a favorite word for critics of big radio) occurs at a moment when the stakes have risen significantly for labels—the urban hybrid has crossover appeal to the *TRL* crowd. Although the practice of "payola"—labels paying radio stations directly to play their music—has been illegal for more than forty years, the practice continues to exist with a twist. As Boehlert asserts, "standing in-between the record companies and the radio stations is a legendary team of industry players called independent record promoters, or 'indies.'"[13] These supposed indies are paid by the labels to "promote" their music, while the stations are paid (sometimes in the thousands) by the "indies" to get songs added to station playlists. The practice costs record labels millions of dollars in promotion every week. There's no doubt that the recording industry's fixation with online music providers was in part fueled by the amount of money spent on this practice. This shuffle-step payola also has ramifications for music criticism, as those organs and critics who are outside the "mainstream" often face difficulties getting access to product in the ways that the press is naturally expected to. It goes without saying that the kinds of "promotion" that occur in radio may also in fact occur within the critical press (you can't really do justice to a recording in a seventy-five-word review).

Neo-payola is apparently even more insidious in urban radio, which replicates the unaccountable gatekeeping system endemic to many black institutions. Boehlert notes (damn, bruh, when the book coming out?) that while the practice is clearly a problem in mainstream commercial radio (he asks, at one point, "Why does radio suck?"), "urban radio remains a world apart, the Wild, Wild West of the music industry," adding that while "indie" cash often ends up in a station's budget, "by contrast, the cash still goes into the personal bank accounts of powerful programmers and consultants."[14] Even Radio One, which is the largest black-owned radio conglomerate, with sixty-five stations in twenty-two markets, has not been above such criticism. The station is owned by Kathy Hughes. In an examination of Radio One's stations in Cleveland, Thomas Francis writes that "Black singers drop off CDs at Radio One stations, but never get called back and never hear their music on the radio. Those decisions . . . are based on the color of green. If you want to play on Hughes's stations, you have to pay."[15]

It is in this kind of competitive (really, noncompetitive) environment that public radio has become such a crucial forum for both "pop and politics" (shout out to Farai Chideya). In 1946, the FCC set aside a range on the FM spectrum that would allow for the creation of "educational" radio outlets. The Public Broadcasting Act, passed in 1967, allowed for the further development of "public" broadcasts by providing federal funds to upgrade "educational" outlets to full-fledged "public" outlets.[16] Many of these stations were staffed by community members and college students and were safe havens for heady public-affairs programming and "out-tha-box" playlists. During the mid-1980s, when hip-hop music was still persona non gratis on commercial radio, the genre found a place on college and public radio. Barlow cites stations like Howard University's cable radio station WHBC and KPVU-FM at Prairie View A&M (both HBCUs) for their "reproduction of hip-hop culture" well before it became lucrative in the recording, radio, video, and clothing industries to promote it.[17]

My own sense of the power of public and community radio was formed a decade ago, when I was programming a public-affairs and music program called *Soul Expressions*, where I very comfortably created a playlist that incorporated artists as diverse as the Highway QCs, Phyllis Hyman, Ronnie Dyson, Clifford Coutler, Valerie Simpson, D'Angelo, Pete Rock, and CL Smooth and the poetry of Nikki Giovanni. I particularly enjoyed those times when I could meld music with politics, mixing the speeches of Angela Davis, Malcolm X, and Martin Luther King, Jr., over the blues instrumentals of Jimmy McGriff and Jimmy Smith. No doubt Deena Barnwell felt that empowerment when she played DJ Vadim's "Your Revolution" during her weekly program "Soundbox" on WBOO-FM in Portland, Oregon, in October 1999.

"Your Revolution" was a collaboration between the Russian-born DJ Vadim and spoken-word artist Sarah Jones. In the song, Jones grabbed a riff from Gil Scott-Heron's "The Revolution Will Not Be Televised" to argue that the "revolution" was not happening between the "thighs." The song is one of the most powerful challenges to the sexism and misogyny in hip-hop as Jones systematically takes on the hip-hop's status quo, dropping nods and disses to Biggie ("Big Poppa"), LL ("Back Seat" and "Doin' It"), Bell Biv Devoe ("Poison"), SWV ("Downtown"), Bobby Brown ("Humpin' Around"), Jay Z and Foxy Brown ("Ain't No Nigga"), Shaggy ("Boombastic"), and Akinyele, who she clowns for his lyrical fantasy of his "six-foot blowjob machine." As Barnwell notes, "The hip-hop game is very misogynistic. . . . I've been disrespected as a woman in this game. Jones's song is inspirational."[18] This aspect of the song was apparently lost on the FCC, who cited WBOO-FM for playing a song that was "patently offensive"—in other words, vulgar. The station was fined $7,000, which is serious money for a station that is largely listener-supported. As Jones herself noted at the time of the fine, the song was a reflection of her life "as a black woman. Growing up in a culture where women of color too often are perceived as oversexed," adding that it was clear to her that the FCC was attacking her "freedom as a person, as a woman, and as a woman of color, to defend [herself]."[19] At the time of her offense, Jones was well known in performance circles for her one-woman show *Surface Transit*, which gave voice to eight very distinct fictional New Yorkers.

Ironically, Eminem's "The Real Slim Shady" was cited for "indecency" at the same time as "Your Revolution," thus equating, in the minds of some, Jones's anti-sexist rhetoric with Eminem's strident misogyny and homophobia. Whereas Eminem became a cause célèbre for free-speech advocates—garnering a "postcoital" hug from Elton John after the two performed together at the Grammy Awards ceremony in 2002—Jones was an afterthought to most. Jones went on the offensive in early 2002, following the dropping of charges against Eminem and KKMG (the station that was cited), on the basis that the song's sexual references "are not expressed in terms sufficiently explicit or graphic enough to be found patently offensive."[20] Thus Jones's attempt to "cockblock" hip-hop's misogyny was deemed more "offensive" than that misogyny itself. At the axis where big business and the FCC meet, perhaps it is clear that "Your Revolution" was a challenge not only to sexist "lyrical flow" but also to the flow of capitalism, as companies like Viacom, Time Warner, and Sony regularly trade in the kinds of sexist and misogynist images of women of color that Jones's song brilliantly critiques. Frankly, it seemed like a blatant case of censorship.

Katia Dunn observed in the magazine *Bitch* that the "FCC has only filed a handful of complaints like this one in the last 20 years and similar cases had been handled differently. . . . [I]t became clear that the

FCC had less tolerance for Jones's case than for Eminem's."[21] Dunn also notes that it seems "particularly convenient that the one station the FCC has chosen to crack down on hardest happens to be one of a handful of independent, non-corporate owned stations in America."[22] As Jones noted as she filed suit against the FCC for violating her First Amendment rights (the suit was thrown out on a technicality in September 2002), "My name was hanging in the air with 'indecent' attached to it in this really problematic way, especially since my work is concerned with social justice and feminist issues. . . . [T]hat it should be associated with sexual indecency and intending to shock is just not something that I can just let sit there"; Jones added that it's the other songs that are "played ad infinitum on mainstream radio airwaves that's really problematic. . . . [L]et's not use a double standard that victimizes certain voices."[23] The attack on Jones suggests that even in the spheres of public and community radio, thought-provoking and diverse music and politics will not find a place on America's airwaves.

This is one of the many issues that Michael Franti and Spearhead confronted on their recording *Stay Human* (2001). Franti is well known among progressive political circles from his days as the lyrical frontman of the Disposable Heroes of Hipocracy in the early 1990s and his current role as lead vocalist and lyricist for Spearhead, whose recordings *Home* (1994) and *Chocolate Supa Highway* (1997) are the musical embodiment of an organic Gramscian tradition in contemporary pop music. *Stay Human* was released on Franti's own label Boo Boo Wax (distributed through Six Degrees Records) after he broke free from Capitol Records. In an interview, Franti tells the story of his meeting with the president of Capitol, who suggested that he should do a track with Will Smith.[24] In such an environment, Franti's move away from major-label-land was a no-brainer. Although *Stay Human* is ostensibly a political broadside against the death penalty, Franti creates a fictional radio program called *Stay Human Radio* that combines a public-affairs-style vision with a melodic musical spectrum that references a broad range of black musical styles. The recording drops nods to Marvin Gaye, Earth, Wind, and Fire (the "Devotion"-inspired "Oh My God"), P-Funk ("All the freaky people make the beauty of the world"), Jean

Knight's "Mr. Big Stuff" (the track "Sometimes" precedes a phone interview with the fictional Governor Shane), and even Bob James's "Angela's
Theme."

The focal point of the recording is the case of "Sister Fatima," who
has been accused of murdering James and Ellen Buchanan, the owners
of a building where Sister Fatima ran a medical marijuana office. As the
recording's liner notes suggest, "Many believe that Sister Fatima, who
had been a police target since the late Sixties because of her outspoken
views on racial equality, police violence, environmental issues, gay, lesbian, bisexual, transgender rights, and the compassionate use of medical
marijuana, was framed."[25] In this context, Sister Fatima becomes a template for a broad-based politics—a radical fluidity, if you will—that transcends race, gender, class, and sexuality. Franti more pointedly notes that
"Sister Fatima is a fictitious character based on a lot of what is going on
in America today," adding that there is now a big prison industrial complex—"people making money out of the penal system. . . . I wanted to
transmit this message without people getting down about it."[26] Franti's
focus on Sister Fatima also deftly flips the longstanding fixation with
male political prisoners. Franti addresses this dynamic in the liner notes:
"Over the past thirty years there have been a large number of high profile cases involving African-American political prisoners in the United
States. . . . So why is it that the case of this one *revolutionary woman* [my
emphasis] has received no media attention?"[27] Franti's comments indirectly reference the "celebrated" cases of the recently freed political prisoners Geronimo Pratt and Mumia Abul Jamal, which have received
international attention.

The recording features a "real-time" radio broadcast with the jocks
the Nubian Poetess (Nazelah Jamison) and Brother Soulshine (Franti)
interspersed between tracks by Spearhead. The duo note in their opening segment that their station is "entirely volunteer staffed and funded"
and that it's the "only one of our kind, since KBLV shut down recently,
being the last federally non-funded station to lose their license." Their
primary target throughout the broadcast is the fictional Governor
Franklin Shane (What else would he be named?), who is portrayed by
Woody Harrelson. Harrelson and Franti have worked together in the

past for the medical marijuana movement. Reportedly, Harrelson had some reservations about his role on the recording, as his father is currently imprisoned for murder and is seeking parole.[28] Within the context of *Stay Human*'s narrative, Shane was trailing badly in his reelection bid and ordered the execution of Sister Fatima on the night of the election to generate support among hard-line anti-crime voters. When Shane is interviewed by the host of *Stay Human Radio*, he spews classic white supremacist rhetoric. In Shane's most insidious commentary, he asserts that "it's desperate times and it calls for desperate measures, and if you think about it too, there's an overpopulation situation, in the world, and we're gonna eliminate the people who do not function within this society." Later in his segment, Shane continues to defend the death penalty on the basis that it "makes more room in our prison systems today and frankly they're overcrowded, so it's actually a much more humane thing to do for the rest of the prison population." Shane's comments imply a connection between the warehousing of "criminals," the death penalty, and "legal" genocide.

Some critics will suggest that Franti is engaging in heavy-handed depictions of those who favor the death penalty, coloring them as "racist"—Shane describes Soulshine and the Nubian Poetess's line of questioning as "left wing, pinko philosophy"—but such criticism misses the point. One of the important dynamics of community-based radio is that it gives voice, in fairly democratic ways, to those outside of the mainstream, including those who may be informed by conspiracy theorists. In the context of *Stay Human Radio*, Shane is allowed access in ways that Soulshine and the Nubian Poetess would never be afforded in the mainstream media. As the two assert early in the recording, they represent what the "others won't say and what the other won't play." This is powerfully represented when Sister Fatima herself, grabs the mike in a telephone interview. During her interview, Sister Fatima asserts that she was a threat because she "wants to unite people, whereas they want to keep people divided. They're afraid of our unity, because we are the overwhelming majority." While Sister Fatima's comments may suggest a natural bifurcation between "white" and "black," Franti's own "fluid" politics suggests that her comments more broadly reflect a struggle between political and economic elites and the masses of folks exploited by them, which transcends race, gender, and ethnicity. Franti, who has mixed-race parentage, asserts that black culture "is a mixed culture. We are not just black or white, you know. A lot of what is positive in our society is a result of the amalgamation."[29]

In the aftermath of Sister Fatima's execution, the real killer of the Buchanans turns himself in. The moment is a classic indictment of the death penalty's insidiousness—innocent people are killed. Shortly thereafter it is revealed that Shane has died of a self-inflicted gunshot wound to the head. While reporting the chain of surprising events, which was apparently not reported by the mainstream press, Soulshine asserts that "it's time, personally, that we start to take the media in its own hands and become the media ourselves." Soulshine is barely able to complete his thought before the station is bum-rushed by federal agents, who quickly shut down the broadcast. There is no doubt that Franti's narrative throughout *Stay Human* reflects his own hardcore radical politics, and he offers very little space for alternative points of view that could challenge his ideological assumptions. But again this is the value of presenting his message in the context of a community-supported radio station: How many sites are there in the mainstream media where left-wing or radical politics can be expressed unadulterated? Even in the context of the shutting down of *Stay Human Radio*, how far removed is this situation from the kind of silencing that Sarah Jones has faced with the FCC? For so many folks hoping to take over the airwaves with some "Radio Free Soul," particularly young folks who are generating radio programming via "pirate radio" and Internet radio, Robert Williams, Sarah Jones, and Michael Franti are powerful inspirations.

CHAPTER ELEVEN

● ●

BIG PIMPIN'

I was pulling into the parking lot of my then two-year-old's day care when I first heard the news that the contract of popular talk-show host Tavis Smiley was not being renewed by Black Entertainment Television (BET). The announcement came courtesy of Tom Joyner, who is the host of the largest syndicated radio program targeted to African-American audiences. The *Tom Joyner Morning Show* is part of my every-day ritual: my daughter and I get to listen to some old-school soul and I get to get my laff-on courtesy of J. Anthony Brown and my inform-on via Smiley's twice-weekly commentaries. For sure I was surprised by the announcement, even letting out a loud chuckle at the irony of the move, as I stood in the parking lot. Hell, it was only two years earlier that *Newsweek* said that Smiley was one of the twenty or so people who were changing how we get our news, and, of course, he had been the winner of the coveted NAACP "I make Negroes look good" Image Award three years running. He had also achieved the distinction of being BET's highest paid on-air talent. But my surprise turned to reservation as I prepared for the inevitable "rally around the race" pitch that Joyner et al. were going to employ to get Smiley reinstated as the host of *BET Tonight*. By the time I had returned to the car ten minutes later, Joyner was giving out the e-mail address and phone number to Viacom's (the parent company of BET) CEO, Mel Karmazin. I had been here before.

Since 1996, Smiley and Joyner have spearheaded several campaigns—known to the world as "air advocacy campaigns"—aimed at "empowering" the black community. Using the visibility that Smiley was afforded on BET and access to an audience of 7 million spread out over one hundred radio markets, Smiley and Joyner had redefined the Chitlin' Circuit for the digital era. At their best, they inspired listeners to send faxes and e-mail to the heads of congressional committees about a range of issues, including providing disaster relief for a North Carolina town that had been damaged by floods, brokering for a Congressional Medal of Honor for Civil Rights–era matriarch Rosa Parks, and, most recently, sponsoring a "take a loved one to the doctor" campaign in concert with ABC Radio (then Joyner's syndicator) and the Department of Health and Human Services. Via promotions like the *Sky Show* (sponsored by Southwest Airlines), the radio crew, which features Joyner, Brown, newswoman Sybil Wilks, and comediennes Ms. Dupree (a psychic) and Myra Jay, appears live virtually every Friday in cities that carry the show. The programs are often showcases for the many charities that Joyner and the show support (they regularly give out money to exceptional fathers and mothers), most notably the Tom Joyner Foundation, which raises money for HBCUs (historically black colleges and universities). Over the past few years, Joyner's show has also sponsored the "Fantastic Voyage," an old-school soul cruise that also raises money for his foundation. Currently the foundation raises about $200,000 a month and has raised over $13 million since its inception seven years ago.[1] Joyner himself is a product of the Tuskegee Institute (where the ghost of Booker T. lives) in Alabama.

At their worst, Joyner et al. were engaged in mundane bourgeois activism that has little to do with the everyday realities of most black folks, such as forcing the Christie's auction house to scrap plans to auction off antebellum-era collectibles (I ain't hatin' on the sentiment, but it's not like Pookie and Nay-Nay, or Arthur or Elsie for that matter, give a damn). In the most celebrated example of their bourgeois activism, Joyner and Smiley spearheaded a boycott of CompUSA (the nation's largest computer retailer) in 1999 for the company's failure advertise to a significant degree with black media (namely *The Tom Joyner Morning*

Show). The morning crew had black listeners who had purchased products from CompUSA send in copies of their receipts to the show, which were then boxed up and sent to CompUSA. At one point during their boycott efforts, Joyner and Smiley read a racist fax on-air that was supposedly from the CompUSA president, only to find out that it was hoax (the duo apologized on-air for the blunder). After some nudging from Joyner's syndicator, Joyner and Smiley sat down with CompUSA's president, James Halpin, to knock out an agreement, which included a 10 percent discount for those folks who had sent in receipts, a promise to hire a black advertising agency, and an appearance by Halpin on the show.[2] Although Halpin blamed the "oversight" on the company's financial troubles, it was quite clear that, as he appeared on the *Tom Joyner Morning Show* to apologize and pledge a commitment to advertise in black media, that he had also acquired a half hour of free publicity for his company—as did Smiley and Joyner for themselves. With the campaign, Smiley and Joyner had became playas, big ballers, shot callers able to leap global conglomerates in a single bound: Look, it's a bird, it's a plane . . . no, it's big pimpin' bourgeois style.

If Smiley and Joyner could be accused of big pimpin, they were inspired by the now legendary example of BET founder Bob Johnson, who has turned big pimpin' into a fine art. The term *pimp*, of course, has a long history at the dark axis of ghettocentric black masculinity and illicit ghetto activities such as prostitution. In its most simplistic (and powerful forms), pimpin' was a constant reminder of black patriarchy's role in the black community, as pimps were the visible controllers and connoisseurs of black female sexuality. It is not far-fetched to suggest that pimps derived negative connotations within mainstream black institutions in part to detract from the fact that black women were also powerfully exploited inside of those institutions. With the publication of Robert Beck's (Iceberg Slim) autobiography *Pimp: The Story of My Life* (1969) and the film *Superfly* (1972), the concept of pimpin' was introduced to mainstream America, so much so that the pimp (I'm thinking Antonio Fargas specifically) became a staple of television drama in the 1970s and early 1980s.

Even as the image of the pimp began to wane in the 1980s, it reemerged with a vengeance via the narratives of hip-hop artists like Too Short, Big Daddy Kane, and, most recently, Jay Z, who despite initial concerns from his management scored a crossover hit with "Big Pimpin'" in 1999. Through the world of hip-hop and, more broadly, American youth culture, a "neo-pimpin'" emerged that was not specifically tied to the exploitation of women (though that remained a powerful subtext in projects like the film *American Pimp* and HBO's *Pimps Up, Hoes Down*), but rather extended into the world of rigid dichotomies— "black" and "white," became pimps and hoes. Rockie Beatty, who is a cofounder of the clothing line Pimpgear, notes that his inspiration was "not to be a pimp who beats down women, not at all, but we think of being a pimp as being empowered—doing your own thing."[3] USC professor Todd Boyd, a self-described "professor of pimpology," adds, "This society is based upon a principle of supply and demand. You are on one side or the other of that equation—you're either a pimp or a ho." It is in this context that the "corporate" and "spiritual" hustle has been conflated with the idea of big pimpin'. While hip-hop artists are dutifully critiqued for their willing circulation of pimp imagery in their music videos, some of the "big pimps" in the black community are shielded from intense scrutiny because they exist in the "respectable" spheres of blackface corporate America and mega-church spirituality (shout out to Otis Moss III for his insightful critique of the black mega-church). Whereas hip-hop artists are sometimes only pimpin' the *imagery* of pimps, the respectable "big pimps" are pimpin' black culture and black misery on the real.

Bob Johnson has performed such a role brilliantly over the last two decades; he first pimped the idea that he could deliver black audiences to the cable television industry in 1979. He has often exploited (that's what pimps do, right?) his position as the black "lone wolf McQuade" in the cable industry to better his own business interests, with the assumption being that he was doing it in the name of the black community at large. As Jonathan Chait notes, "Johnson has spent his career converting the moral capital of the black struggle for equality to his own personal advantage," adding that Johnson's "genius lies in finding certain corners of the economy where he can guarantee himself a steady stream of risk-free profit without having to provide goods or services of any special value."[4] Over the past five years, Johnson has, specifically, provided access to distortions of black life and culture via the music videos that dominate his network. Apparently such imagery does have special value to the Viacom corporation, which paid $3 billion in stocks and cash to acquire the network and its holdings from Johnson in late 2000. Currently, Johnson has traded his perceived "leadership" role (leader and gatekeeper are not interchangeable roles) within the black community into influence within the Bush administration, as witnessed by his appointment to Bush's Commission to Strengthen Social Security. Johnson became Bush's "nigga" after publicly siding with Bush's proposed abolition of the estate tax. While big-moneyed centrists like Bill Gates opposed Bush's plan, Johnson argued that the estate tax disadvantaged a generation of black millionaires, who, unlike their white counterparts, came to their wealth "on a different path, a different road than they have."[5]

Johnson has for a long time escaped serious scrutiny in the black community because of his "race man" status, the black community's unwillingness to "air dirty draws" (and thus hold folks publicly accountable), and Johnson's innate ability, as Chait notes, to make his business interests "legitimate" civil rights issues. It is in this context that I was, quite frankly, offended that Joyner et al. would ask listeners to hold Viacom accountable in Smiley's "firing" in a way that they had never held Bob Johnson (big pimpin' spendin' cheese) accountable when he owned BET. I was offended that black listeners were asked to fight for a program that had significantly underachieved as a legitimate vehicle of progressive thought and critique. In support of Smiley, there were clearly restraints placed on him at BET. Even a casual listener to *The Tom Joyner Morning Show* could discern the freedom and passion that Smiley brought to his twice-weekly commentaries that were absent in his role at BET. In a world dominated by heady conversations that include a notable absence of black commentators and critics, *BET Tonight with Tavis Smiley* gave its audiences a regular view of black public intellectuals such as Michael Eric Dyson and Cornel West, prominent black clergy such as Bishop T. D. Jakes, and popular authors like the "high priestess" neo-Afrocentric mystic Ilyant Vanzant.

Like *The Arsenio Hall Show* in the late 1980s and early 1990s, Smiley's show allowed black folk to see themselves taken seriously, while Smiley himself, with his forays into "big mama" wit and ebonically authentic diction, created a comfort zone for some audiences—an intelligent, savvy Foghorn Leghorn on the black-owned ghetto-fabulous version of *The Firing Line.* At a moment when black public intellectuals have to work as hard and even harder at promoting themselves than at promoting the actual scholarly work they do, Smiley redefined self-promotion, using both BET and *The Tom Joyner Morning Show* as vehicles to promote his books and his numerous speaking gigs and trips to Krispy Kreme (can't hate on him for that). One of the running jokes on *The Tom Joyner Morning Show*—courtesy of J. Anthony Brown, who in my mind is the show's real intellectual—was the fact that Smiley's commentary was often just an opportunity to tell listeners what the next stops were on his book tour. These aspects aside, if *The Charlie Rose Show* can be identified as the model for heady liberal talk on television, then *BET Tonight with Tavis Smiley* was a legitimate, though significantly flawed, black equivalent.

Part of the problem with Smiley's show was that it was often reduced to cronyism. During one appearance by attorney Johnnie Cochran and Cornel West, Smiley introduced the duo as his good friends, effectively undermining his value and authority as a host, since he was unlikely to really challenge them in any significant way. It's similar to the numerous softball interviews that Ahmad Rashad did with Michael Jordan, in which most audiences were not privy to the fact that Rashad was part of Jordan's inner circle (shout out to Stuart Scott in that regard). For the record, Cochran and West were on the show to discuss the acquittal of Sean "P. Diddy" Combs, as BET and MTV (both Viacom networks) became "Diddy Central" for the duration of the trial. In comparison, Smiley once invited Russell Simmons onto the show, seemingly just to berate the mogul for calling Smiley a "sell-out Uncle Tom" when the host requested an interview with him hours after the death of Tupac Shakur. The incident spoke volumes about the way Smiley used the show to craft and protect his image, as if his audiences should have been as offended by Simmons's quip as Smiley was.

Although West and Dyson were prominently featured (often!), and rightfully so, on *BET Tonight*, Smiley rarely invited black scholars and intellectuals who were not known quantities to his audiences. Thus black scholars and public intellectuals such as Joy James, bell hooks, Tricia Rose, Cathy Cohen, Jill Nelson, Michelle Wallace, Barbara Smith, Farah Jasmine Griffin, Beverly Guy-Sheftall, Hazel Carby, the late June Jordan (there's a pattern here, huh?), or male thinkers such as Phillip Brian Harper, Robin D. G. Kelley, Houston Baker, Derrick Bell, and others who are just as engaging and knowledgeable as West and Dyson were rarely, if ever, given regular forums on the program. In retrospect, it seems as though Smiley would only invite thinkers who were already accepted by his audiences as being smarter than he was. This reading is supported by the fact that Smiley often—and dramatically—genuflected to the likes of Dyson and West, admitting that he didn't quite understand what they were saying. On other occasions, when Smiley was forced to deal with issues of popular culture, particularly hip-hop, he seemed terribly out of touch. Granted, he was forced to do such shows so that the network could attract younger audiences, but he rarely seemed to come up to speed with the issues germane to those audiences and noticeably tried to protect his inadequacies by framing the conversation in very specific terms. On a show that featured Common, Dead Prez, and writer Kevin Powell (check *Step into a World: A Global Anthology of the New Black Literature*), Smiley spent more than twenty minutes asking *all* of the panelists individually how they defined "conscious" hip-hop, even as they simply stated that they were in agreement with the previous answers, wasting a unique opportunity to have a more serious conversation with some of the more progressive voices in hip-hop (Common's homophobia notwithstanding). The reality is that it is hard to come up to speed with your guests if you are on one seemingly continuous fifty-city book tour—just ask Diddy when was the last time he was behind the boards.

The day after Joyner first announced that Smiley's contract was not being renewed by BET, Smiley appeared on *The Tom Joyner Morning Show* during his regularly scheduled commentary and publicly expressed his dismay that his contract was not being renewed and that word had been delivered to his agent via a four-sentence fax. Despite protests from his staff, many of whom suggested that Smiley resign immediately because BET didn't "deserve" him, Smiley also announced that he would stay with the station until his contact actually ended in the fall. While Smiley remained silent, Joyner and company continued their assault on Viacom, suggesting that Smiley's contract had not been renewed in retribution for his political stances. One caller even suggested that Viacom had gone after Smiley in response to his efforts to get the struggling black hospital drama *City of Angels* renewed for the 2000–1 television season, despite the fact that the quality of the show was at best uneven and not widely supported even by African-American audiences. Bob Johnson et al. responded very quickly to the old-school wolf tickets being sold by Joyner and Smiley by publicly affirming that it was an in-house decision made by Johnson himself to pull the plug on Smiley's term with the network. In a press release issued hours before Smiley's appearance on *The Tom Joyner Morning Show*, the network stated that it was a "creative decision made by BET as part of our regular planning process for the new season debuting in September."[6] Nearly forty-eight hours after that statement, BET issued another statement that Smiley's contract would be terminated immediately. Bob Johnson himself would suggest that "recent actions by Mr. Smiley left us little recourse but to make this move."[7]

Popular opinion was that Smiley had become too politically hot for the more conservative Bob Johnson. Some industry insider suggested that Johnson and BET/Viacom moved on Smiley in response to Smiley's selling of an exclusive interview with former Symbionese Liberation Army member Sara Jane Olsen to ABC's *Primetime Live*. This was later corroborated by Johnson, who asserted that there was a "lack of mutual business respect" between the network and the former host, adding that the network had had "something of a difficult relationship with Tavis over the last five years."[8] Johnson was also likely personally offended by the end-around criticism by Joyner et al. that suggested that it was a decision made over Johnson's head. Although Johnson sold BET for $3 billion in October 2000, the company is still run on a day-to-day basis by Johnson and his management team. Johnson has proven to be very sensitive to public criticism, hence his very public disputes with cartoonist Aaron McGruder, who regularly clowns BET and a host of other black folk in his strip *The Boondocks*. From Johnson's vantage point, the criticism that suggested that he didn't make the decision may have infuriated him as much as or more than the criticisms of the move itself. Johnson admitted during his unprecedented appearance on a special one-hour *BET Tonight*, where viewers were able to call in or e-mail one of the most prominent gatekeepers of black intellectual and entertainment property, that the specific reason for Smiley's removal was because of the interview with Sara Jane Olsen. Johnson is disingenuous, though, when he suggests that Viacom did not play a part in his decision-making process, particularly because Smiley's appearance on *Primetime Live* helped ABC trounce the debut of the heavily promoted urban cop drama *Big Apple* on the Viacom-owned CBS—a show that was likely to attract a significant black urban audience before its quick cancellation.

Culling perceptions from radio appearances by Al Sharpton and Cornel West on New York City's WRKS, *The Tom Joyner Morning Show*, and various listservs dedicated to African-American issues, the general consensus was that Smiley was in fact being punished for his political views. While such a view is an obvious response to Smiley's firing, Smiley's body of political work has not suggested that he is pushing for any ideas that are not already part of the status quo of black mainstream political activity. Given the choices offered to the American public during the 2000 presidential election, Smiley's efforts to increase voter registration and increase voter consciousness, albeit to the flavor of old-school soul, did little more than popularize the efforts of traditional black-elected leadership. Given the age range of Tom Joyner's core audience, and the relevance of the term *old-school*, those efforts did little to reach out to the youngest segment of the African-American electorate and instead preached to a choir who had been preached the same sermon consistently over a twenty-year period, since the first election of Ronald Reagan. Even Smiley's highly publicized "State of Black America" events, the first held on the eve of the Democratic National

Convention in August 2000, give a portrait of how mainstream Smiley's sensibilities are. Nearly all of the participants were the kind of known quantities that had made regular appearances on his show and the numerous other "talking heads" programs on television. While Smiley should be commended for including a wide range of political voices, including conservative stalwarts such as Armstrong Williams, Stanley Crouch, and Rev. Kirbyjon Caldwell (he of Bush inauguration fame), scholars Lani Guiner and Mary Frances Berry, and "young" voices like Aaron McGruder and Farai Chideya, there were no major radical voices such as those of Black Radical Congress leaders and scholars Manning Marable and Bill Fletcher, no major leaders from within the black gay and lesbian communities, and no one doing the kind of grassroots organization of welfare recipients. It was the classic coming together of policymakers and policy informers, but no one who was policy affected. The gathering spoke to the general disconnect of bourgeois mainstream black political activity from the people they hoped to impact. I say all this to suggest that Smiley has not posited anything in his formidable body of political work that would suggest that he is at all a threat to the political status quo. If anything, he has himself become a media commodity, which does not guarantee that his politics travel with him.

Smiley emerged out of this "crisis" more influential than he was as the host of *BET Tonight*, signing deals with ABC's *Primetime Live*, CNN's *Talk Back Live*, and, most important, National Public Radio, where he hosts and produces a daily radio program. Black folks, though, are still left with the problem of BET, which was able to deflect criticism in the past because of Smiley's presence. Since 1996, when longtime *Video Soul* host Donnie Simpson was put out to pasture, Johnson has aggressively tried to cultivate a more youthful audience. In 1998, Bev Smith's show *Our Voices* also separated from the Johnson plantation. Johnson has shown a distinct pattern of pulling public affairs and "adult" programming when they do not reach the kinds of audiences and, more important, generate the kind of ad revenue that BET desires. In this regard, Smiley's departure had likely been plotted the previous year, when the show was reduced to a half hour instead of the one-hour call-in *BET Talk* that it debuted as in 1996.

What troubles me now is that suddenly BET's moves are being aggressively criticized because it is now owned by Viacom. Black audiences have been disappointed, dismayed, and disgusted by BET's primary programming for more than five years, which is why Aaron McGruder's critiques of BET in *The Boondocks* resonated so powerfully with many. In another example of his questionable decisions, Johnson ceased publication of George Curry's *Emerge* magazine, arguably the preeminent source of political commentary about black America. Where was the outcry and public disdain for that decision? Did Tom Joyner et al. give out fax numbers and e-mail addresses at BET and Vanguarde Media in response to the demise of *Emerge*, or to the removal of Donnie Simpson and Bev Smith, or to the network's reliance on those damn "bling, bling and booty shaker" videos that run all day? Because BET was then a "black-owned" company, Bob Johnson was protected as audiences and supporters closed ranks around the "premiere" black media outlet. Ultimately, the Viacoms of the world can and will make decisions detrimental to black audiences if only because of the general inability or unwillingness of those audiences to hold themselves accountable—and there is unfortunately no fax number or e-mail address that can rectify that.

CHAPTER TWELVE

●●●●●●●●●●●●●●●●●●●●●●●●

BUT IT'S N●T A RAP CD

During the summer of 1992, it seemed as though hip-hop music and culture were on trial, as black youth culture was under indictment for a series of incidents, including the so-called L.A. Riots. While hip-hop was not directly implicated in the insurrections that occurred in the aftermath of the acquittal of the four police officers accused of beating motorist Rodney King the year before, it was clear that the music of artists such as Ice Cube, NWA, and Public Enemy reflected the rage that many black youth felt in response to issues of police brutality and political disenfranchisement. In the weeks shortly after the riots, rap activist Lisa Williamson (known in rap circles as Sister Souljah) reflected on the "riots" with the controversial statement that "if black people kill black people every day, why not have a week and kill white people," adding that white folks were "well aware of the fact that black people were dying every day in Los Angeles under gang violence. So if you're a gang member and you would normally be killing somebody, why not kill a white person."[1] Sister Souljah's point was that in the aftermath of the "riots" it seemed as though the lives of white people—Reginald Denny as one example—were of more value than the black lives that were lost every day in the context of gang violence and at the hands of the LAPD.

Then Democratic presidential hopeful Bill Clinton referenced Williamson's statement in a speech at the annual convention of Jesse

Jackson's Rainbow Coalition. It was a calculated attempt by Clinton to show the nonblack wing of the Democratic party, particularly those aligned with the Democratic Leadership Council (DLC), that he was not beholden to the Civil Rights "lobby," while also suggesting that he held more moral authority than the "moral" leadership of the black community. At the time of the attack, Sister Souljah was little more than a fringe artist whose association with the seminal political rap group Public Enemy validated her within the ranks of hip-hop culture. Clinton's attack portended his often problematic political uses of black women, such as Lani Guinier and Jocelyn Elders, the "quota" and "condom" queens who were jettisoned from Clinton's sphere when their declining "value" to him politically no longer deemed them worth of his protection.

By the summer of 1992, it was the music of Ice T and his band Body Count that was under scrutiny as the recording "Cop Killer" was cited for advocating attacks on law enforcement officers.[2] Although the controversy was used to highlight the violent nature of some rap lyrics and the violence within black youth culture (which in the American imagination was all too often conflated with gang violence), the fact of the matter was that "Cop Killer" was not a rap CD. Body Count was Ice T's thrash metal band, and there was nary a black kid in the hood (yes, I'm being essentialist here) listening to that joint. The power of the recording was not in its effect on black kids—KRS-One's "100 Guns" (*Edutainment*) was released a year earlier to little scrutiny, and the very same summer of "Cop Killer's" release Dr. Dre and Snoop Dogg blatantly rapped about doing "187 on an undercover cop" on the soundtrack to *Deep Cover*—but rather its impact on white kids, some of whom know that police brutality is an cross-racial affliction.

A decade later it was another so-called rap CD that was under scrutiny, but for vastly different reasons. This CD was at the center (so we think) of a very public dispute between Harvard's president, Lawrence Summer, and the "preeminent" black public intellectual, Cornel West. According to senior faculty members at the university and sources close to West, in a private meeting with West in October 2001, Summers "chided" West for recording a "rap" CD, for his prominent role in Al Sharpton's likely presidential bid in 2004, for his overly "accessi-ble" scholarly work, and for grade inflation. By all standards, West is an academic "star" whose scholarly image had transcended the academy and found its way onto episodes of *The West Wing* (where Dule Hill read a copy of West's *Keeping the Faith*), film sequels for *The Matrix*, and pro-files in *Vanity Fair*; the fact that he was offended by Summers's charges is not surprising. The story was leaked to the *Boston Globe* in late December 2001.[3] In Summers's defense, he had had similar "critical" discussions with other Harvard University faculty, particularly with regards to grade inflation. But Summers's purported comments and the various schools of response to the controversy raise troubling questions about general perceptions of black intellectual production, the increas-ing gaps—real or perceived—between elite black intellectuals and the larger black public they "speak" for, and the often bankrupt strategies of mainstream Civil Rights activists and sycophantic black conservative commentators alike.

Now, I had known a little bit about this "rap" CD some months before the "controversy" as a copy of West's *Sketches of My Culture* sat somewhere on a shelf in my office. I had gotten a copy of it from West's people and had only listened to it once—and only the first six tracks at that. I have all too vivid memories of hearing those first six tracks in Starbucks one night, and quietly and shamelessly chuckling my ass off as I returned the disc back to its jacket and into the far, far recesses of my consciousness. Although I had initially wanted to write a full-length feature about West and the CD for the online magazine Popmatters.com, after that initial listen I decided to take a "Lauryn Hill." The term is a reference to the artist of the same name and critical response to her *Lauryn Hill Unplugged* disc. Rather than pan the dreadful double-disc, many critics chose not to say anything about the disc out of respect for Hill and her talents. While I appreciate West's desire to broaden his influence as a public intellectual, the CD was a major misstep of aes-thetic judgment. I have had mad respect for Cornel West for more than a decade and had been in the game myself, in part because of his role modeling, so I wasn't gonna write disparagingly about what was simply an atrocious performance (kind of like W. E. B. Du Bois doing Joe Tex—

he of the Chitlin' Circuit favorites "You Said a Bad Word," "Bad Feet," "Skinny Legs and All," and "My Papa Was"). *Sketches of My Culture* was a lot of things, but rap CD was not one of them.

Cornel West began his scholarly career a little more than twenty years ago as a self-defined postmodern Marxist black philosopher. At that time there was no public language to support even the idea of a Cornel West and the generation of black poststructuralist and feminist literary and cultural critics and theorist that emerged during the late 1970s and 1980s. Names like Barbara Christian, Houston Baker, Jr., Hortense Spillers, and Henry Louis (Skip) Gates, Jr., were simply not part of the public lexicon, particularly in relation to the ebbs and flows of everyday black life in America. Nevertheless, many of these figures would emerge as powerful forces within the American academy, Gates being the most prominent, with his groundbreaking study *The Signifying Monkey* (1988). During this period, West published three philosophical tomes: *Prophecy Deliverance: An Afro-American Revolutionary Christianity* (1989), *The American Evasion of Philosophy: A Genealogy of Pragmatism* (1990), and *The Ethical Dimensions of Marxist Thought* (1991). He also published *Prophetic Fragments* (1988), a collection of short essays that more easily distilled West's idea of a prophetic democratic vision. Scholarly in his work, West's real power came from his lay-preacher style that was part Emersonian (DuBoisian), and Franklin-ian (as in Rev. CL, Aretha Franklin's father). As West admitted in an 1990 interview with Bill Moyers (*A World of Ideas*), he believed that the "vocation of the intellectual as trying to turn easy answers into critical questions and putting those critical questions to people with power."[4] On the brink of intellectual stardom, West was described by Robert Boynton (who would later write an influential essay on the black public intellectual for *Atlantic Monthly*) as bringing "religious zeal to intellectual issues" and making the "life of the mind exciting."[5]

West's initial breakthrough to popular audiences came with *Breaking Bread: Insurgent Black Intellectual Life* (1991), his collaborative "conversation" with bell hooks that was published by South End Press in 1992. Hooks already had a rather prolific career, specializing in presenting "popular" black feminist theory and criticism to "alternative" audi-

ences in books like *Ain't I a Woman* (1981) and *Talking Back: Thinking
Feminist, Thinking Black* (1989). Arguably, at the time of their collaboration hooks was the more visible of the two. *Breaking Bread* primed
West for the widespread acceptance of *Race Matters* (1993), his collection of very accessible essays on race and African-American culture. The
book officially ushered in the era of the black public intellectual. Nattily
dressed in navy three-piece suits and an even nattier (not nappier) Afro,
West became the poster boy for a generation of black scholars, including Gates and hooks and others such as Michael Eric Dyson, Patricia
Williams (who writes consistently brilliant articles for *The Nation*),
Todd Boyd (*The New H.N.I.C.: The Death of Civil Rights and the Reign
of Hip-Hop*), and Tricia Rose (author of the groundbreaking book on
hip-hop, *Black Noise: Rap Music and Black Culture in Contemporary
America*), whose seeming sole purpose for mainstream (literate) white
America was to interpret the signs and sounds of hip-hop, black youth
culture, the O. J. Simpson trial (which made Dyson a star), the Million
Man March, and the murders of Tupac Shakur and the Notorious
B.I.G. (Biggie Smalls/Christopher Wallace). While this generation of
black public intellectuals has been alternately celebrated and scorned,
they were not a "new" phenomenon, as some argued in the mid-1990s,
but rather the latest of a long tradition of black public intellectuals that
included seminal figures such as Ida B. Wells Barnett, W. E. B. Du Bois,
and the legendary C. L. R. James.

At the time of *Race Matters*'s publication, West was directing the
Afro-American studies program at Princeton. By 1996, West was firmly
ensconced as a member of the "dream team," the collection of black
scholars that comprised the faculty of the W. E. B. DuBois Institute for
Afro-American Research. By the late 1990s, this group also included
folks like Gates, who ran the institute, sociologist William Julius Wilson
(*The Truly Disadvantaged*), Evelyn Brooks Higginbotham, and K.
Anthony Appiah. The DuBois institute is synonymous with the field of
African-American studies, often eclipsing the profile of equally important programs and departments like those at Yale, NYU, Duke, Berkeley,
Columbia, and Brown. According to Jacqueline Trescott in a 1996 arti-
cle on the institute, the dream team was "in terms of critical mass . . . the

most prestigious group of black intellectuals since Thurgood Marshall gathered his team three decades ago" in preparation for *Brown vs. Board of Education*.[6] In the article, *Black Issues in Higher Education* publisher Frank Matthews admitted that the stakes were high: "We have the right to expect something from them in terms of solutions . . . some answers to the very vexing problems we have—from freedom of speech and rap music to how do we deal with the AIDS crisis. We have to expect more than business than usual."[7] While the institute has fallen short of such lofty expectations—how can any individual department be expected to change the world?—its high visibility has had, generally speaking, a positive impact on the field of African-American studies. While Gates wields real gatekeeper power within African-American studies, it is West who has been the most visible embodiment of the field.

It is against this backdrop that Lawrence Summers, former treasury secretary in the Clinton administration and brand-new president of Harvard University, sat down with West in October 2001. After the story broke in late December, the reactions were swift. The "attack" on West was conflated with the larger issue of Harvard's commitment to affirmative action, leading the battling reverends Sharpton and Jackson (in mortal combat over leadership of the mainstream Civil Rights movement) to enter the fray. In a phone conversation with the *Boston Globe*, Jackson asserted that the "tension at Harvard is having an impact across the country. . . . It is America's flagship university. And the tension at Harvard over the equivocation or lack of clarity about affirmative action and inclusion is very disturbing."[8] Jackson apparently intervened against West's wishes. According to West, "Jesse's got a right to come. I just told him he didn't need to come. And when he did come and said, 'Would you appear with me?' I said, 'oh no, no, no brother. I don't do that stuff on my behalf like that.'"[9]

In a separate conversation with the *Boston Globe*, Sharpton stated that he didn't want to see faculty members "intimidated."[10] Given the myriad crises faced by people of African descent in the United States—police brutality, racial profiling, the erosion of civil liberties, lack of meaningful health care, and a near state of economic depression in some black communities, particularly after 9/11—the decision of Sharpton and Jackson to use whatever political and social capital they possess to mediate a dispute between an elite Ivy League president and a six-figure-salaried elite black public intellectual (in colloquial terms, a "six-figure nigga") seems particularly problematic. One has to wonder if either Jackson or Sharpton would extend the same energy in support of black faculty and staff at historically black colleges and universities who, depending on the institution, are treated as little more than chattel. But to raise questions about black faculty who are "intimidated" by gate-keepers within black institutions is to risk access to and influence within those very institutions. No politically astute black mainstream politician (or black intellectual) is willing to do that.

In another questionable response, *The Tom Joyner Morning Show* initially reported that Harvard was attempting to "fire" Cornel West. West was, of course, a tenured university professor at Harvard (one of fourteen at the institution) who, short of being convicted for a role in the 9/11 attacks, was not likely to be "fired" by the institution, as is the case with most tenured professors. The mistake on Joyner's part speaks to the fact that the general public has very little understanding of the ebbs and flows of academic life, though that didn't keep the show from mounting one of their famous "air advocacy" campaigns in support of West. The "air advocacy" campaigns (the hosts urge listeners to fax and e-mail complaints/protests), which are largely the brainchild of commentator and National Public Radio host Tavis Smiley, are a mixed bag. On the one hand, they have been instrumental in assisting flood victims in North Carolina and pushing through the appointment of Roger Gregory to the federal courts. On the other hand, the campaigns have been bogged down in symbolic minutiae such as protesting the flying of the Confederate flag in South Carolina (as opposed to actually helping to address the economic and educational inequities in the state). Accordingly, it was on the debut edition of Smiley's NPR show in January 2002 that West first spoke publicly about his dispute with Summers, acknowledging that he doesn't "tolerate . . . disrespect, being dishonored and being devalued."[11] West was particularly offended by Summers's suggesting that he had missed three weeks of class in the fall of 2000 campaigning for Bill Bradley and his request that West periodically show him works in progress. In response to the latter request, Nobel Prize–winning novelist Toni Morrison chimed in, "You don't do that unless you're dealing with an uppity slave. The owner can monitor [academic papers] because he owns you."[12] Nevertheless, one has to wonder that if this had been another era, and Smiley and Joyner were positioned as they are now, whether they would have extended such forums to the institute's namesake, W. E. B. DuBois, when the influential black intellectual—the template for the tradition, really—was carted out in front of McCarthy's House Un-American Activities Committee (HUAC) in the early 1950s and asked to renounce his ties to radicalism.

The efforts to rally around Cornel West are likely unprecedented in the history of the black intelligentsia in the United States, with only the early 1990s controversies surrounding the suspect Afrocentric "scholar" Leonard Jeffries coming close. The sudden attention given the black intelligentsia raised consciousness among the black masses about the role of black intellectuals in their lives. During an extraordinary three-hour call-in program broadcast on C-Span 2 in early January 2002, West fielded a wide array of questions about himself and the field of African-American studies. One caller raised the question as to why scholars such as West and others teach at elite "white" institutions instead of teaching at HBCUs. West did what so many of us know as the poststructuralist two-step (I've done it more than a few times), with a lot of references to "teaching loads," "research budgets," and "financial rewards." Of course, many of the HBCUs, especially elite institutions like Howard, Hampton, Spelman, Morehouse, and Fisk, were largely responsible for nurturing most of the black intelligentsia well into the 1980s.

With the "integrating" of traditionally "white" universities and colleges post-1970, there has effectively been a brain drain of the best and brightest black thinkers from HBCUs. Black scholars and intellectuals have been effectively integrated out of black institutions. Still, more than half of the black Ph.D.s in the United States are products of HBCUs, and those Ph.D.s most often pursue careers at HBCUs. In some cases, those faculty members are forced into a state of peonage, where they teach eight and ten courses per year (in comparison, most faculty at public and private research institutions teach two to four courses), leaving them unable to become productive scholars and thus making them less marketable to other institutions. This reality has broader implications beyond HBCUs when the experiences of community college faculty and adjunct faculty are more closely examined. There is effectively a two-tier system of higher education, where students and faculty at elite research institutions simply derive greater rewards than those at nonresearch (teaching) and community colleges. Courtland Milloy makes such a point in his biting commentary about the lack of "elite" black intellectuals in Washington, D.C., as he opines that the reason "Gates and West give for considering leaving Harvard is that they don't always feel respected. However, the discomfort they are experiencing ought to serve as a reminder of how much worse it must be for blacks who have no power to leverage."[13]

Part of the leverage that West possessed was a longstanding offer to return to Princeton. Part of the public discourse surrounding his flap with Summers had been threats by West and fellow dream-teamers Gates and Appiah to leave Harvard. Months after the flap, West and Appiah had in fact bolted to Princeton. This is part of the academic star system: elite scholars are recruited from one elite institution to another all the time, and the dream team is no different. In her scathing critique of Gates in the *Village Voice*, Thulani Davis suggests that the controversy was little more than a "power play" on the part of West to help him secure a more lucrative deal from Harvard (or Princeton).[14] While such tactics are not unusual (some elite scholars pursue offers from other institutions for just that reason), Davis notes that in this instance West's power moves may create a "backlash for academics, black and white, in African American Studies all over the country."[15] She adds, "These thousands of scholars, some doing brilliant and unheralded work, have struggled for respectability for years, and they don't need the kind of fallout that comes when privileged men call the race troops to arms for no greater reason than to enhance their already cushy careers."[16] In Davis's essay, NYU historian Robin D. G. Kelley raises the point that "if the president of Harvard could bring the country's top Afro-American department down a notch, I can't imagine what deans might do at other institutions where there is no respect for what we do."[17]

Barely two weeks after the *Boston Globe* first broke the story, Summers affirmed his commitment to "create an even more open and inclusive environment that draws on the widest possible range of talents."[18] Summers was, of course, within his right to try and hold his faculty accountable—college and university presidents regularly do this—but this particular incident with West is unique because of West's high profile and the historic devaluation of black intellectual thought (and, more explicitly, the devaluation of the intellectual capabilities of people of African descent) and, more recently, a general skepticism about the rigor and significance of African-American studies and its various incarnations (black studies, Africana studies). There was a general consensus, especially among right-leaning commentators, that Summers had capitulated to the "evil" forces of white liberal guilt, political correctness, black victimology, and old-school race pimping. In this regard, the very backlash that Davis and Kelley suggested was happening became real-time narratives in press organs like *National Review*, the *Wall Street Journal*, and even the "liberal" *New York Times Magazine*. Roger Kimball, for instance, made such a point in *National Review*, where he argued that Summers "learned . . . that if he dares to criticize black professors at Harvard, he will face the wrath of The [New York] Times, Jesse Jackson, and the whole steamroller smear machine of racialist political correctness. . . . It is the textbook of liberal intimidation at work."[19]

Commentary about the West-Summers fray ranged from public examinations of West's income from public lectures to general perceptions that West was "crying wolf."[20] In the very *New York Times Magazine* that Kimball accused of liberal bias, Kate Zernike wrote an article on the controversy, titled "Can Crying Race Be Crying Wolf?"[21] In the Sunday *Times* (London), Andrew Sullivan derisively titled his commentary on the flap "When Being Black Is an Excuse for Taking the World for a Ride." In the article, Sullivan states that West is "phenomenally rich . . . it's hard to argue that he is a victim of the racist, sexist, homophobic, bourgeois elites he so often invokes and condemns." The premise of both articles is that West's economic status not only supersedes his feelings of insult in the aftermath of Summers's comments, but also bankrupts, in their minds, his more legitimate disgust over racial, sexist, and queer discrimination and economic exploitation. Both essays exhibited, in general, a profound ignorance of the black intellectual traditions, and more specifically a fundamental misunderstanding of the field of African-American studies.

Nowhere was such ignorance more profound than in *National Review* contributing editor John Derbyshire's ridiculous article, "Af-Am Nonsense." Early in the article, Derbyshire admits suggesting that he was a "modest authority" on the subject of the dispute because he "once read a book by Cornel West . . . standing in the aisle in one of the bookstores on midtown Fifth Avenue in New York."[22] He adds that "*Race Matters* was a small book, I am a fast reader, and I won't swear that I read every word. I read enough, though, to know that the book was irredeemably awful . . . it was so badly written and constructed that you couldn't tell what it was trying to say."[23] The reality that he might have been ignorant of the field of African-American studies is lost on Derbyshire, who felt he could and should legitimately critique a book that he skimmed while standing in line at a Barnes and Noble store—a book written by a scholar in a field of study that he has no real knowledge of. (I guess we can call this "white privilege," the same thing that Summers demonstated when he criticized West for a CD Summers hadn't listened to.) Derbyshire in fact later admits that, "like most non-black people" he "always thought that 'Afro-American Studies' is a pseudo-discipline, invented by guilty white liberals as a way of keeping black intellectuals out of trouble and giving them a shot at holding professorships at elite institutions without having to prove themselves in anything really difficult."[24] It is exactly this kind of uninformed and condescending "bullshit" that West was reacting to in the first place.

In *Breaking Bread*, West writes that the "central task of postmodern Black intellectuals is to stimulate, hasten, and enable alternative perceptions and practices by dislodging prevailing discourses and powers. This can be done only by intense intellectual work and engaged insurgent praxis."[25] West's quote has effectively become a mantra for a whole generation of black intellectuals, particularly those who work in the fields of cultural studies and critical theory. In other words, it has been partly the job of these scholars to render traditional discourses of black life and culture as unrecognizable from those traditions in an effort to create a space for alternative visions of black life and culture, on the one hand countering white-supremacist doctrine and, on the other, challenging the hegemony of mainstream black institutions. The written work of scholars such as Hortense Spillers, Houston Baker, Jr., Paul Gilroy, and Michael Awkward, as well as the public lectures of West and Michael Eric Dyson, are textbook examples of how difficult it can be to follow many of these themes. Some would recognize this as representing a certain complexity of thought among these scholars or, at least, an overreliance on poststructuralist jargon. Derbyshire just calls it "bad" writing.

Race Matters was a particularly perplexing book for some readers because it attempted to shorthand some of West's more erudite commentary. In short, if the goal of Beacon Press and even West was to make *Race Matters* a best-selling commentary on matters of race, then that would more likely be achieved in a 150–page book as opposed to a 500-page one. It is well known within the field of African-American studies that *Race Matters* was heavily edited for just that reason—to make West a viable crossover star. This is not to say that five-hundred page nonfiction books cannot be best-sellers, but five-hundred page nonfiction books by black intellectuals might be a difficult sell for audiences who are largely unaware that a black intellectual tradition exists. Such readers probably regard public figures like Jesse Jackson, Louis Farrakhan, Magic Johnson, and Ja Rule as being the only purveyors of black intellectual thought.

The reality is that even in the era of the black public intellectual, black thinkers and artists are rarely allowed a public complexity, but rather are reduced to the smallest possible racial box in order to sell them and their ideas to a mainstream audience, black and nonblack, who have never thought of "blackness" as being complex at all. Thus there is no language, for example, to think of Jay Z as an "entrepreneurial Gramscian thug" instead of just a "gangsta rapper." In this environment, John McWhorter's largely anecdotal *Losing the Race: Self-Sabotage in Black America* (2000) is hailed as a "brave intellectual achievement" instead of just a collection of uncritical perceptions of black life. The small space allowed black public intellectuals was made painfully clear recently when Michael Eric Dyson appeared on *Book Notes with Brian Lamb* to promote his book *Holler if You Hear Me: Searching for Tupac Shakur* (2001). Admittedly, Lamb's audience is not the type that would be familiar with Shakur (or with Dyson for that matter), but rather than letting Dyson do his thing (and when given time and freedom, he can "perform" like the good Rev. Green), Lamb reduced Dyson to answering simply inane questions like: "What's a homie? . . . OK, then what's a ho [whore]? Then what's a bitch?"

In his article, Derbyshire doesn't grant black intellectuals and the field of African-American studies much complexity. Of the presence of a German-born literary critic at the Du Bois institute at Harvard, Derbyshire writes, the "presence of Prof. Sollors is encouraging, suggesting that this is not entirely a boondoggle for otherwise-unemployable black intellectuals."[26] (As an aside, Derbyshire rails against the fact the institute was named after a communist, again showing his ignorance about the complexity of even Du Bois's legacy.) In other words, the department can be validated only by the presence of a white and therefore presumably objective scholar. Derbyshire, finally, suggests that African-American studies is bankrupt because it doesn't engage in a formal mode of peer review. He writes, "You publish a paper in a learned journal, or read it at a scholarly conference, and scholars in your field then scrutinize it. Does this actually happen in 'Afro-American Studies'? My guess is that it doesn't."[27]

Derbyshire should guess again. *Phylon* and the *Journal of Negro History* were pillars of black intellectual life for much of the first half of the twentieth century at a time when many black intellectuals did not have access to white-run scholarly journals. Even today, journals such as *African American Review, Callaloo, Black Renaissance, The Western Journal of Black Studies* and *Transition* (which is housed at the DuBois institute), as well as "nonblack" journals such as *Social Text* and *Public Culture* (which published a groundbreaking issue on the black public sphere in the mid-1990s), are some of the places where black scholars do in fact face rigorous forms of peer review. Clearly, there was no form of peer review for Derbyshire before he provided such an ignorant and condescending commentary on the field of African-American studies.

While Derbyshire can ultimately plead ignorance, Shelby Steele presumably knows better. His mean-spirited diatribe against West et al. in the *Wall Street Journal* is not so easily dismissed. There is a long history of difference between West and Steele, who are the most visible poles of liberal and conservative ideology in blackface. Like the black minstrals who continued to blacken their faces well into the twentieth century, both men could be accused of "blackening" up to represent their respectives ideologies. Currently a research fellow at the hyper-conservative Hoover Institution, which also houses fellows Thomas Sowell, Dinesh D'Souza, and National Security Advisor Condoleeza Rice, Steele, who is trained in literature, earned the National Book Critic's Circle Award for his largely anecdotal *The Content of Our Character: A New Vision of Race in America* (1990). (Steele is John McWhorter's intellectual father.) Steele has been the consistent voice of blackface commentary against affirmative action and multiculturalism. In classic form, Steele used the West controversy to attack white liberal guilt. In the article, he describes West as an "academic lightweight."[28] (To put his statement in perspective, Steele has published two books, while West has written or edited close to twenty.") Steele's argument is that West is a university professor at Harvard only as a function of affirmative action policies. Of course, Steele doesn't openly discuss whether he is allowed a voice at *The Wall Street Journal* because he, too, might be a mediocre scholar who has been given a "conservative pass" as the most visible (and decidedly uncritical) apologist for black ambition.

Steele goes on to describe "white guilt" (which he accuses Lawrence Summers of) as "best understood as a vacuum of moral authority. . . . [I]t means whites lack the authority to say what they see when looking at blacks and black problems."[29] Apparently, Steele is unaware of the moral authority of white (and black) law enforcement officers who racially profile black, Latino, and Arab people throughout the country. I'm pretty sure that the family of Amadou Diallo (an unarmed man who was shot to death by New York police) or Sherae Williams (who was "quietly" beaten by NYPD officers) would agree that there is a vacuum of moral authority and privilege among whites. While I concur to some degree that Jackson and Sharpton function as enforcers of white guilt and silence, I am hard pressed to find examples where that has translated into real institutional or political power.

Now, thanks to this debate, America has some idea of the black intellectual tradition, though figures like Steele, Derbyshire, and Kimball will have you believe that it is at best mediocre and at worst bankrupt. On the other hand, "spokespersons" such as Sharpton, Jackson and Joyner and Smiley have in some ways undermined the self-critical functions of the black intelligentsia by brokering perceptions within the mainstream that there really is some connection between the efforts of these bourgeois political spokespersons and the work being produced in the field of African-American studies. This is simply not the case, unless you count the recent hip-hop summit as an example (which I don't). One hopes that such energy will be used in the future to support the efforts of those folks who actually do meaningful, scholarly work in the field, instead of simply supporting (and celebrating) those who show up regularly on *Nightline*, *Charlie Rose*, and C-Span 2. With real support for African-American studies (and Afro-Diasporic studies) and the scholars in the field, the kinds of attacks on the tradition made by the folks identified above will be seen as nothing more than racist attacks on the intellectual capabilities of the black community, for they are certainly not insightful commentary.

CHAPTER THIRTEEN

●●●●●●●●●●●●●●●●●●●●●●

THREE THE HARD WAY

> When you're entrusted with something, man, and I speak as an artist, you're supposed to try to bring out the best in people, not the worst in people. See if you're gonna get entrusted to a language, you're supposed to take the language to a level, at its best where it's heightened.
>
> —Umar Bin Hassan

> Tolerance is getting thinner / Cause Iraq never called me a "nigger" / So what I wanna go off and fight a war for?
>
> —Paris, "Bush Killa"

> I spit verbs because my word is bond / like James, Barry, and crazy glue.
>
> —Gino Morrow, "I Spit Verbs"

Roc-A-Fella Entertainment, the Jay Z, Damien Dash, and Kariem Biggs entity, has grossed more than $300 million—$100 million in record sales with over $150 million generated from the Roc-A-Wear fashion entity. The success of Roc-A-Fella earned Dash and Jigga a cover story in a recent edition of *Black Enterprise*, the longtime bible of black capitalist ambition. Published by Earl Graves, (who was part of a group of black publishers including *Essence* magazine publishers—Earl Lewis and Clarence O. Smith, and former *Vibe* magazine publisher and current *Savoy* magazine Publisher Keith Clinkscales—who supported NYC mayor Michael Bloomberg), *Black Enterprise* has kept a close eye on hip-hop's burgeoning economic empire since it profiled Russell Simmons in a cover story in 1992. (Simmons was the cover story for the June 2002 issue of that magazine, which listed the top one hundred black-owned companies.) Although Simmons is no longer intimately connected to the recording industry (his ace boon, Lyor Cohen, currently heads Island/Def Jam, which has direct lineage to the Def Jam label Simmons founded with then ace boon Rick Rubin in 1983), his own clothing line, Phat Farm (and Baby Phat), which Jay Z used to hawk, grossed $120 million in 2000—twice as much as in 1999. In this environment (and with such dutiful roles models), it's easy to understand why shorties still on the block ain't tryin' to hear nothin' 'bout art, instead tryin' to get their entrepreneurialisms on. ("What the fuck I wanna be an artist for if I get my own label like Jigga?")

It is this very mindset—replicated as a generational divide—that Bay Area artists Idris Ackamoor and Kamau challenge in their moving performance "The OG and the B-Boy." The mini-play captures the transformation of public space in black communities over the past three decades as Ackamoor, who plays the saxophone while tap-dancing, personifies previous generations of black male artists who claim the "street" as the site of their creative expression. The music of doo-wop, in which black, Latino, and whites congregated on urban street corners to harmonize, and later hip-hop, in which artists constructed lyrical ciphers on those same streets, decades later, are prime examples. As Ackamoor portrays, such men—think of those "old southern men filled with northern pain," to quote Umar Bin Hassan, who still stand on street corners playing standards on their thirty-year-old saxes—are seen as little more than creative have-beens who have no relevance to contemporary black life. Ackamoor's character is juxtaposed with that of Kamau, who embodies the kind of "juvenocratic terror" that has taken over public spaces in black communities. Kamau literally steps on the stage with boom box blaring and cell phone ringing, encapsulating the way that even the sound of hip-hop and the technologies that the form has been shaped by have created a soundscape of terror for some urban dwellers. It is in the context of this "noise" (Tricia Rose's *Black Noise* and Tony Mitchell's *Global Noise* are good reads in this regard) that Ackamoor confronts Kamau, beginning an exchange of perceptions that ultimately have to do with the ability of each to make money from his "art." While Ackamoor's character still believes he can make meaningful art and stake out a living tap dancing and playing the sax for small coins, Kamau, who is exposed as a brilliant spoken-word artist, has chosen to give up on the possibility that his art could provide, and instead has chosen a career in street pharmaceuticals. For Kamau's character, the choice was clear: neither performing art on the street nor taking a low-level nine-to-five was going to help him take care of his kids.

Now I ain't tryin' to romanticize about artists. On the real: them original cats like Grand Master Flash and the Furious Five and the Cold Crush used to sell mix tapes at a dollar a minute. Ain't nothin' wrong with cats payin' the bills with their art. But there's always a real cost associated with stayin' true to your art when market demands suggest that there's more money available following trends. This is what Angie Stone was talking about in "Soul Assurance" when she went after those neo-soul denizens who ain't got no love for or skill at soul music but found a niche in the market by having somebody who sounds like the Soulquarians or Touch of Jazz produce their tracks. Folks need to ask Dionne Farris and Sandra St. Victor what happened when they tried to do their own shit with one of the major labels (three companies, really, with hundreds of boutique and vanity labels in the mix) or why Prince was rolling around industry functions with the word *slave* scrawled on his cheek. Over the last decade, with the development of user-friendly recording equipment and the emergence of the Internet as a primary site of commerce, folks committed to decidedly independent distribution of their art have been able to find a niche. Recently, three of these artists, Umar Bin Hassan, Paris, and Gino Morrow, have stepped up with projects that represent the possibilities that artists have to remain "true to the game" without having to be sanctioned by the Big Three or Viacom-land.

Umar Bin Hassan (born Jerome Huling) has been in the game for a while. The Akron, Ohio, native was raising hell the old-fashioned way in his hometown when he caught a performance of the Last Poets at Antioch College in Yellow Spring, Ohio, in the spring of 1968. The Last Poets were "formed" on May 19, 1968, when Abiodun Oyewole (then a student at Hunter College), David Nelson, and Gylan Kain took the stage and "read" poetry during a Malcolm X celebration (his birthday is May 19) in Mount Morris Park (now Marcus Garvey Park) in Harlem. By the time the group came to Antioch College, Nelson had left the group and was replaced by Felipe Luciano (he of Young Lords fame). Bin Hassan was eventually invited to join the group and trekked to NYC later that year (his moment of arrival is immortalized on the track "Forty Deuce"). As Bin Hassan told Timothy White a few years ago, "All I had was 22 cents, my suitcase, and a book of my own poetry. And I wasn't gonna leave until they let me join. My poetry with the group was naïve at first, but my influences were Miles Davis and Marvin Gaye singing "Stubborn Kind of Fellow."[1]

After bumrushing a performance at the East Wind, the Last Poets' loft on 125th Street in Harlem, and performing a piece called "Motherfucker" (which Oyewole banned him from reading again), Bin Hassan joined the groundbreaking spoken-word group that, along with Gil Scott-Heron and the Watt Prophets, is generally recognized as the forefather of hip-hop. Classic Last Poets tracks like "Niggers Are Scared of Revolution" (which Hassan inspired six months after being in NYC) and "This Is Madness" all have the mark of Bin Hassan's signature venomous wit and soulful cadences. With the emergence of "political" hip-hop in the late 1980s, the Last Poets, who have had seven different members over the past thirty years (and many contentious skirmishes about who the real Last Poets are), reemerged to record several new discs, including *Holy Terror* (1995) and *Time Is Coming* (1997). Bin Hassan, in particular, was introduced to the hip-hop generation after a cameo performance of "Niggers Are Scared of Revolution" in the film *Poetic Justice* (1993).

After struggling with drug addiction and homelessness (according to Bin Hassan, he knows "every homeless shelter from Springfield, MA to Alexandria, VA and each one throughout the Midwest"), he released his first solo disc, the brilliant *Be Bop or Be Dead* (Axiom/Island, 1994), which was produced by Bill Laswell. *Be Bop or Be Dead* included remakes of "Niggers Are Scared of Revolution" and "This Is Madness" and "AM" (as in *after Miles*) his remarkable tribute to Miles Davis. On the latter track, Bin Hassan drops lines like these:

> Up jumps Miles, Up jump Miles, bobbing and weaving sticking moving
> going against traffic on a one-way street . . .
> Miles turning his back on guaranteed death and low life insinuations
> perpetuated by the perverted fantasies of the founding fathers of these
> United States of fuck you muthafuckas, fuck you muthafuckas
> Miles was our gators and lizards
> Our silk shirts and hickey freemans
> He was our cool walks in the wind

Bin Hassan's lyrics speak, obviously, to the genius of Davis, but also to the way that his performance helped present an image of pride and resistance and the quintessential example of high urban style in the 1950s. The song was also a broader tribute to the be-bop tradition; Bin Hassan suggests an explicit connection between bop and hip-hop: "Somewhere I hear a revival / somewhere I hear bop playing / It is playing in the hip-hop walks of young boys who hit strange notes with hands on triggers / Bam! Bam! Bam! / Max [Roach] picks up the beat / Rhythms from the bush / Passionate and vital information." Despite his belief in hip-hop's potential, Hassan recently admitted some disappointment with hip-hop: "I mean, it's just like the same thing over and over again, man. It's like whose bitch you fucking, how many niggers you killed and don't fuck with my shit and nigger, nigger this."[2] Bin Hassan's comment may sound ironic coming from someone who is best known for the song "Niggers Are Scared of Revolution," but Hassan reminds folks that the song was "not used to degrade black people the way white writers like Hemingway used it. . . . It's used to awaken and enlighten."[3]

Countering the proverbial "bling-bling" of corporatized "soul music," in early 2002 Bin Hassan released *Life Is Good* (Stay Focused Records), his long-awaited follow-up to *Be Bop or Be Dead*. Despite the critical acclaim of *Be Bop or Be Dead*, Bin Hassan was wary of the "big" labels. In an interview with Stephen Slayburgh, Bin Hassan says, "I had become disgruntled with big record companies, who didn't seem to want to put out a record with old men telling the truth. They'd put out records about getting that booty or shooting that nigger, but they couldn't deal with a truthful album."[4] With *Life Is Good*, Bin Hassan not only gets at the necessary truths, but also dabbles in styles of music not usually associated with the Last Poets, such as house, reggae, and acid jazz. The opening track, "Redbone," is a three-part tribute to the "redbone" women (what some folks call hi-yello) who have inspired his art at various points in his life. In the opening section he talks about how such women inspired his initial commitment to black struggle. In a later section, he discusses how the "high art of snapping and popping" by "redbone" women became part of his art. On the reggae-tinged "For the People" (backed by the Black Roots Band), Bin Hassan urges folks to "Take your time with the dreams, for this is for the people / take your time with the music, for this is for the people / take your time with the revolution, for this is for the people." The song is a product of Bin Hassan's willingness to own up to the ways that the revolutionary generation of the 1960s and 1970s failed to build the kinds of institutions that those behind them could take advantage of and a reminder that even in the midst of struggle it's always about recovering humanity.

The speed-balled "Personal Things" (originally recorded on *Be Bop or Be Dead*) powerfully addresses the ways that crass materialism and commercialism have altered our sense of perception and thus life as Bin Hassan chants, "Idle chatter become reality while problems go unsolved / Prearranged, prefabricated, preconditioned / We're baptized, advertised and posthumously mentioned." The true highlight of *Life Is Good* is the "hidden" remixed version of "Epic" (the last track listed). Running more than twelve minutes, the song begins with soulful "gothic" chants before giving way to a solid backbeat and trunk-thumping bass lines. The mesmerizing groove, later joined by searing guitar lines, rolls forward for more than five and a half minutes before Bin Hassan's signature melismatic spoken-word flourishes are heard. In the song's most brilliant moment, Bin Hassan says,

The creative process begins to turn ugly
vandalizing and robbing graves of child prodigies
turning into serious discussions of mass murder
and the therapeutic value of Saturday morning shopping sprees
the betrayal of genius is burning at the stake
the spider descends
the violence is always there
the web embraces us all
more insidious than drugs, more pleasurable than sex
slightly entangled, slightly confused
that possible criminal element awakens you to the terror and loneliness
of running in to the silent pain of someone else looking to you for
    answers
glamorous and well financed pools of blood profiling on neighborhood
    corners
while smiling at and tempting the boldest gangsta rap

In this section, Bin Hassan poignantly describes how genius has been reduced to celebrations of mass murder in film and literature and how real redemption and good health are thought to be found during so-called personal health days, in which books by personal gurus (creative hacks) are consumed. His reference to the spider is, of course, a reference to the Internet ("the web embraces us"), implying that the Internet has become as addictive and therapeutic as drugs and sex. Lastly, he takes a quick shot at the stylized violence that emanates from black urban spaces. He describes gangster rap and music videos as "glamorous and well financed pools of blood." The song serves as a fitting metaphor for the struggles of being a creative artist at the moment, when little that circulates as black culture can actually be seen as anything more than a marketing ploy to sell blackness to the most willing bidders.

Umar Bin Hassan is part of a tradition in America of "angry black men," and while black rage and anger had commercial value in the mainstream (see Norman Mailer's "White Negro" essay), very rarely has detailed analysis of the objects of black rage found its way comfortably into the mainstream. So while angry black men (and people) can be detected everywhere in popular culture—from Eddie Griffith's "Undercover Brother" to Alan Keyes (presumably pissed off because we all find him so damn funny)—detailed critiques of white supremacy and American imperialism are often divorced from the stylish nature of black rage. Thus the Chuck Ds and KRS-Ones of the world become media poster boys for leftist urban agitprop without any fundamental consideration of the issues that inspired their rage in the first place.

Paris, the self-described "Black Panther of Rap" (he is a San Francisco Bay Area native), was part of a historic generation of hip-hop Gramscians, like Chuck D (of Public Enemy) and KRS-One and others such as X-Clan, Poor Righteous Teachers, and the artist formerly known as Ice Cube. Although Paris's first disc, *The Devil Made Me Do It* (1990), initially sold 250,000 copies and earned him a solid reputation among "conscious" folks, it was the release of his controversial follow-up, *Sleeping with the Enemy* (1992), that made his music a national topic. Included on the disc were several powerful political tracks including "Assata's Song" (a tribute to activist Assata Shakur) and "Coffee, Donuts, & Death" (about police brutality). But it was the track "Bush Killa" that piqued the interests of a wide range of folks, including record executives and the Secret Service, as the song was interpreted as a threat on the life of then president George H. W. Bush. The song featured a figure who identifies himself as "P-Dog the Bush killa" who drops lines like "I'm steady waiting for the day I get to see his ass / and give him two from the barrel of a black guerrilla / and that's real coming from the motherfucking Bush killa." The initial cover art for *Sleeping with the Enemy* featured P-Dog making his move on the White House.

Sleeping with the Enemy was recorded at a particularly volatile moment for hip-hop and black folk in general, thus the disc was conceived as a response to the Gulf War (which "Bush Killa" explicitly addresses), the Rodney King beating and subsequent acquittal of four LAPD officers, the 1992 L.A. insurrections, and right-wingers (and at least one postmodern Dixiecrat from Arkansas) attacks on Sister Souljah, Ice T, and Tupac Shakur. With the release of "Bush Killa," which featured a deconstruction of Bush's own comments during the Gulf War, Paris hoped to have some impact on the 1992 presidential election. When the disc was turned in to his label Tommy Boy, it was politely returned. Tommy Boy's distributor, Warner Brothers, was still dealing with the fallout of Ice T's "Cop Killer," and was in no mood to court more scrutiny. Although he was still signed to the label, Paris was allowed to shop the disc to 4th and B'Way and Rick Rubin's Sex Records (also distributed by Warner), which also passed on the project. After a low-six-figure settlement with Warner, Paris finally released *Sleeping with the Enemy* on his own Scarface Records (distributed independently by INDI), weeks after Bill Clinton won the 1992 election. Shortly before Clinton's inauguration, Paris published an open letter to the president elect in the *Washington Post* in which he urged Clinton to socialize health care, address the crisis in public education, and develop a "comprehensive urban plan that addresses unemployment and job creation."[5] He also used the letter to explain that he understood that "Bush Killa" would be "disturbing to many, but what I hoped to call attention to—the real-life economic violence visited upon millions of African-American people every day of their lives—is more disturbing and more real."[6] He added that George Bush was a "ready-made symbol of politics and policies that have assaulted black America for nearly half of my life."[7]

Unable to make the kind of music he wanted (and get the airplay and support he needed), after two follow-up discs Paris "retired" from the scene. Paris earned an economics degree from UC-Davis in 1990 and spent his "retirement" as an investment consultant. Armed with some financial freedom (courtesy of smart investments on Wall Street), Paris returned from "retirement" with the track "What Would You Do?" (*Sonic Jihad*). The song takes strident aim at G-dub, John Ashcroft and the Patriot Act, which Paris (and many others, I might add) feels is an attack on American civil liberties, including freedom of speech, protection from unreasonable search and seizures, and due process. Davey D describes "What Would You Do?" (which was available for free download at the site) as "one of the best Hip Hop songs . . . heard in years. The intensity of the song and the subject matter is a breath of fresh air at a time when so many insist on bringing us bling bling material."[8]

Paris begins "What Would You Do?" with a nod to PE's "Black Steel in the Hour of Chaos," with the lyric "I see a message from the government, like every day / I watch it, and listen, and call 'em all suckas / they warnin' me about Osama or whatever / Picture me buyin' this scam I said never." While the opening reconnects Paris to the radical rap tradition he retired from in the mid-1990s, it also lays out his belief that the 9/11 attacks were fabricated to dupe the American public to willingly hand over their civil freedoms; he adds later in the song that "the oldest trick in the book is MAKE an enemy / Of fake evil now the government can do it's dirt / and take away ya freedom lock and load, beat and search." Later in the song, Paris addresses the proclivity of black folks to close ranks around Bush ("'fore 9/11 motherfuckas couldn't stand his name / Now even brothas wavin' flags like they lost they mind") and Rudolph Giuliani ("Fuck Giuliani ask Diallo how he doin'"). Countering criticisms of "political" rap in the mainstream, Paris hits back: "So now you askin' why my records always come the same / Keep it real, ain't no fillers, motherfuck a blingin'." On the CD single (which Paris handed out for free at the Berkeley hip-hop conference in 2002), Paris includes a version of "What Would You Do?" that features a deconstruction of Bush, Jr.'s voice, much like the one that appeared on "Bush Killa." It goes without saying that "What Would You Do?" represents the kind of critical rhetoric rarely found in mainstream popular music, particularly hip-hop.

Although Gino L. Morrow is not as well known as Umar Bin Hassan and Paris, the thirty-year-old poet, painter, and graphic designer is clearly a product of the world that both of those artists imagined. Born and raised in Buffalo, New York (whose natives include Ishmael Reed, Rick James, the late Frankie Crocker, and the late Grover Washington, Jr.), Morrow earned a BFA from SUNY-Fredonia, where he was a founding member and artistic director of a small collective known as the Genesis Project. It was in that capacity that Morrow opened for the Last Poets (with Bin Hassan) at a 1994 concert that featured the pianist Onaje Allan Gumbs. After a move to Kansas City, Morrow founded the Black Poets Collective and eventually won three Slam championships in the region for his stirring performances. Feeling a need to have greater control over his art and its distribution, Morrow and his wife created the Grassroot Literary Movement Press, which published his first collection, *Spitfire: Poetry and Prose*, featuring 34 original pieces. One highlight of the collection is "N.I.K.E." (short for "Nigga Ignorantly Kneel to Exploitation"). In his stinging critique of the sneaker industry, Morrow writes, "I can finally see through the debris of famous faces / flashing lights and sound bites, none of which is right / I can see Indonesian sweat shops and 9mm glocks / blood spots and black bodies outlined in white chalk," adding that "Of course it's no coincidence that stock in Nike has increased / CEO's pockets get deeper / youth morale decline / and self-esteem gets weaker."

Later in the collection, Morrow pays tribute to Gil Scott-Heron (a seminal influence) and issues a potent critique of the commodification of blackness in popular culture. Referencing Scott-Heron's classic "The Revolution Will Not Be Televised" throughout, Morrow writes,

> Oh yeah, and those of you who own basic cable
> are able to watch the revolution on COPs
> and America's Most Wanted.
> Those with extended video digital cable
> can learn 230 reasons why the government
> legalizes slavery in the form of privately-owned
> penitentiaries on the Learning Channel;
>
> 470 ways to pimp broke bitches on HBO;
> 543 ways to maintain the status-quo on CNN;
> 666 reasons why niggas should rap, do comedy
> and play basketball on BET and 913 reasons
> why white folks will always consider you a slave
> on the History Channel

On the back jacket of Morrow's *Spitfire*, I write, "Call this the era of the 'gangsta truth'—an historical moment where any 'truth,' be it bred by the need for scrutiny, critique or just straight up resistance, is demonized, challenged and illegalized." Against the flows of black popular capital at

Viacom, AOL-Time Warner, Sony, Rush Communications, Roc-A-Fella and even Starbucks, Umar Bin Hassan, Paris, and Gino L. Morrow are poised to bring the "gangsta truth" at a moment when their voices and their examples are so needed.

NOTE*S*

INTRODUCTION: MU*S*IC ON MY MIND

1. John F. Callahan, ed., *The Collected Essays of Ralph Ellison* (New York: Modern Library, 1995), 279.

2. Ibid., 278.

3. Wray Herbert, "The Making of a Hip-Hop Intellectual", *U.S. News & World Report* (November 4, 1996), 48.

4. Norman Kelley, *Rhythm and Business: The Political Economy of Black Music* (New York: Akashic Books, 2002), 8.

5. It has been in the context of e-mail exchanges, letters, cards, forwarded articles, and phone calls, that De Veaux and I have had an ongoing dialogue about her concept of "newblackness." My definition of newblackness is drawn from this dialogue.

CHAPER ONE

1. Timothy Finn, "Power to the Spoken Word," *The Kansas City Star*, May 4, 2001, 14.

2. Shawn Edwards, "Heroes Never Die," *Pitch Weekly*, May 16, 2001. Online

3. Finn, "Power to the Spoken Word," 14.

4. Edwards, "Heroes Never Die." Online

5. Russell Potter, *Spectacular Vernaculars: Hip-Hop and the Politics of Postmodernism*, (Albany: State University of New York Press, 1995), 36.

6. Richard Harrington, "Wake up Call," *Washington Post,* February 13, 1994. 61.

7. Nicole Moore, "Last Woman Standing," *OneWorld Magazine,* February–March 2002, 42.

8. Ibid.

9. Etheridge Knight, *Poems from Prison* (Detroit: Broadside Press, 1968).

10. Quoted in *Call and Response: The Riverside Anthology of the African American Literary Tradition,* ed. Patricia Liggins Hill (New York: Houghton Mifflin, 1998), 1482.

11. Greg Tate, *Flyboy in the Buttermilk* (New York: Fireside Press, 1992).

12. Bill Leigh, "Me'Shell Gets Real," *Bass Player,* March 2002, 81.

CHAPTER TWO

1. Aine Ardron-Doley, "She's Due," *Philadelphia City Paper,* January 31, 2002, online.

2. De La Soul, "Baby Phat," *AOI: Bionix* (Tommy Boy, TBCD1362, 2001).

3. Lois Najarian, press release, "Angie Stone to Unveil Breakthrough Video for First Single 'Brotha,'" J Records, September 14, 2001.

4. See *Soul Babies: Black Popular Culture and the Post-Soul Aesthetic,* (New York: Routledge, 2002), 56–64.

5. Ardron-Doley, "She's Due."

CHAPTER THREE

1. Robin D. G. Kelley, "A Jazz Genius in the Guise of a Hustler," *New York Times,* May 13, 2001, AR1.

2. Liner notes, *1st Born Second* (2001).

3. Jim Farber, "Bilal Set to Wow," *Daily News,* June 24, 2001, 12.

4. Russell Simmons with Nelson George, *Life and Def: Sex, Drugs, Money, and God* (New York: Crown Publishers), 26.

5. Kelley, "A Jazz Genius," AR1.

6. Farber, "Bilal Set to Wow," 12.

7. Arnold Rampersad, ed., *The Collected Poems of Langston Hughes* (New York: Vintage Classics, 1994), 23.

8. Steve Jones, "An Insightful, Creative 'Second Child' of Jazz," *USA Today,* April 20, 2001, E1.

9. Liner notes, *1st Born Second.*

10. Bakari Kitwana, *The Hip-Hop Generation: Young Blacks and the*

Crisis in African-American Culture (New York: Basic Civitas Books, 2002), 184–85.

CHAPTER FOUR

1. Angela Davis, "Race and Criminalization: Black Americans and the Punishment Industry," in *The House That Race Built: Black Americans, U.S. Terrain*, ed. Wahneema Lubiano (New York: Pantheon Books, 1997).

2. Benedict Anderson, *Imagined Communities: Reflections on the Origin and Spread of Nationalism* (London: Verso Books 1991).

3. Libby Copeland, "Kemba Smith's Hard Time," *Washington Post*, February 13, 2000, F1.

4. Liner notes *Who Is That Bitch, Anyway?* (1975).

5. Michael Eric Dyson, *Race Rules: Navigating the Color Line* (New York: Addison Wesley, 1996), 140–45.

6. I-Lien Tsay, "Keys to the City: Alicia Goes on Location in Brooklyn, NY," *In Style*, December 1, 2001, 289.

7. Ibid.

8. You-me Park and Gayle Wald, "Native Daughters in the Promised Land: Gender, Race, and the Questions of Separate Spheres," in *Masses, Classes, and the Public Sphere*, ed. Mike Hill and Warren Montag (London: Verso Books, 2000), 234.

CHAPTER FIVE

1. Vanessa E. Jones, "Hit Song a Touchy Subject with Some Radio Listeners; Tweet's 'Oops (Oh My)' Takes on a Taboo," *Boston Globe*, March 23, 2002, D1.

2. Ibid.

3. Gail Mitchell, "The Gold Mine: Elektra's Tweet Is 'Humming,'" *Billboard*, March 2, 2002, 73.

CHAPTER ƒIX

1. Julianne Malveaux, "Selling the Dream," *In These Times*, May 28, 2001, 10.

2. Transcript, *CNN Talkback Live*, March 29, 2001.

3. Ibid.

4. Letta Taylor, "A Postscript to a Legacy," *New York Newsday*, June 10, 2001, D6.

5. Quoted in David Ritz, "The Queen in Waiting," liner notes, *The*

Queen in Waiting: The Columbia Years (1960–1965) (Columbia/Legacy, AC2K 85696, 2002).

6. Tai Moses, "The Rebirth of Marvin Gaye," *Creative Loafing*, March 28–April 3, 2002.

7. David Ritz, "Midnight Love and Sexual Healing Sessions," liner notes, *Midnight Love and Sexual Healing Sessions* (Columbia/Legacy, C2K 65546, 1998), 11.

8. Ibid.

9. Ibid.

10. Harry Weinger, "Finding the Groove: Adventures in the Vault," liner notes, *Let's Get It On (Deluxe Edition)* (Motown Records, 440 014 758–2, 2001).

11. "Marvin Gaye Set for Pullman Bond," *Business Wire*, September 20, 2000.

CHAPTER ſEVEN

1. Quoted in Michele Kort, *Soul Picnic: The Music and Passion of Laura Nyro* (New York: Thomas Dunne Books, 2002), 7.

2. Paul C. Taylor, "Funky White Boys and Honorary Soul Sisters," *Michigan Quarterly Review* 36, no. 2 (spring 1997): 320–336.

3. Kort, *Soul Picnic*, 13.

4. See Richard Harrington, "Laura Nyro: A World to Carry On," *Washington Post*, April 13, 1997, G1; Vince Aletti, "Arty as Heaven," *Village Voice*, April 22, 1997, 70.

5. "Laura Nyro: Poetic Passionate Voice of Pop Music," *Pittsburgh Post-Gazette*, April 10, 1997, B6; Pierre Perrone, "Obituary: Laura Nyro," *The Independent*, April 11, 1997, 20.

6. Harrington, "Laura Nyro," E1.

7. Stephen Holden, "Laura Nyro, Intense Balladeer of the 60s and 70s, Dies at 49," *New York Times*, (April 10, 1997), D29.

8. Don Butler, "Singer's Legacy More Than Mere Songs," *Ottawa Citizen*, April 15, 1997, B11.

9. Patti LaBelle with Laura B. Randolph, *Don't Block the Blessings: Revelations of a Lifetime* (New York: Riverhead Books, 1996), 159–63.

10. Ibid., 79–101.

11. Ibid., 154.

12. Kyra Gaunt, "Translating Double-Dutch to Hip Hop: The Musical Vernacular of Black Girls' Play," in *Language, Rhythm, and Sound: Black Popular Cultures into the Twenty-First Century*, ed. Joseph

Adjaye and Adrianne Andrews (Pittsburgh: University of Pittsburgh Press, 1997).

13. Suzanne Smith, *Dancing in the Street: Motown and the Cultural Politics of Detroit*, (Cambridge, MA: Harvard University Press, 1999), 170.

14. David Ritz, *Divided Soul: The Life of Marvin Gaye* (New York: De Capo Press, 1991), 107.

15. Smith, *Dancing in the Street*, 2.

16. Quoted in Smith, *Dancing in the Street*, 2.

17. Smith, *Dancing in the Street*, 130.

18. Ray Allen, "Shouting the Church: Narrative and Vocal Improvisation in African-American Gospel Quartet Performance," *Journal of American Folklore* 104 (1991): 309.

19. Ibid., 313.

20. Kort, *Soul Picnic*, 128.

21. Quoted in Kort, *Soul Picnic*, 30.

22. Ibid., 73.

23. Quoted in Kort, *Soul Picnic*, 13.

24. Michele Kort, "Laura Nyro (1947–1997)," *The Advocate*, January 20, 1998, 80.

25. Michele Kort, "Laura's Legacy," *The Advocate*, April 30, 2002, 58.

26. Ibid.

27. David Roman, "Comment: Theatre Journals," *Theatre Journal* 53, no. 3 (2001): iv.

28. Bruce Vilanch, "Partying for Pride," *The Advocate*, July 7, 1998, 53.

29. Reid Davis, "What WOZ: Lost Objects, Repeat Viewings, and the Sissy Warrior," *Film Quarterly* 55, no. 1 (winter 2001): 4.

30. See recent Garland biographies Gerald Clarke, *Get Happy: The Life of Judy Garland*, (New York: Random House, 2000), and Lorna Luft, *Me and My Shadows: A Family Memoir* (New York: Simon & Schuster, 1998), by Garland's daughter.

31. Michael Joseph Gross, "The Queen Is Dead," *Atlantic Monthly*, August 2000, 63.

32. Davis, "What WO2,", 3.

33. Paul Outlaw, "If That's Your Boyfriend (He Wasn't Last Night)," *African American Review* 29, no. 2 (summer 1995): 349.

34. Ibid.

35. Sylvester was backed by the female duo Two Tons of Fun, who a few years later, as the Weather Girls, recorded the track "It's Raining Men," which has become an anthem within gay male culture.

36. Quoted in Vince Aletti, "LaBelle," liner notes, *LaBelle: Something Silver* (Warner Brothers Records, 9 46359–2, 1997), 8.

37. LaBelle, *Don't Block the Blessings*, 155.

CHAPTER EIGHT

1. Juan Flores, *Divided Borders: Essays on Puerto Rican Identity* (Houston: Arte Publico, 1993), 151.

2. Flores, 151.

3. Miguel Algarin and Miguel Pinero, eds., *Nuyorican Poetry: An Anthology of Words and Feelings* (New York: Morrow, 1975), 9.

4. Juan Flores, *From Bomba to Hip-Hop: Puerto Rican Culture and Latino Identity* (New York: Columbia University, 2000), 179.

5. Ibid., 63.

6. Ibid., 65.

7. Flores, *Divided Borders*, 147.

8. Flores, *From Bomba to Hip-Hop*, 68.

9. Flores, *Divided Borders*, 89.

10. Ibid.

11. Flores, *From Bomba to Hip-Hop*, 88.

12. Manuel Perez-Rivas, "The Lords of East Harlem," *New York Newsday*, January 24, 1990, 3.

13. Jennifer A. Nelson, "'Abortions under Community Control': Feminism, Nationalism, and the Politics of Reproduction among New York City's Young Lords Party," *Journal of Women's History* 13, no. 1 (spring 2001): 158.

14. Quoted in Flores, *From Bomba to Hip-Hop*, 112.

15. Eric Demby, "Boys from the Hood," *URB* (January–February 2002): 97.

16. Carol Cooper, liner notes, *Nuyorican Soul*.

CHAPTER NINE

1. Brad Cawn, "There She Goes," *UR Chicago*, June 2001: 67.

2. Ibid., 68.

3. Kimberle Crenshaw, "Demarginalizing the Intersection of Race and Sex: A Black Feminist Critique of Antidiscrimination Doctrine, Feminist Theory, and Antiracist Politics," in *The Black Feminist Reader*, ed. Joy James and T. Denean Sharpley-Whiting (Malden: Blackwell Publishers, 2000), 216.

4. Hortense Spillers, "Mama's Baby, Papa's Maybe: An American

Grammar Book," *The Black Feminist Reader*, ed. James and Sharpley Whiten, Publisher 57.

5. Joy James, *Shadowboxing: Representation of Black Feminist Politics* (New York: St. Martin's Press, 1999), 9.

6. Elisa Ludwig, "Guided by Voices," *Philadelphia Weekly*, April 26, 2002, 24.

7. Kendall Thomas, "Ain't Nothin' like the Real Thing: Black Masculinity, Gay Sexuality, and the Jargon of Authenticity," in *The House That Race Built: Black Americans, U.S. Terrain* ed. Wahneema Lubiano (New York: Pantheon Books, 1997), 129.

8. Craig Roseberry, "'Supa Sista' Ursula Rucker Makes Poetic Debut of K7," *Billboard*, September 8, 2001, 42.

9. Kevin Powell, liner notes, *The Iron Pot Cooker* (Vanguard Records 79356, 1999).

CHAPTER TEN

1. Timothy B. Tyson, *Radio Free Dixie: Robert F. Williams and the Roots of Black Power* (Chapel Hill: University of North Carolina Press, 1999), 149.

2. Quoted in Tyson, *Radio Free Dixie*, 287–88.

3. William Barlow, *Voice Over: The Making of Black Radio* (Philadelphia: Temple University Press, 1999), 53.

4. Ibid., 115.

5. Quoted in Barlow, *Voice Over*, 209.

6. Barlow, *Voice Over*, 214–16.

7. Eric Boehlert, "One Big Happy Channel?" *Salon.com*, June 28, 2001.

8. Ibid.

9. Denny Lee, "Disc Jockeys Are Resisting Taking the Local out of Local Radio," *New York Times,* August 25, 2002, Section 14, 4.

10. Lynnley Browning, "Making Waves on Air: Big Radio's Bad Boy," *New York Times*, June 19, 2002, C1.

11. Eric Boehlert, "Suit: Clear Channel Is an Illegal Monopoly," *Salon.com*, August 8, 2001.

12. Marian Liu, "Radio Listeners Protest Firing of Popular DJ," *San Jose Mercury*, November 29, 2001, online.

13. Boehlert, "Pay for Play," *Salon.com*, March 14, 2001.

14. Boehlert, "Payola City," *Salon.com*, July 24, 2001.

15. Thomas Francis, "Hip-Hopcrisy," *Cleveland Scene*, August 28, 2002, online.

16. Barlow, *Voice Over*, 279–80.

17. Ibid., 284.

18. Chisun Lee, "Counter Revolution" *Village Voice*, June 26, 2001, 40.

19. Lee, "Counter Revolution," 40.

20. Bill McConnell, "Slim Shady Slips By," *Broadcasting and Cable*, January 14, 2002, 42.

21. Katia Dunn, "Rap Sheet," *Bitch: Feminist Response to Pop Culture* (summer 2002): 24.

22. Ibid.

23. Neil Strauss, "Songwriter, Citing First Amendment, Sues FCC over Radio Sanctions," *The New York Times*, January 30, 2002, E1.

24. Fiona Sturges, "And for My Next Rhetoric . . . ," *The Independent*, May 4, 2001, 13.

25. Liner notes, *Stay Human* (Boo Boo Wax/Six Degree Records [PRCD 1048–2]). 2001.

26. Sturges, "And for My Next Rhetoric . . . ," 13.

27. Liner notes, *Stay Human*.

28. Michael Odell, "You're Tuned to Death Row," *The Guardian*, April 30, 2001, 10.

29. Ishmael Reed and Michael Franti, "Hiphoprisy," *Transition* (no. 56 (1992): 158.

CHAPTER ELEVEN

1. Kathy Bachman, "When Tom Joyner Speaks, People Listen," *Media Week*, July 1, 2002, 22.

2. Erin Texeira, "CompUSA Agreement Seen as Victory for Black Stations," *Baltimore Sun*, October 21, 1999, 1C.

3. Quoted in Lisa Richardson, "The Pimp Phenomenon," *Los Angeles Times*, December 3, 2000, E1.

4. Jonathan Chait, "Painted Black," *New Republic*, August 27, 2001, 30.

5. Ibid., 31.

6. Lisa de Moraes, "BET Bumps Talk Host Tavis Smiley," *Washington Post*, March 22, 2001, C1.

7. Lisa de Moraes, "BET Terminates Contract of Talk Show Host Tavis Smiley," *Washington Post*, March 24, 2001, C7.

8. Greg Braxton, "Smiley, BET's Chairman Take to the Air over Firing," *Los Angeles Times*, March 28, 2001, F3.

CHAPTER TWELVE

1. David Mills, "Sister Souljah's Call to Arms," *Washington Post*, May 13, 1992, B1.

2. Chuck Phillips, "'Cop Killer' Controversy Spurs Ice T Album Sales," *Los Angeles Times*, June 18, 1992, F1.

3. David Abel, "Harvard 'Dream Team' Roiled Black Scholars, Summers in Rift," *Boston Globe*, December 22, 2001, A1.

4. Cornel West, *Prophetic Reflections*, (Monroe, Maine: Common Courage Press, 1993), 103.

5. Robert S. Boynton, "Princeton's Public Intellectual," *New York Times Magazine*, September 15, 1991, 40.

6. Jacqueline Trescott, "Harvard's Dream Team," *Washington Post*, February, 26, 1996, B1.

7. Ibid.

8. Scott S. Greenberger, "Jackson Steps into Harvard Dispute," *Boston Globe*, December 31, 2001, B4.

9. Lynn Duke, "Moving Target," *Washington Post*, August 11, 2002, F1.

10. Megan Tench, "2 Black Leaders Confront Harvard," *Boston Globe*, January 2, 2002, B1.

11. Howard Kurtz, "Black Scholar Chides Summers for 'Attack,'" *Washington Post*, January 7, 2002, A3.

12. Sam Tanenhaus, "The Ivy League's Angry Star," *Vanity Fair*, June 2002, 222.

13. Courtland Milloy, "D.C. Should Find Ways to Attract Black Scholars," *Washington Post*, January 9, 2002, B1.

14. Thulani Davis, "Spinning Race at Harvard," *Village Voice*, January 22, 2002.

15. Ibid.

16. Ibid.

17. Ibid.

18. Pamela Ferdinand, "Harvard President Acts to Quell Furor," *Washington Post*, January 3, 2002, A3.

19. Roger Kimball, "Dr. West and Mr. Summers: A Harvard Tale," *National Review* (January 28, 2002).

20. Rob Dreher, "Top Dollar Prof.," *National Review Online*, January 11, 2002.

21. Kate Zernike, "Can Crying Race Be Crying Wolf?" *New York Times*, January 13, 2002, 4, 6.

22. John Derbyshire, "Af-Am Nonsense," *National Review Online*, January 11, 2002.

23. Ibid.

24. Ibid.

25. Cornel West and bell hooks, *Breaking Bread: Insurgent Black Intellectual Life* (Boston: South End Press, 1991), 145.

26. Derbyshire, *National Review Online*.

27. Ibid.

28. Shelby Steele, "White Guilt = Black Power," *Wall Street Journal*, January 8, 2002, A18.

29. Ibid.

CHAPTER THIRTEEN

1. Timothy White, "Music to My Ears," *Billboard*, July 3, 1993, 5.

2. Eric K. Arnold, "What Does It Mean to Be a Last Poet," *Aricana.com*, March 2, 2001.

3. Robert Santiago, "Having Won His Battle, He Doesn't Fear the Revolution, " *Cleveland Plain Dealer*, January 31, 1994, 3D.

4. Stephen Slayburgh, "Beats, Rhyme, and Revolution," *Columbus Alive*, January 17, 2002. Online.

5. Paris, "Yo, a Rapper's Domestic Plan," *Washington Post*, January 3, 1993, C2.

6. Ibid.

7. Ibid.

8. Davey D, "He's Back w/a Vengeance: Paris Returns," *DaveyD.com*, March 21, 2002.

INDEX